D1110116

Underwater Warfare in the Age of Sail

INDIANA UNIVERSITY PRESS BLOOMINGTON & LONDON

Underwater Warfare in the Age of Sail

Alex Roland

Published in Canada by Fitzhenry & Whiteside Limited, Don Mills, Ontario
Manufactured in the United States of America

Library of Congress Cataloging in Publication Data

Roland, Alex, 1944–
Underwater warfare in the age of sail.

Bibliography
Includes index.
1. Submarine warfare—History. I. Title.
V210.R64 1977 359.8'3 77–74436
ISBN 0–253–31824–6 1 2 3 4 5 81 80 79 78 77

To
Robert Seager II
and
Elizabeth A. Aiken

Contents

Illustrations

ACKNOWLEDGMENTS

This study owes whatever merits it might have to many hands besides mine. The footnotes and bibliography attest to the debts I have accumulated in its preparation. For lack of space they must also attest to my gratitude. To only a handful of my benefactors can I give explicit thanks.

Theodore Ropp and I.B. Holley, Jr. were my two principal mentors when I was preparing the original manuscript. Only those who have had the privilege of studying under both men can fully appreciate how thoroughly they complement each other and how completely they train and educate their charges. To both I am deeply grateful.

Part of the research for this study was supported by a Woodrow Wilson Dissertation Year Fellowship. I am grateful to the Woodrow Wilson National Fellowship Foundation, not only for the much needed financial support but also for the courtesy, consideration, and efficiency with which it was dispensed. Similar thanks are due to the Graduate School of Duke University for scholarships in academic years 1971–72 and 1972–73.

Among the many institutions and individuals particularly helpful in my research, three warrant special mention. Dr. Philip K. Lundeberg, Curator of Naval History at the National Museum of History and Technology, generously made available to me his wide knowledge of the history of underwater warfare, as well as the resources of his office and library. He directed me to many leads I might otherwise have missed. Mr. Thomas J. Dunning, Curator of Manuscripts at the New York Historical Society, helped me to root out some especially obscure material, as did Mr. James W. Cheevers, Curator of the U.S. Naval Academy Museum.

Among those who read the entire manuscript and made helpful criticisms were Theodore Ropp, I.B. Holley, Jr., Harold T. Parker, Albert F. Eldridge, Jr., Monte D. Wright, Wallace S. Hutcheon, Jr., and Andrew Patterson, Jr. What mistakes remain are a triumph of error over good counsel. Elizabeth Aiken, Irene Cromer, and Jean Reeder typed the manuscript through several reincarnations. Helmuts A. Feifs did heroic sundry service beyond the call of friendship.

Finally, my thanks go out to two special sources of help and inspiration. Robert Seager II sparked my interest in history more than a decade ago and provided much help and encouragement in the intervening years. Elizabeth Aiken sustained me through the research and writing of this book and paid as dearly as I for its completion. To these two important people in my life this study is dedicated with appreciation and affection.

Introduction

For two thousand years or more, Western man has been attempting to strike his enemies unawares from the concealment of the ocean's depths. Swimmers, mines, torpedoes—all manner of underwater warfare has been employed. All were drawn from the same conceptual well; only the advance of technology made today's submarine more successful than the divers of ancient Greece.

Almost fifty years ago, in his classic *Technics and Civilization*, Lewis Mumford taught us how to evaluate stories like this. In the Greeks, he would tell us, was the "dream of power." In our modern submarines, we drive the "engines of fulfillment." As is so often the case, the wish was the father of the machine, the dream gave birth to the engine. And magic was the womb in which the engine grew. Or, as Mumford put it, "magic was the bridge that united fantasy with technology."

This history of the evolution of underwater warfare is set in the age of sail because that era separated the dreams of power from the engines of fulfillment. The magic that filled those years included the romantic magic of the sailing ship and the physical magic that was then transforming itself into modern science and technology. More than coincidentally, a Trident and a Poseidon stand at either end of the story, symbolizing the common urge that has moved underwater warriors throughout Western history. The modern Trident submarine and its Poseidon missiles drew their names from Greek mythology—and their symbolism as well.

Poseidon was the god of the sea, a realm he won by casting lots with his brothers: Zeus, who won the heavens, and Hades, who won the underworld. The trident, with which Poseidon is invariably pictured, is the three-pronged spear he carried. In his hands it was a tool for fishing; its name meant simply three teeth. But by the time it passed through Latin to English, it had taken on the connotation of sea power. At first this was a sea power of a special sort—sea power that strikes from beneath the surface. Poseidon's domain was, after all, the entire sea, from the boundary of the underworld to the juncture with land and sky, which he and his brothers shared in common. The surface of the sea was not so much his haunt as his border. He lived beneath the surface and came up only to consort with other gods and to influence the affairs of men.

Poseidon personified—or rather deified—for the Greeks the dream of power. In this book I have consciously separated the modern Poseidon from the ancient, the dreams of power from the engines of fulfillment. I have focused on the magicians who wrought the transformation between the two in the belief that this segment of the story has a logic and a unity of its own, independent of what preceded it and what followed.

What preceded the age of sail was almost two millennia of toying with the dream of power. In the fourth century B.C., Alexander the Great reportedly dived to the ocean's floor in a glass

Figure 1. An artist's concept of tomorrow's engine of fulfillment, the Trident submarine.

barrel. He is pictured thus in numerous prints, seemingly content in his crude diving bell while his aides wait anxiously on the surface. So much apocrypha surrounds Alexander that one must accept such stories cautiously. Still, the idea of underwater warfare was current in his time, and there is no reason to believe he wasn't

Figure 2. Poseidon and his trident reach up from behind the seal of the U.S. Naval Academy, symbolizing a dream of power as old as recorded Western history. The men who advocated and advanced underwater warfare in the age of sail were moved by that dream, and they would have endorsed as well the Academy's motto: "From science, seapower."

attracted by it. We know that Greek swimmers were used to remove underwater obstructions, cut ships's cables, bore holes in enemy hulls, and even attach their infamous Greek fire—a secret mixture of sulphur, pitch, nitre, petroleum, and perhaps gunpowder that could burn even underwater. So reliable a source as Thucydides tells of divers being used to remove underwater stakes planted by the Syracusans in front of their dockyards during the siege of their city. Herodotus, Pliny, and Philo of Alexandria reported similar uses of underwater warfare. Surely the sea was important to the ancient Greeks, for both commerce and defense, and they were no more reluctant to conduct war beneath its surface than they were to people it with gods.

Nor was their example lost on their Mediterranean neighbors. For as long as the Mediterranean basin was the center of the Western world, underwater warfare was conducted there much as the Greeks had done it. Bohaddin, the Arabian historian, tells of a submarine apparatus being used to get a messenger into Acre when that city was besieged by the Crusaders. In early editions of his classic *De Re Militari*, Vegetius pictured armed and helmeted divers—underwater warriors—walking on the ocean floor and breathing through air tubes to the surface. The most sophisticated dream of power to issue from the Mediterranean, Leonardo da Vinci's sketches of a submarine, appeared on the eve of the age of sail.

After the age of sail came the now familiar history of the growing refinement and importance of underwater warfare in the twentieth century: the World War I submarine attacks by the Germans, the wholesale submarine warfare of World War II in the Atlantic and the Pacific, the nuclear submarines and guided missiles of the cold war, the Trident and Poseidon of tomorrow—all accompanied, of course, by mines and torpedoes of like sophistication.

The leading figures of the last one hundred years, the men who gave underwater warfare its present shape and importance, have not been unmindful of the debt they owed the magicians of the age of sail. John P. Holland was an avowed admirer of David Bushnell, who designed and constructed a submarine in the American Revolution. Simon Lake read Jules Verne as a boy and early determined to make Captain Nemo's *Nautilus* a reality—perhaps not realizing that Verne had the idea and the name of that submarine from Robert Fulton, the most important magician in the evolution of underwater warfare. Admiral Hyman Rickover paid tribute to Fulton by naming the world's first nuclear submarine *Nautilus*.

There were countless contributors to the development of underwater warfare in the age of sail. Many more could be added without upsetting the thesis of this book. The purpose of concentrating on a few and looking closely at their careers is to gain perhaps some new insights into the human predicament, especially into how and why men have sought to increase their power over the forces of nature to serve the uses of war. There is other matter here as well. This book tells of a small technological revolution in naval weaponry and how it came to pass. It speaks of how ideas traveled in the age of sail, how concepts of international law and morality sprang from the ashes of chivalry, how states went about buying new weapons, especially weapons tainted with dishonor. But always at the heart, this is the story of magicians and their motives—their dreams of power, their engines of fulfillment.

Underwater Warfare in the Age of Sail

I

Underwater Warfare and the Age of Sail

THE AGE OF sail, that era in maritime history when the dominant vehicle of naval warfare was the wooden-walled, multimasted, square-rigged, side-gunned sailing ship of the line, was a time of rapid growth in the development of naval warfare. More versatile and effective than the galley which preceded it and more aesthetically pleasing than the steam and iron fortress which replaced it, the ship of the line, as a war machine, lent distinctive characteristics to naval warfare under sail. Not the least important of these was what Professor Theodore Ropp calls the "hierarchy of power."[1] Warships in the age of sail came to be classified by the number of guns they carried, and a ship of a given rating was all but invulnerable to ships of lesser power. A seventy-four gun ship of the main battle line could be engaged and defeated by ships of similar or superior bulk and firepower, but not by inferiors. This characteristic put a premium on large numbers of large ships; and the exorbitant costs of this arms race coupled with its built-in resistance to change put a premium—at least in the minds of some men—on a way to undermine, literally and figuratively, the hierarchy. Thus, the concurrent development of underwater warfare.

This simultaneous evolution—conventionally bracketed, at least for the age of sail, between the late sixteenth and the mid-nineteenth centuries—is the only constant factor in the story. In all other respects naval history and the history of underwater warfare sailed different courses to the same port. Naval warfare reflects the cultural milieu of the combatants, but, unlike land warfare, it presents a blurred and wrinkled image. Too much time at sea puts mariners out of touch with the societies they represent. Naval warfare in the age of sail lumbered along as ponderously as the enormous machines in which it was conducted. When it altered course at all because of winds from shore, it did so reluctantly, almost in spite of itself. Not so underwater warfare, which mirrored almost perfectly the rapid transformations of science, technics, law, and morality in the three centuries of its gestation.

To place this image in proper context it must be noted that underwater warfare has intrigued imaginative warriors since the beginnings of recorded history. Large measures of accurate prophecy and utter nonsense predate the catalytic influence provided by the age of sail. But by beginning in the interval between the battle of Lepanto in 1571 and the defeat of the Armada in 1588, most of the nonsense can be avoided without scrapping all of the prophecy.[2] Thus we embark in midpassage—and in turbulent waters at that.

The turbulence was being caused by nothing less than a shift in the center of Western history. The nucleus around which the world seemed to turn was migrating from the Mediterranean to the English Channel, from the Renaissance to the Reformation, from Italy to the Low Countries, from Spain to France and England—and with it went the seeds of underwater warfare. At the end of the sixteenth century this migration was well under way; a caravan of cultural baggage stretched from Venice to Dover, and in it were included many of the intellectual furnishings of the modern world. The tail end of this caravan would not arrive until late in the seventeenth century, but as if to mark out the course of future events, Spain ended its most important century by turning from the victory of Lepanto in the Mediterranean to the defeat of the Armada in the English Channel.

Within this larger geographical shift, other facets in the evolution of underwater warfare were also in flux. War was changing from medieval to modern garb, undergoing a "military revolution" in which "the modern art of war [came] to birth."[3] So too were the laws and morals of Western man changing, particularly his concept of the role and process of war; and from this change would issue the modern law of nations. Science and technics[4] were beginning to shed their magical mantle in anticipation of the scientific revolution of the coming century. All of these transformations were to affect the evolution of underwater warfare, and all were to be reflected in the two battles which ushered in the age of sail, and in the work of two men between these battles.

The battle of Lepanto symbolizes far more than it ever accomplished. Tangibly it ended Turkish ascendancy in the Mediterranean and placed a Spanish-dominated Christianity temporarily in control of that sea. But symbolically it marked and mirrored momentous courses in Western history. Subsequent events proved it to be the last great galley battle, the last major engagement in which oared vessels rammed and grappled and troops stormed across narrow planks to win enemy ships in hand-to-hand combat. As such it became a watershed in naval history, one of two events describing the birth of the age of sail. And it was furthermore a mirror of the "century of atrocious warfare"[5] in which it occurred. No less than 25,000 Turks and 8,000 Christians perished in that one day's fighting,[6] far more than in any single battle in the comparatively bloodless age of sail. If the body count seems unusually high, even in the midst of the Wars of Religion and on the eve of the Massacre of Saint Bartholomew, the explanation lies in the peculiar ferocity and abandon with which men fight ideological "outsiders" and the dangers of close combat on a floating platform.

As a final gift to history, Lepanto crippled and instructed a prescient student of warfare, Miguel de Cervantes Saavedra (1547–1616), who in turn drafted some history of his own. The adventures of Cervantes's immortal Don frame a series of epitaphs and prophecies, not only about those "depraved and miserable times"[7] at the end of the sixteenth century but also about the specific forces which had to advance or retire to make way for underwater warfare.

The largest, most eloquent epitaph was for chivalry. "Know, Sancho," proclaims Quixote, "that I was born in this age of iron to restore the age of gold."[8] More than simply Spain's *siglo de oro*, this was the age of chivalry, to be "smiled . . . away" by Cervantes and lamented by knights errant ever since. As well he should have, Quixote mocked and lauded chivalry with the same stroke, for however ridiculous its excesses may have been, it nonetheless did humane service in tempering the conduct of war. In honoring a code of ethics, it nurtured and brought to flower a law of nations.[9] In fostering a brotherhood in arms, it created an institution which survived all battles and judged all combatants.[10] And most importantly for the evolution of underwater warfare, it undertook to judge how and with what tools a Christian knight could undertake to kill his fellow man.

When Quixote discourses on the "danger" and "distress" to which the soldier is subjected, he selects two examples which speak volumes about the twilight of chivalry into which underwater warfare was born. First he asks his listeners what can compare to the soldier

> who, being besieged in some strong place, and at his post or upon guard in some ravelin or bastion, perceives the enemy carrying on a mine under him, and yet must upon no account remove from thence, or shun the danger which threatens him so near? All he can do is to give notice to his commander, that he may countermine, but must himself stand still, fearing and expecting, when on a sudden he shall soar to the clouds without wings, and be again cast down headlong against his will.[11]

A horrible spectacle this, especially when viewed with the roseate nostalgia of an age of gold. The only danger Quixote can conjure to compare with it is

> when two galleys shock one another with their prows in the midst of the spacious sea. When they have thus grappled, and are clinging together, the soldier is confined to the narrow beak, being a board not above two feet wide; and yet though he sees before him so many ministers of death threatening, as there are pieces of cannon on the other side pointing against him, and not half a pike's length from his body; and being sensible that the first slip of his feet sends him to the bottom of Neptune's dominions; still, for all this, inspired by honor, with an undaunted heart, he stands a mark to so much fire, and endeavors to make this way, by that narrow passage, into the enemy's vessel. But what is most to be admired is, that no

> sooner one falls, where he shall never rise till the end of the world, than another steps into the same place, without suffering any interval of time to separate their deaths; a resolution and boldness scarce to be paralleled in any other trials of war.[12]

Though Cervantes's own experience led him to value the latter enterprise the more dangerous and hence the more honorable, the common evil he finds in both is gunpowder. "Blessed be those happy ages," continues Quixote, "that were strangers to the dreadful fury of these devilish instruments of artillery, whose inventor I am satisfied is now in hell, receiving the reward of his cursed invention."[13] This coupled fear and condemnation of gunpowder weapons reflects a common sentiment at the end of the sixteenth century. "There is no doubt," said one military commentator, "that Powder is a diabolical invention, the effects of which are no less dangerous than frightening."[14] Even Galileo attributed the speed of cannonball and bullet to supernatural forces, and the exclamation "son of a gun" lingers still to remind us of superstitious minds that saw the devil in every breech and chamber.[15] From this source the term "infernal machine" came to be applied to all sorts of military explosives, particularly to early naval mines, torpedoes, and exploding ships. So prevalent was this usage in the fifteenth and sixteenth centuries that the word *machina* was used almost exclusively in this sense, just as an infernal was so understood in later centuries. But the connotation of evil remained long after the association with the devil had disappeared.[16]

Of still more memorable symbolism in the Don's adventures are the famous jousts with the windmills. No mere arbitrary features of the Spanish countryside were these towering, grinding automata, for as A. Rupert Hall reminds us, the "fully developed windmill . . . was the most elaborate large-scale machine before the steam engine."[17] As such it represented all too clearly the "age of iron" Quixote so detested. His attack was a defense of the "golden age" against these "outrageous giants"[18] Pausing only to declare them "lawful prize" (for even in the heat of battle he is true to his code), he charges gallantly and is smitten by the machinations of a world he doesn't understand and cannot change. Many such romantic charges against the modern engines of war would be made before the relentless course of "progress' unseated all such defenders of chivalry. Not the last of these battles would be waged over the issue of underwater warfare.

Cervantes did not actually write *Don Quixote* until the sixteenth century had run its course. In the meantime work was well under way on a weapon system "infernal" enough to enrage any self-respecting knight errant. Underwater warfare consists of two facets: the detonation of an explosive charge adjacent to the soft underbelly of a ship, and the delivery of that charge at the proper time and place. Both problems were addressed between the battle of Lepanto and the defeat of the Armada.

The most important delivery system in the age of sail was the submarine, and according to the dean of submarine historians, "the earliest complete plan for a submarine boat that is known" is number eighteen of William Bourne's *Inuentions or Deuices . . .* (1578).[19] Bourne (c. 1535–1583) styled himself "a poore Gunner,"[20] a calling just then beginning to emerge from the "atmosphere of necromancy"[21] attached to it since the fourteenth century. More accurately he was a popularizer for artisans, transforming French and Italian treatises on gunnery, navigation, and allied arts into the English vernacular. A succession of tracts between 1565 and 1590 won for him a considerable local reputation and a permanent place in the history of geography, arms, and technics.[22]

Evidence abounds that Bourne was particularly familiar with the writings of Nicolo Tartaglia (1499–1557), the famous Italian mathematician and engineer. Aside from testifying to the movement of ideas from the Mediterranean to the English Channel, this familiarity reveals the source of two pertinent features of Bourne's writing. As Edgar Zilsel has pointed out,[23] Bourne and Tartaglia both subscribed to a cumulative view of technical progress, feeling that publication and accumulation of knowledge were the path to advancement. Introducing his *Inuentions or Deuices*, Bourne apologized for "this rude and barbarous volume," explaining that "the writer . . . is most unlearned and simple" but nevertheless motivated "to profit the common wealth." Noting that "all Artes, Sciences, or faculties, had a beginning before they came unto their perfection," he hoped that his modest offerings could serve as such a stepping-stone.[24] This sounds much like Tartaglia's dedication in *Questi et Inventioni* . . . (1554) in which he states that the man who discovers something new "and wants to own it for himself alone deserves no little blame. For if all our ancestors had behaved this way we should today differ little from irrational animals."[25]

Tartaglia's *Questi et Inventioni* also contained a proposal for a diving bell,[26] the most likely source of Bourne's idea for his submarine. When combined with the instruction on weight, volume, and displacement Bourne claimed to have had from John Dee,[27] all the essentials of his invention are present. His scheme encompassed little more than a sealed vessel with contractible sides to vary displacement and a hollow mast for air resupply when submerged, but it lacked only a means of propulsion to render it a workable, if crude, submarine.

The other side of the underwater warfare coin was stamped by the Italian engineer Frederico Gianibelli in 1585. Controversy abounds over Gianibelli's seniority in the history of mine warfare, and more than one expert agrees with J. S. Cowie that "it is a matter of good manners rather than of technical accuracy to state that the first recorded use of mines was in 1585."[28] But one fact remains. During the age of sail, Gianibelli was generally credited with producing "the first example in the history of war of a real sea mine."[29]

At the end of the sixteenth century Gianibelli's title of engineer was still synonymous with military engineer—reflecting the term's origins in the Roman *ingenia*. In the days of the Empire these had been catapults, ballistas, and other such siege weapons, but by the seventeenth century the machines with which engineers made their reputations were incendiary and explosive devices—the more spectacular the better.[30] In fact one such pyrotechnic contraption, the petard, became so closely associated with the engineer's profession that it crept into the literature as a frequent example of the craft. Thus in his *Battaille of Agincourt* Drayton had his "Engineer providing the Petar to break the strong Percullice"; and Shakespeare's Hamlet observed

> 'tis sport to have the enginer
> Hoist with his own petar.[31]

This petard was "an Engine (made like a bell, or Morter) wherewith strong gates are burst open"—another of those infernal machines Quixote railed against. Its appearance in the late sixteenth century coincided closely with the use Gianibelli made of its essential principle in the siege of Antwerp.[32]

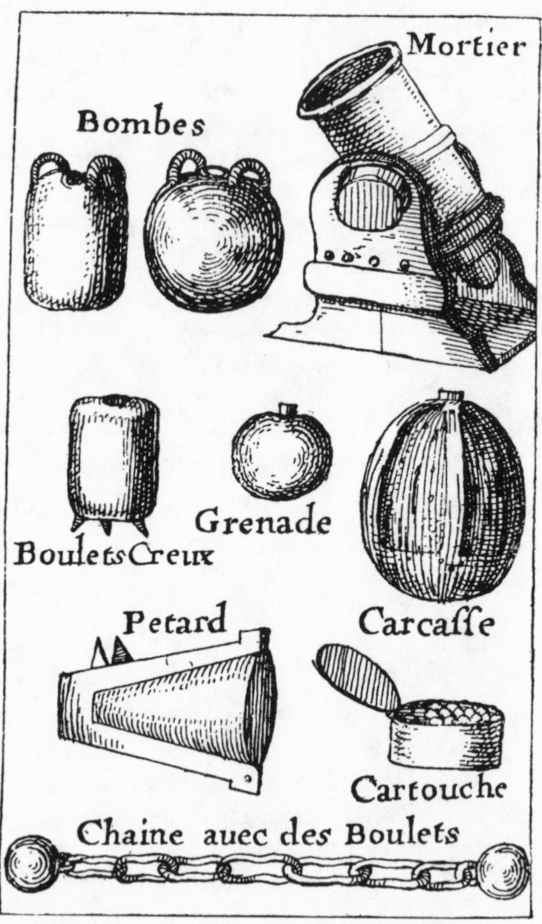

Figure 3. The staple exploding weapons of land warfare in the seventeenth century, as pictured in Louis de Gaya's *Traite de Armes* (1678). Most who used similar devices in underwater warfare called them bombs or carcasses, though the constraining effect of the water really made them more like the directed charge of the petard.

A native of Mantua, Gianibelli first had tried to sell his engineering talents in Spain, but, rebuffed and indignant, he settled instead in the Low Countries amidst the turmoil of the revolt of the Netherlands.[33] In 1585, the Duke of Parma, commander of the Spanish forces in that struggle, had blockaded Antwerp by erecting a bridge across the Scheldt River. Slightly more than half of

Figure 4. As this illustration from Louis de Gaya's *Traite de Armes* (1678) clearly shows, emplacing a petard could be just as complex and hazardous as emplacing an underwater explosive.

this 2,400-foot span stood on piles; the rest floated on boats chained together. To raise this blockade, Gianibelli proposed to send a fleet of exploding ships drifting into the bridge. In spite of the skepticism of the town elders which reduced his grand scheme to several fireboats and two exploding ships, Gianibelli accepted the challenge and made the best of his limited resources. Aided by a pair of local artisans—Peter Timmerman, "a mecanician," and Jan Bovy, "a clockmaker"[34]—Gianibelli covered a hold-full of powder in each vessel with a 6-foot-thick roof of "blue tombstones" topped by "a pyramid of heavy marble slabs . . . filled with mill-stones, cannon balls, blocks of marble, chain shot, iron hooks, plough-coulters," and more.[35] Most chroniclers then and since considered this pile of rubble to be so much antipersonnel debris. In fact, it did for Gianibelli's ships what the bell or mortar did for the petard—it directed the force of the explosion horizontally, so that when the seven thousand pounds of powder in one of the ships went off next to the bridge, a 200-foot hole was blown in the barricade. The eight hundred or more Spaniards cut down by the storm of missiles or blown away by the blast were simply an added bonus. We have no conclusive evidence that Gianibelli understood the principle of the shaped or directed charge, but neither do we have evidence that he did not. What we do know is that he employed that principle to great effect against the Spanish. What water pressure beneath the hulls of enemy ships would do for later underwater miners, Gianibelli accomplished with tonnage piled atop his explosion. Perhaps the nineteenth-century historians of underwater warfare were more astute than their twentieth-century counterparts when they dubbed Gianibelli the father of mine warfare.

One of the problems faced by Gianibelli—and all subsequent dabblers in underwater warfare—was what to call these strange devices. Chroniclers of the siege referred to them variously as "bomb ships," "fire ships," "infernal ships," "mines," and "infernal machines," but the name most often applied by contemporaries—especially the singed and unstrung Spaniards—was "the hell-burners of Antwerp." Associated with the devil (as all such engines were), and drawn larger than life in countless war stories, these mines acquired an infamy of far more power and reach than the unexploited spectacular at Antwerp that broke the bridge but not the siege.

But before looking to the powerful afterglow of the hell-burners of Antwerp, it might be well to note in passing the legal world into which these Mephistophelian machines were introduced. Balthazar Ayala (1548–1584), the Prince of Parma's "jurisconsult," prepared for him during the siege of Antwerp *Three Books on the Law of War. . . .* [36] Much of this classic volume is a "how-to" handbook on military discipline, strategy, and theory, but some is concerned with the nascent law of nations, and even with the *jus in bello*—the law *in* war. Ayala begins by asserting that contrary to much current opinion, "There are laws of war just as much as of peace."[37] From this revelation he launches into a discussion of the "just war," obviously referring to Spain's endeavor against the heretic Netherlands. Only by indirection does he finally get around to addressing the weapons and tactics that may be used legitimately in war. Assassination and poisoning are condemned, but all else is sanctioned under the indiscriminate umbrella of "necessity." The rule of thumb is "custom in peace and expediency in war"; and "that [is not] reckoned a breach of law which is done under the stress of necessity and at the instance of public expediency."[38] Of course one man's necessity is another man's war crime, and the devil can cite "public expediency" for his own purposes. But until the *jus in bello* was spelled out more clearly than this, Gianibelli's machines could be labeled Mephistophelian and unchivalrous, but not strictly illegal. This early breach between military consensus and what passed for international law in the age of sail was to be a continuing feature of the development of underwater warfare.

In many respects the "Archimedes of Antwerp," as Schiller styled Gianibelli,[39] was a mold from which his successors were cast. In portraying the Mantuan engineer, John Motley unwittingly described latter-day miners better than he knew, and his account merits quotation at some length:

> Gianibelli was no patriot. He was purely a man of science and of great acquirements, who was looked upon by the ignorant populace alternately as a dreamer and a wizard. He was as indiffer-

> ent to the cause of freedom as of despotism, but he had a great love for chemistry. He was also a profound mechanician, second to no man of his age in theoretic and practical engineering.
>
> He had gone from Italy to Spain that he might offer his services to Philip, and give him the benefit of many original and ingenious inventions. Forced to dance attendance, day after day, among sneering courtiers and insolent placemen, and to submit to the criticism of practical sages and philosophers of routine, while he was constantly denied an opportunity of explaining his projects, the quick-tempered Italian had gone away at last, indignant. He had then vowed revenge upon the dulness by which his genius had been slighted, and had sworn that the next time the Spaniards heard the name of the man they had dared to deride, they should hear it with tears.[40]

But even in Antwerp, when he presented his plan to the Senate,

> Ignorance and incredulity did their work, as usual, and Gianbelli's [*sic*] request was refused. As a quarter-measure, nevertheless, he was allowed to take two smaller vessels of seventy and eighty tons. The Italian was disgusted with this parsimony upon so momentous an occasion, but he at the same time determined, even with these slender materials, to give an exhibition of his power.[41]

The final result was his "floating marine volcanoes," which were intended " to deal destruction where the Spaniards deemed themselves most secure."[42] This whole description outlines in many respects the careers of future underwater warriors, and, as will be seen shortly, this last feature is the key to understanding all of them.

Antwerp fell to Parma later in 1585, and Gianibelli went to work for Queen Elizabeth. He busied himself with the defense of the Thames, but his reputation sailed the English Channel and contributed to the defeat of the Spanish Armada. Appropriately enough that naval engagement closed out not only Gianibelli's flourish on the stage of Western history but also the gestation period of the age of sail. From that point on, all of the Atlantic powers "regarded the sailing ship as the backbone of the fleet."[43] Thus was underwater warfare provided with windmills of its own.

On its way to disaster, the Armada entered the English Channel in July of 1588, fenced indecisively with the English fleet, and put into Calais Roads to resupply and make contact with the invasion force led by Parma. While the Spanish were failing in the latter two endeavors, Admiral Sir William Winter, afloat with the English fleet, recalled Gianibelli's famous exploits at Antwerp and suggested a fireship attack on the Spanish.[44] Preparations were quickly made and the attack came off on the night of 6/7 August. King Philip had repeatedly warned the Duke of Medina Sidonia, commander of the Spanish fleet, that the English were preparing some such mischief, but neither of them knew that the ships' crews lived in dread of the same eventuality. Gianibelli's hell-burners were "a common item of gossip in the fleet," and the "magician-scientist" himself was rumored to be embarked with the English.[45] When the attack came, panic spread quickly behind cries of "The Hell-burners of Antwerp!" The Spanish fleet broke into disarray; cables were cut precipitously; some ships grounded, most fled in diverse directions never again to regain successfully the crescent formation which had marked their entry into the Channel. The English chased them into the North Sea and then abandoned them to the weather, the rocky coast of the British Isles, and the shortage of supplies which completed the disaster.

But that was not the end of it. Just as Lepanto provided an introduction to recurring themes in the history of underwater warfare, so did the defeat of the Armada presage the future. Garrett Mattingly, the battle's most eloquent historian, has noted that

> as the episode of the Armada receded into the past it influenced history in another way. Its story, magnified and distorted by a golden mist, became a heroic apologue of the defense of freedom against tyranny, an eternal myth of the victory of the weak over the strong, of the triumph of David over Goliath.[46]

The analogy with David and Goliath settles as comfortably with the twentieth-century mind as it did with that of the sixteenth century. It is a familiar, recurrent concept in the Christian-Hebraic world, one whose historical accuracy is no more important than the Armada's. It is what R. R. Palmer would call a "good myth," one which "reflects a belief about the human predicament or human behavior."[47] The importance of the David and Goliath story is not whether the encounter on the plains of Elah ever occurred, but whether the myth has provided or reflected a conceptual framework within which men are wont to view the problem of human conflict. Like Arnold Toynbee, I believe that it has.

Toynbee felt that the triumph of mind over matter, of wit over brawn, is "ideally exemplified" by David and Goliath. For him this was a "philosophic truth" also to be seen in the "unfolding history of human competition in armaments."[48] Goliath is the massive, armored warrior, disdainful of the clever, deceptive David. They meet and the giant is smitten, not by superior strength, but by forces he never deigned to recognize. The key to the encounter is "the act of idolization,"[49] Goliath's crippling infatuation with his own imagined invincibility. While the giant should have been protecting himself and attacking David, he scoffed instead and left his vulnerable temple exposed.

Similarly, underwater warfare was the Davidic response to the hierarchy of power in the age of sail. The underwater explosion next to the soft underbelly of the ship was the sling and the stone with which maritime Davids attacked ships of the line. Cleverness and deception were pitted against mass and armor. The very existence of Goliaths, proclaimed invulnerable by the conventional wisdom, aroused a succession of cerebral warriors who were forever telling counterpart Sauls that they could fell the giant.

Of course the essential precondition was the "act of idolization." Just as Gianibelli attacked "where the Spaniards deemed themselves most secure," so did his successors prey upon the sailor's love affair with the ship of the line. The peculiar warmth of this infatuation—the necessary catalyst of underwater warfare—is hard to gauge or appreciate in the twentieth century. John Ruskin gives perhaps a taste of the reverence with which otherwise sane and sober men viewed these vessels in the age of sail:

> Take it all in all, a ship of the line is the most honorable thing that man, as a gregarious animal, has produced. By himself, unhelped, he can do better things than ships of the line; he can make poems and pictures, and other such concentrations of what is best in him. But as a being living in flocks and hammering out, with alternate strokes and mutual agreement, what is necessary for him in these

> flocks to get or produce, the ship of the line is his first work. Into that he has put so much of his human patience, common sense, forethought, experimental philosophy, self-control, habits of order and obedience, thoroughly wrought hard work, defiance of brute elements, careless courage, careful patriotism, and calm expectation of the judgement of God, as can well be put into a space 300 feet long by 80 feet broad. And I am thankful to have lived in an age when I could see this thing so done.[50]

Nor was this allure fortuitous, for as John U. Nef reminds us,

> men-of-war were designed to charm the beholder. The masts, spars, and yards formed, with the hull of the ship, a sketch worthy of a great draftsman. Both masts and hull were richly embellished: the mast with streaming, many-colored pennants, as well as billowing sails; the hull with elaborate decorations at bow and stern and all along the sides. These sides were punctured with rows of cannon's mouths, looking more like the oval windows in the lofts of castles than the belching muzzles of flame which they became when, in sight of enemy vessels, they spit out their balls of destruction.[51]

It is little wonder that these machines turned the heads of naval officers and lulled them into the pleasing conceit that they were vulnerable only to their peers. In this case, the "act of idolization" was almost irresistible—and almost fatal.

II

Cornelius Drebbel and the Uses of Magic

LOOKING BACK across three and a half centuries of Western history, it is almost impossible to make out the figure of Cornelius Drebbel (1572–1633), let alone say for sure what he was. His performances commanded a wide audience in his day, and indeed for some time after his death. As late as 1672, if his editor is to be believed, he was still highly regarded by "all those who presume to know the good Authors in [chemistry]."[1] But now only his biographers remain to plead for him that he was "undoubtedly the best known of the numerous inventors we find in Europe at the beginning of the 17th century and [that] his fame . . . spread over the whole of the civilized world of that day."[2]

Recovering Cornelius Drebbel from the obscurity into which he has fallen is necessary to an understanding of the evolution of underwater warfare, for not only was he the next major figure after Bourne and Gianibelli, he was also one of the most important in the whole story. More than any single man before the nineteenth century, Drebbel acted out or personified all the main themes that dominate the development of underwater weaponry. In particular, his career revealed the complex relationship between early technics, magic, and science; his dealings with government and the military forebode many conflicts between later inventors and the state; and the personal motivations that impelled him likewise touched many other early Davids. To the extent one can pierce his obscurity and resolve the enigma of Drebbel himself, one can catch a glimpse of the future course of underwater warfare.

Born and raised in the Netherlands during the war with Spain, Drebbel trained as an artisan from an early age. From the Antwerp refugees who settled in Middleburg after 1585 he learned glassmaking, and from the famous artist Hendrick Goltzius (1558–1617) (whose sister he married in 1595) he learned engraving and alchemy. After a speckled career of invention and manual labor in various cities of his native land, he arrived in England shortly after, and probably because of, the accession of James I. He caught the new king's eye with a "*perpetuum mobile*" of uncertain construction and purpose and won for himself, as he termed it, "the position of paid servant to His Imperial Majesty," Henry, Prince of Wales.[3] After some years of entertaining young Henry, and a three-year sabbatical at the court of Rudolph II in Prague (during which absence Henry died), Drebbel returned to the employ of James I, survived the accession of Charles I, went to work for the Admiralty in 1626, and thence departed royal service under a cloud, to live out his remaining four years as a poor brewer and innkeeper.

Drebbel's more sympathetic contemporaries called him "philosopher," "inventor," "engineer," "naturalist," and "mathematician." His critics were wont to ascribe him a "sorcerer," an "alchemist and charlatan," a "jackass, braggart and windmaker," and—amongst the more common and superstitious folk—a "strange Monstar," whose beer they would drink for the thrill of viewing him.[4] Before the end of the seventeenth century, Robert Boyle, the greatest chemist of the scientific revolution, eulogized Drebbel as a "deservedly famous Mechanician and Chymist."[5] Modern historians have titled him "empiric and inventor," "civil and military engineer," "technologist," "showman," even "artist"; and G. N. Clark has gone so far as to call him a "true scientist."[6] Add to this catalogue the title *courtier* and one would have a fair collection of the various facets of his career.

But attempts to lift from these labels a silhouette of the man are confounded by two features of the labels themselves. The first is etymological. The seventeenth century's philosopher is the twentieth century's scientist—the former cursed only with a wider range of interest and an infinitely narrower range of method, knowledge, and apparatus. An engineer then was a military engineer in the Leonardo-Gianibelli mold, about to become a civil engineer in the mold of Colbert's *Corps des Ponts et Chaussees*. The title *alchemist* accused Drebbel of chasing the philosopher's stone (which he did), but the next generation save one dubbed him chemist and credited his researches. In spite of its modern connotations, a charlatan then was nothing more evil than "a pratler, a talkative fellow."[7]

This problem of terminology is particularly troublesome in Drebbel's case, for he stood on the shifting border between magic and science, with one foot in each realm—and neither he nor his contemporaries knew it. When Cervantes referred to "the magic art" as "a science" he was only confessing his inability to discern any difference between the two. And what Cervantes couldn't see in "those depraved times" was likely to escape most observers. So great a scientist as William Harvey (1578–1657) took part in the examination of witches, and Johannes Kepler (1751–1630) was a mystic and an astrologer whose only apology was that "Mother Astronomy would certainly starve if daughter Astrology did not earn the bread of both."[8]

Nor can these giants of the early scientific revolution be slighted for failing to see what has only recently come to light from the perspective of the twentieth century. In his classic study of anthropology, Sir John Frazer opened the door by noting that magic is "next of kin to science."[9] Upon this foundation Lynn Thorndike built his monumental *History of Magic and Experimental Science*. His central idea was that "magic and experimental science have been connected in their development; that magicians were perhaps the first to experiment; and that the history of both magic and experimental science can be better understood by studying them together."[10]

Viewed in this light, Drebbel comes into sharper focus. To contemporaries, as well as to later generations, he could easily appear to be both chemist and alchemist, technologist and sorcerer, philosopher and wind maker—for in fact he was all of these things at once, the archtype "magician-scientist" that timorous

Spaniards in the Armada had imagined Gianibelli to be. As Thorndike describes him, he "was probably the most pretentious, secretive and magical figure in the scientific and technical world of the early seventeenth century."[11] Thorndike as well might have said that he was the most scientific figure in the magical world, for in that age they were opposite sides of the same coin. In either case he was a man who walked in the parallel worlds of intellectual science on the one hand and practical invention on the other, and to that degree he is representative of most succeeding Davids.

The second factor that blurs Drebbel's silhouette is our twentieth-century preoccupation with career and vocation. We ask little children what they want to *be* when they grow up, impressing upon them the peculiar notion that one's career somehow defines what one *is*. Of course no such easy label fits Drebbel, and the safest title to give him is the one he claimed for himself —inventor—perhaps adding only that he was a court inventor, directing his primary energies toward the pleasure of whatever prince seemed most likely to reward his efforts. When returning from Prague in 1613, he wrote to James I: "I have always burned, and still burn, with a great desire to serve your gracious majesty and to divert you with my inventions"[12] —of which an exaggerated list followed in close order. The obsequious posture of the courtier coupled with inflated claims for his "inventions" provides a fair glimpse of the man at his worst, but even so no worse than Leonardo and countless other court performers before him. Nor was he in this regard much worse than his successors in underwater warfare.

Today we would call much of Drebbel's "invention" plagiarism, but not so at the beginning of the seventeenth century, "when plagiarism was practiced with the most cynical impudence."[13] Peter Gay has noted that "if there were a debtor's prison for intellectuals who have failed to acknowledge their obligations, it would be filled with natural philosophers of the scientific revolution."[14] William Bourne would surely have done some time, as would Cornelius Drebbel, but stature in the history of science and technics was no proof of innocence either. As Lynn Thorndike observed, even the father of the scientific revolution, the venerable Francis Bacon (1561–1626), made "a virtue of not citing authorities."[15] So again, in context, Drebbel is no worse than his contemporaries.

One reason for the spate of plagiarism that marked the seventeenth century was the flurry of scientific ideas then swirling across the state and language borders of Europe, propelled largely by the correspondence of the learned men of the time. Increased book production and the travels of these same men contributed to this rapid propagation of knowledge, but the correspondence of the initiate was the most important medium. Letters served the function later taken over by newspapers and journals, and the speed of transmission was truly remarkable. The Dutch States General heard Hans Lippershey's application for a patent on a telescope on October 2, 1608; by the end of the year the glasses were on sale in Germany; Galileo heard about them in 1609, and in 1610 his observations of Jupiter's satellites were being repeated in France.[16]

In this era of comparatively rapid-fire information, Drebbel did his share of stealing and contributing. He is rightly credited with some original inventions, particularly in the field of optics, dyeing, and incubation. He is just as rightly accused of borrowing "extensively the honours of preceding discoverers."[17] In presenting his *perpetuum mobile* to James I, he made a standard disclaimer of the age, avowing that he "used neither the writings of the ancients nor anyone's aid, but . . . discovered these things only by assiduous observation and scrutiny of the elements."[18] One can't help feeling that he was protesting too much.

He would have been hard pressed to make the same claim for the submarine he built and sailed on the Thames in the early 1620s, for in this he had ample opportunity to draw upon the work of others. While he was still in Holland three countrymen from a village near his birthplace of Alkmaar invented, demonstrated, and won a patent for a diving bell. Still closer in time to his own invention was the work of John Napier (1550–1617), the famous mathematician, who shared a common friend with Drebbel. Henry Briggs (1556–1631), a mathematician in his own right and a confidant of both men, visited Napier in 1615 and 1616, shortly before the latter's death, and may well have become privy to Napier's plans for a submarine. This would at least account for the year 1618 being the earliest reported date at which Drebbel was at work on his own submarine.[19]

But like Leonardo before him, Napier was cautious and secretive about his submarine plans, even with friends like Briggs. The most likely source of Drebbel's ideas in this field remains William Bourne's *Inuentions or Deuices. . . .* Later editions of Bourne's works appeared all through the first half of the seventeenth century, and, as has already been stated, he enjoyed a considerable popularity in England. A leading authority on submarine history has observed that " it is more than probable that the Dutchman had read [Bourne's] account," and even Drebbel's biographers allow that "he must have known of Bourne's ideas."[20] In fact, the connection to Napier through Briggs suggests yet another path to Bourne, for Briggs was corresponding with a Mr. [John?] Clerke of Gravesend (Bourne's hometown) on the subject of a special kind of ruler.[21] Bourne was an expert on navigational instruments, including one of his own invention, and his name would be sure to arise. It was in just this manner that ideas then circulated among like-minded men of curiosity.

Accounts of Drebbel's submarine are scarce and contraditory, but it seems to have differed somewhat from Bourne's, being in effect an elongated diving bell with no communication to the surface when submerged. But the principle of varied displacement was the same, and Drebbel's chief contributions (aside from the air supply to be mentioned later) were the addition of oars protruding through leather gaskets and the use of compass and pressure gauge for navigation. The submarine made several successful dives in the Thames River, at least one in the presence of James I, and thus won considerable public attention. But were it not for a clue given by Drebbel's close friend, Constantyn Huygens (1596–1687), father of the famous scientist Christiaan, it would seem hardly different from the numerous schemes for diving bells advanced throughout the seventeenth century. Following a description of the boat, Huygens said:

> From all this it is not hard to imagine what would be the usefulness of this bold invention in time of war, if in this manner (a thing which I have repeatedly heard Drebbel assert) enemy ships

> lying safely at anchor could be secretly attacked and sunk unexpectedly by means of a battering ram—an instrument of which hideous use is made now-a-days in the capturing of the gates and bridges of towns.[22]

By "battering ram" he of course meant petard. Not only does this establish Drebbel as the originator of the spar torpedo, it also suggests the source of his ideas on underwater explosions—his second contribution in underwater warfare.

The "water petard" or "water myne," as Drebbel's devices were styled, recall the principle of the shaped or directed charge used so effectively by Gianibelli at Antwerp. There can be little doubt that Drebbel was well acquainted with these exploits, for not only were they notorious all over western Europe, but firsthand accounts were carried by the refugees of Antwerp to the town of Middleburg where Drebbel was learning the glass trade in the 1590s. Knowledge like this in the hands of a man like Drebbel was a volatile mixture—especially when set in the "golden mist" of the English generation looking back on the Armada. Drebbel's penchant for wonder-working, his public posturing, his exhibitionism and obsequiousness, his overweening self-confidence, his taste for victories over the forces of nature—these are the characteristics that send romantic iconoclasts charging against the reigning order of things. All that was lacking was an enemy worthy of his powers, and, as Don Quixote knew, such monsters are seldom wanting. In this case they arose in 1626 in the form of ships and fortresses defending the besieged Huguenot stronghold at La Rochelle.

In January 1626, the Master of Ordnance received a royal warrant "for the making of divers water mines, water-petards, and boates to goe under water." This warrant was echoed and expanded on January 26 in the "Orders of Buckingham's Expedition" for the relief of La Rochelle. There an entry appeared "for the making of dyvers watermines, water petards, forged cases to be shot with fireworks, and boates to go under water." The following June 29, Buckingham expanded this still further to include "360 forged iron cases with fireworks, 50 watermines, 290 water petards and two boates to conduct them under water, for H.M.

special services to go with the fleet." Within a week Drebbel was set up with "lodgings and workshops" in the Minories, the former abbey just outside the London walls then serving as the laboratory of the Ordnance Department.[23] How he came to this enviable position in government employ warrants some attention, for in seventeenth-century England his particular approach to underwater warfare had severe obstacles to overcome.

What distinguished Drebbel from Bourne and Gianibelli was the use each of them made of their inventions. Bourne freely published his ideas "to profit the common wealth," confident that progress derived from the accumulation and refinement of knowledge. Gianibelli turned his talents to an immediate demonstration of his powers—a demonstration splashy enough to echo across the English Channel, intimidate the Spanish, and secure his reputation. In contrast, Drebbel's course of action was to sell his ideas, or, as his biographer put it, to "make science pay."[24] In a petition to James I in 1621, Drebbel openly avowed that he was "not less inclined to render my services to Your Majesty by profitable, than by ingenious and gratifying inventions."[25] This, in fact, was his role as a court inventor, the calling by which he supported himself, a profligate wife, and several children. In applying this philosophy to underwater warfare, he became in effect an arms peddler, the third and most important role in which maritime Davids would dispose of their weapons in the age of sail. And he also became a truer model of the wandering Italian engineer than even Gianibelli had been.

Unfortunately for Drebbel, Parliament was then taking a rather dim view of James's generous endowment of court favorites. In 1623, about the time Drebbel was demonstrating his submarine on the Thames, Parliament passed the "Statute of Monopolies." This legislation, the model for most succeeding patent regulations, was intended as much to curb the king's disbursements as to reward or encourage inventors. Huygens reported that Drebbel's inventions were widely believed to be worth much less than James invested in them, so it may well be assumed that the Dutchman was one of the targets of the law.[26] As if these legal shackles were not bad enough, James died in 1625 and was succeeded by his less indulgent son, Charles I. In the funeral procession, according to a contemporary account, "Drebbel the Engeneere walked between Baston le Peer the dauncer, under officers of the Mynte, Actors and Comedians"[27]—an ominous indicator of his status in the new pecking order.

Nor was his diminished brilliance and influence at court the only impediment to Drebbel's military designs. Not much encouragement was given to the development of weapons in seventeenth-century England, partly because contrivances still so closely associated with the devil were not considered worthy of protection and nurturing, and partly because there was no one particularly qualified to evaluate them. Inventions like Drebbel's were referred to the Board of Ordnance, where the Master Gunner and the Fire-Master passed on the advisability of testing them at crown expense.[28] Generally, new and better recipes for gunpowder were most likely to attract court and military interest. Cannon and other ordnance were left to the discrimination of the gunfounders, who were expected only to produce a weapon no worse than its predecessors. Occasionally an artisan would earn a patent from Charles I if he presented a particularly worthy innovation, as, for example, one Arnold Rotispen did in 1626.[29]

In spite of these institutional and traditional obstacles, Drebbel won a niche in the Minories and a chance to prove his ideas. The same Rotispen who pulled off the similar coup in cannon manufacture provided the artisan's skill for the endeavor, as Timmerman and Bovy had done for Gianibelli at Antwerp. Joined by Abraham Kuffler, one of Drebbel's sons-in-law, they set about preparing the "water engines" for the relief of La Rochelle.[30] After laboring a year, they delivered the required machines and were rewarded in the amount of £100.[31] Presumably these engines were intended for use in the expedition of October 1627, but neither in that futile effort nor in its equally futile sequel the following June is there any evidence that they were employed—in spite of the fact that Kuffler sailed with both expeditions. So Drebbel himself signed on for the third attempt at the handsome salary of £150 a month, while Kuffler embarked yet again at 20 shillings a day. Several attempts were made with Drebbel's machines, against French ships and against the sea forts, but all—like the expedition itself—failed. When the fleet returned to England the War Council held an investigation and halted further payments to Drebbel and Kuffler.[32] The details of this unhappy failure are not known, but the results are: it ended Drebbel's public career. Over his shoulder, as he withdrew from the halls of government, he blamed it all on the "fear and cowardice" of the leaders of the expedition,[33] but that apparently made little impression on the Admiralty, the War Council, or the King. They held Drebbel personally and solely accountable for the failure of his devices; his excuses fell on deaf ears. Many of Drebbel's successors in underwater warfare would make the same futile attempts to blame their failures on circumstances.

Some time later Drebbel's inventions were demonstrated successfully for the Dutch, but they too turned them down, apparently on moral grounds.[34] Though there is no evidence that English chivalry had been particularly offended by Drebbel's machines, there were probably some moral objections abroad —especially within the navy. Artillery and firearms were gaining acceptance, but less familiar gunpowder weapons were still closely associated with the devil. The Gunpowder Plot, the failed attempt by Roman Catholic extremists to blow up King James I and his Parliament in 1605 by exploding twenty barrels of gunpowder beneath the House of Lords, was so labeled because it struck a frightening, resonant chord in the popular imagination. Even mines in the conduct of sieges had come to be associated with the primary goal of blasting a hole in the fortress, and in this context Shakespeare warned that "the Mynes is not according to the disciplines of the Warre."[35]

But there was more than this to the prejudice against underwater warfare. A real clue to the specific chivalric objection appeared about this time in Alberico Gentili's *De Iuri Belli Libri Tres* ([1598] 1612 ed.).[36] In the chapter entitled "Of Arms and Counterfeit Arms," Gentili approached the issue indirectly by putting to rest the lingering classical notion that powerful war machines were illegal because they "deprived men of an opportunity to show courage."[37] This had been one of Don Quixote's favorite laments, but one now buried (if not forgotten) along with his chivalry. It was in his argument against banning such machines that Gentili uncovered the prejudice against underwater warfare. "Those things are not of an exterminating character," he said, "which are so open that they may be avoided."[38] In other words, weapons which can be seen and thus defended against are lawful because they do not tend to invalidate war's role as a reasonable international arbiter. War was a continuation of the medieval judicial duel, and for the institution to fulfill this useful social function it was necessary for all to agree that snipers in the woods would not be tolerated. By the same logic, in Gentili's discussion of the fifteen reasons why poison was illegal, not the last important was "because it is clandestine, and therefore not proper in war."[39] This is the very same constraint which caused Francis Bacon to condemn experiments in noiseless gunpowder, "for," he said, "it may cause secret murder."[40] "Clandestine" and "secret" were the pith and core of the objection to underwater warfare throughout the age of sail.

Military men seldom perceived this line of reasoning clearly, but here was the lingering spectre of chivalry which haunted them throughout the age of sail and disposed them to eschew underwater warfare. Its twin moral restraint was the association with the devil, which itself came to be "included under the head of poisons." The "magic arts," said Gentili, are "another kind of poisoning," and, as such, "unlawful in war, because war, a contest between men, through these arts is made a struggle of demons."[41] For as long as the term *infernal machine* was in common usage, military men throughout the Western world would stiffen at the thought of "clandestine warfare" or "exploding engine."

However active such moral reflexes may have been in England at the time, they did not stop Drebbel's heirs from using up the rest of the century peddling his invention. Johannes Kuffler, another son-in-law, visited Samuel Pepys in March 1661 trying to sell Drebbel's "engine to blow up ships." Pepys resolved to take it up with the Duke of York the next day, but his diary gives no indication what took place—a reflection perhaps of Kuffler's insistence that only the king and his heirs could be privy to the details of the secret. In the same month, Kuffler and his brother-in-law, Jacob Drebbel, petitioned the crown for a £10,000 reward if the same invention be proven effective, and included a veiled threat to sell it abroad if they were refused. But refused they were; or at least there is no evidence that their proposition was taken seriously, beyond the fact that Pepys was still discussing it in 1663. By 1689 a third generation had entered the picture. One of Abraham Kuffler's sons visited Constantyn Huygens, Jr. (1628–1697), another son of Drebbel's close friend, and told him that Cromwell had promised him a great sum for the invention to sink ships but had died before the deal was closed. Six years later, one of Drebbel's daughters was asking the same Huygens for assistance in gaining a subsidy from the king in return for the same invention.[42]

But this was a dead end. No substantive result ever came of the Kufflers' efforts to sell Drebbel's engines. What they did do was spread the story of Drebbel sufficiently far so that it could be taken up by another group for another reason. Drebbel claimed to have invented a means whereby he could renew the air in his submarines, allowing, by one account, two dozen men to stay submerged for twenty-four hours without any surface contact. This he allegedly did by releasing from time to time within the submarine a "liquor" which cleansed and refreshed the air. This claim intrigued the learned men of Europe and kept Drebbel under their pens all during the seventeenth century.

Representative of the kind of men who sustained and propagated Drebbel's reputation in these years was Father Marin Mersenne (1558–1648), a Minimie friar who has been well described as "*secretaire de l'Europe savante*."[43] Educated at the *Collège du Mans* and the University of Paris, traveled in France, Spain, Italy, and the Low Countries, centrally located in Paris, and well connected with most of the great minds of his day, Mersenne was a catalyst of intellectual activity. Through his hands passed the important books, letters, and conversation of the day, to be sorted, classified, and redirected. A true college of scholars existed then, and Mersenne was the dean—supervising, suggesting, connecting. He was just the sort of man to ensure that news of Drebbel's "liquor" reached the right people.

Not a productive original thinker himself, Mersenne was an honest compiler of the works of others, "the good thief," as one contemporary called him.[44] In 1634 he posited, apparently without prior knowledge of Drebbel's work, that underwater navigation was possible. His discussion then was incomplete and raised more questions than it answered. However, in 1644, having learned about Drebbel, he became clear and expansive. He cited Drebbel's work, noted the features of the Dutchman's submarine, and added several important suggestions of his own, including copper hull, gimlets for piercing enemy ships, underwater cannons, ventilators and tubes to the surface, and so on.[45]

More importantly, he introduced Drebbel to his fellow scholars. Some, like George Fournier (1595–1652), with whom Mersenne wrote *Questiones theologiques* . . . in 1634, simply accepted the master's opinion on Drebbel's ability to renew the air in his submarine.[46] Others, like the abbé de Haute-Feuille, using Mersenne's version of Drebbel's experiments to attack the Dutchman, maintained that Drebbel's claim to have discovered "*une essence volatile*" was just a smoke screen to disguise his real method of renewing the air. This, said the abbé, was nothing more than a bellows with an intake and exhaust valve and two pipes to the surface.[47]

At least one observer stated that there were no pipes to the surface, so Haute-Feuille's supposition seems unlikely. The mistake, however, is understandable, for Drebbel was given to using what Huygens called "studiedly ambiguous words."[48] In this case he claimed to have discovered the "quintessence of air," though even he had conceded that quintessence was a term of many meanings among scholars. In contemporary medicine it could mean an addition to the four elementary qualties—hot, cold, dry, moist—or to the four body juices—blood, phlegm, black bile, yellow bile. In the alchemist's bag it could be another element to add to earth, fire, water, and air. Or it could be used as Drebbel used it, to define a constant property—an essence—of all elements.[49] This last was the way Paracelsus (1493–1541), the dominant chemical authority of the time, used the term, and his own vagueness of definition suggests that he was Drebbel's source.

So secretive and mysterious was Drebbel about the nature of his inventions that few if any of his successors ever learned exactly how he renewed the air in his submarine. In an obscure publication in 1604 he claimed that "saltpeter, broken up by the power of fire, [is] thus changed into something of the nature of air."[50] Other rumors also circulated in his wake, and it is entirely possible that the secret may have been passed on to experimenters who significantly advanced the search for oxygen. But that was not Drebbel's real importance. He was rather an impetus by example, the proof that submarine navigation was not only possible but had in fact already been accomplished—and by a sorcerer at that. As Lewis Mumford has observed:

> . . . magic was the bridge that united fantasy with technology: the dream of power with the engines of fulfillment. The subjective confidence of the magicians, seeking to inflate their private egos with boundless wealth and mysterious energies, surmounted even their practical failures: their fiery hopes, their crazy dreams, their cracked homunculi continued to gleam in the ashes: to have dreamed so riotously was to make the technics that followed less incredible and hence less impossible.[51]

While rendering submarine navigation less incredible and less impossible, Drebbel was also serving as an homunculus of sorts for future Davids. The shifting and indefinable combination of magician, technician, and scientist; the battle record of practical failure with ingenious and feasible weapons; the career capped by financial failure; the uses made of science and the curious interest of the scientific community in return—all these themes and more recur frequently in the history of underwater warfare. That all of them converged in the brief career of this nearly forgotten inventor is a measure of both Cornelius Drebbel and the uses of magic.

III

Robert Boyle and the Oxygen Connection

IN HIS monumental *Study of War*, Quincy Wright marked an important feature of the *jus in bello*. Discussing the conditions under which such restraints are likely to obtain, he noted that "when war is fought for broad, ideological objectives, such rules have tended to break down because the end is thought to justify all means and war has tended to become absolute." [1] This generalization suits particularly well the century in European history spanning the wars of religion. Protestants and Catholics unleashed upon each other all manner of atrocity in Christ's name, and engaged in an intracultural savagery normally reserved for outsiders. As if to draw that very comparison, Pope Gregory XIII declared the Saint Bartholomew Massacre "more agreeable than fifty Lepantos" and had a commemorative medal struck.[2]

Perhaps in that "degenerate age," as Quixote called it, the new machines of underwater warfare seemed less objectionable than they might have otherwise. But during the fifth decade of the seventeenth century the temperature of war in Europe cooled. In the year of Mersenne's death, Christianity concluded with itself the Peace of Westphalia and ushered in a century in which Cervantes might have taken some comfort. As John U. Nef describes it:

> After more than a hundred years of atrocious warfare the Europeans bound up their wounds, scowled at, cursed, and dreaded each

> other, and even continued to fight, but with diminishing fierceness and less destructive consequences. The hundred years preceding the War of the [Austrian] Succession . . . were an age during which, in spite of occasional setbacks, the tendency was continually toward more pacific conditions.[3]

Professor Nef has perhaps overstated his case, but his evaluation is nevertheless a fair assessment of the progress of underwater warfare between the Wars of Religion and the age of the democratic revolutions. During this time not a single machine to compare with Gianibelli's or Drebbel's did battle in Europe. Many were devised, some even constructed; but nothing like the hell-burners of Antwerp appeared to spread the news of underwater warfare.

One of the peculiarities of underwater warfare is that its essential ideas were always more important than any prototype constructed during the age of sail. Particularly is this true of the seventeenth century. Only the vaguest reconstruction of Drebbel's submarine is possible today, but its conceptual features have defied the worst workings of time. Propagation of these ideas in the peaceful years following the Wars of Religion was effected partly through the unstructured correspondence of Mersenne, partly through the peripatetic petitioning of the Kufflers. But more important still was the burgeoning scientific revolution and its concomitant institution, the scientific society. To understand how these milestones in the history of science contributed to the evolution of underwater warfare it is necessary to retreat briefly to the work of one of Drebbel's contemporaries.

Francis Bacon (1561–1626) flourished during Drebbel's years in England, and indirectly he contributed as much as did the Dutchman to the development of underwater warfare—or at least to the dissemination of its ideas. The essential facts of his political, literary, and scientific activities are well known, but his role in the emergence of modern science and technics is currently the subject of warm debate.[4] Part of the problem stems from the undifferentiated nature of science in the early seventeenth century. Natural philosophy, the contemporary term closest in meaning to the modern word science, was not yet clearly distinguishable from other intellectual disciplines—let alone from technics and magic. Bacon's philosophy was a mix of all of these, and it suffers today as much from etymological difficulties of interpretation as from any other. Herbert Butterfield has cut through the verbiage and provided enough of the essential features of the argument to satisfy this investigation. Said Butterfield:

> Bacon did not support a dead kind of empiricism; the empirics, he said, were like ants merely heaping up a collection of data. The natural philosophers still generally current in the world, however, were rather like spiders spinning their webs out of their own interior. He thought that the scientists ought to take up an intermediate position, like that of the bees, which extracted matter from the flowers and then refashioned it by their own efforts.[5]

The hive Bacon would have constructed for his scientists was sketched out as the House of Salomon in *New Atlantis*, written in 1623 and published posthumously in 1627. In this scientific utopia one of the Fathers of Salomon's House explained: "The end of our foundation is the knowledge of causes, and secret motions of things; and the enlarging of the bounds of human empire, to the effecting of all things possible."[6] In pursuit of this end the thirty-six fellows of Salomon's House performed distinct but cooperative tasks. The largest group of fellows consisted of the Merchants of Light, who traveled abroad collecting information. Three Depredators, or Pillagers, collected experiments from books; three Mystery-Men collected experiments from the crafts; three Compilers arranged and codified results, and so on.[7]

Among what Bacon's successors would call the philosophical apparatus of Salomon's House were all manner of laboratory and experimenting equipment and models of machines and devices. All was intended to contribute, directly or indirectly, to useful knowledge, but the definition of useful was extremely broad. Contrary to John U. Nef's picture of the seventeenth-century scientist as a pacifistic, intensely moral soul reluctant to use his skills for purposes of war, the Father of the House pointed out:

> We represent also ordnance and instruments of war, and engines of all kinds: and likewise new mixtures and compositions of gunpowder, wild-fires burning in water, and unquenchable. Also fire-works of all variety both for pleasure and use. We imitate also flights of birds; we have some degrees of flying in the air. We have

> ships and boats for going under water, and brooking of seas; also swimming girdles and supporters.[8]

Finally, Salomon's House contained two galleries: one to hold replicas and diagrams of all famous inventions, and one for the statues of all principal inventors. "For every invention of value," remarked the Father, "we erect a statue to the inventor, and give him a liberal and honorable reward."[9] Writing amidst the rubble of his political career and close upon the passage of the Statute of Monopolies, Bacon might well have been commenting here upon the stricter reins with which Parliament was then controlling such "inventors" as Drebbel.

Bacon never finished *New Atlantis*, nor did he see the House of Salomon realized. But within a half-century of his death there sprang up in its image the Royal Society of London, soon to be followed by similar academies all over Europe. Bacon used the expression "he rang the bell which called the wits together"—a fair assessment of his own role in the emergence of modern science. But one suspects he would have been more pleased to hear it said of him that he was "the veritable apostle of the learned societies."[10]

The origins of the Royal Society presaged its entire history. Shortly after the restoration of Charles II, the new monarch was called upon to grant a royal charter to an informal group of Englishmen interested in science. This club, a strange mixture of amateurs and academics, had been meeting for some years at Oxford, and later in London, to discuss current topics of scientific interest and to exchange news, ideas, and experiments.[11] The request for a charter was not just a bid for royal patronage, but was also an effort to institutionalize their activities on the Baconian model. As described in 1663 by Robert Hooke, one of the Society's most active and productive members, the corporate goals at the outset were very similar to those of Salomon's House:

> The business and design of the Royal Society is—
>
> To improve the knowledge of all naturall things, and all useful Arts, Manufactures, Mechanick practices, Engynes and Inventions and Experiments.. . . .
>
> To attempt the recovering of such allowable arts and inventions as are lost.

> To examine all systems, theories, principles, hypotheses, elements, histories and experiments of things naturall, mathematicall, and mechanicall, invented, recorded or practiced, by any considerable author ancient or modern.[12]

In pursuit of these ambitious goals the Society began publishing its *Philosophical Transactions* in 1665. This remarkable journal, published continuously to this day, is perhaps the most useful single record of the course of science in the Western world over the last three centuries.[13] Henry Oldenburg (c. 1615–1677), the first secretary of the Society and the first editor of its *Transactions*, sketched the purpose and design of the journal in terms fully as grand as Hooke's:

> It is . . . thought fit to employ the *Press*, as the most proper way to gratify those whose engagement in [Philosophical Matters], and delight in the advancement of Learning and profitable Discoveries, doth entitle them to the knowledge of what this Kingdom, or other parts of the World, do, from time to time, afford, as well as the Progress of the Studies, Labors, and attempts of the Curious and Learned in things of this kind, as of their complete Discoveries and Performances; To the end, that such Productions being clearly and truly communicated, desires after solide and useful knowledge may be further entertained, ingenious Endeavors and Undertakings cherished, and those, addicted to and conversant in such Matters, may be invited and encouraged to search, try, and find out new things, impart their knowledge to one another, and contribute what they can to the Grand Design of improving Natural Knowledge, and perfecting all Philosophical Arts, and Sciences.[14]

To fulfill this function Oldenburg carried on a correspondence that literally circled the globe. Sailors, colonists, adventurers, and explorers were encouraged to send back reports which would contribute to the pool of knowledge in London. Foreign publications were collected and reviewed. Articles were exchanged with the journals of foreign academies. An unsuccessful attempt was even made to have the Royal Society made into a patent review board for the crown. Failing this, the Society encouraged the "projectors" who haunted the halls of government in the seventeenth century to run their schemes by the fellows for unofficial approval. Scientists, artisans, and magicians alike were given a hearing, if only their offerings contributed some "solide and useful knowledge."

Abroad, the scene was much the same. The Royal Society had in fact been proceded by several short-lived academies in Italy, one of which was disbanded for a while because its members were suspected of poisonings and incantations.[15] But the continuing legacy really unfolded in France, where the *Académie des Sciences*, "the intellectual side of Colbertism,"[16] was formed in 1666 in the image of the Royal Society. A lineal descendant of Descarte's theories of scholarly collaboration (hardly distinguishable from Bacon's) and Mersenne's circle of friends and correspondents, the *Académie* imitated the Royal Society in many of its goals and activities, even to producing the rival *Journal des sçavans.*[17] Combined with the German academies which soon followed, the Royal Society and the *Académie des Sciences* helped to form the loom on which, in Herbert Butterfield's words, there flew a "shuttle running to and fro and weaving what was to become a different kind of Western culture."[18]

But all was not progress and light in the meeting rooms and laboratories of the new academies. For every two steps forward there was at least one back. Lynn Thorndike has noted that the spirit of the societies was "curious and credulous rather than skeptical and critical,"[19] and the very volume of the material they attracted and accumulated tended to preclude discriminating evaluation. Part of the problem stemmed from the large number of curious amateurs who peopled the academies, but the scientists were hardly less to blame. In the seventeenth century these men still indulged marvelous and wondrous notions of reality and were as anxious as their less sophisticated fellows to pursue the most fanciful experiments. Nevertheless, the societies should not be judged by standards of modern invention. In their own goals of collecting and disseminating knowledge they succeeded admirably.

The work of the Royal Society, and especially its contribution to underwater warfare, can perhaps best be understood through the work of Robert Boyle (1627–1691). Like the Society, Boyle was not especially interested in underwater warfare—except perhaps as a noteworthy curiosity. . Nevertheless, the record of this arcane weaponry intruded itself upon his work in the contributions it made to the study of air, respiration, explosives, and the natural history of the ocean. As underwater warfare crept into Boyle's work, so too did it creep into the proceedings of the Royal Society and the course of the scientific revolution. And through these channels it would be preserved and passed on to succeeding generations.

In many ways Boyle was the English counterpart of Marin Mersenne. He flourished in the second half of the seventeenth century instead of the first, and he operated in the institutional world of the academies. but in most else their careers were strikingly similar. Both were widely traveled and just as widely read, and both were recognized centers of vast circles of collaboration. Mersenne was a protégé of Descartes, Boyle the heir of Bacon. In their times and countries they were required visiting for all travelers of note. And both were important catalysts of scholarly activity, though Boyle had by far the larger list of credits for original work.[20]

Boyle's specialty was chemistry—of a much more modern variety than that practiced by Gianibelli or Drebbel.[21] In fact, he—along with Paracelsus in the preceding century and Lavoisier in the next—was largely responsible for leading modern science out of the alchemical maze. He dared to question the assumptions upon which the elaborate theories of medieval potion-making were erected. He pioneered thorough and carefully documented experiments which found the old theories wanting. And he contributed the notion of a *Skeptical Chymist* to the vocabulary of the scientific revolution.

The nature of air was one of his pet projects, indeed the one for which he is best remembered. In his day chemists were trying to discern what is was about air that made it conducive to burning and breathing. Several experimenters, including Boyle and Robert Hooke, had remarked upon the composite nature of air, but none had yet succeeded in identifying its components. Drebbel's procedure of isolating the then unknown oxygen by the burning of nitre had been tried inconclusively by several men. William Harvey's (1578–1657) discovery of circulation and its concomitant respiration had provided new and intriguing evidence, but no theoretical breakthrough. Boyle and his contemporaries were closer to the truth than the succeeding phlogiston school was to be, but they had no Lavoisier to synthesize the evidence.

Boyle's description of air, published in 1660, in fact sounds very similar to Lavoisier's more than a century later. Boyle said:

> there is in the air a little vital quintessence (if I may call it so) which serves to the refreshment and restoration of our vital spirits, for which uses the grosser and incomparably greater part of the air [is] . . . unserviceable.[22]

Of course this also sounds like Cornelius Drebbel, whose work was quite familiar to Boyle. Relying on the testimony of Johannes Kuffler and an intermediary who had talked to one of Drebbel's passengers, Boyle pieced together a fair understanding of the Dutchman's scheme. As he saw it,

> *Drebell* conceived, that it is not the whole body of air, but a certain quintessence . . . that makes it fit for respiration; which being spent, the remaining grosser body, or carcasse, if I may so call it, is unable to cherish the vital flame in the heart: . . . [Drebbel] had a chymical liquor, which he accounted the chief secret of his submarine navigation. For when . . . he perceived that the finer and purer part of the air was consumed . . . he would, by unstopping a vessel full of this liquor, speedily restore to the troubled air such a proportion of the vital parts, as would make it again . . . fit for respiration. . . .[23]

Boyle concluded by saying that "*Drebell* would never disclose the liquor unto any, nor so much as tell the matter whereof he had made it, to above one person, who himself assured me what it was." In 1604 Drebbel had published one scheme for releasing oxygen: burning saltpeter. But the method that Boyle was referring to was probably "burning of the spirits of wine."[24] Whichever method Boyle had in mind, Drebbel's use of it seems to have stimulated the great chemist in his own attempt to isolate oxygen.

Whatever Drebbel's role in the discovery of oxygen, this episode reveals another important feature of Boyle's career. He harbored no qualms whatsoever about dealing with artisans and mechanicians and engineers and magicians in his search for useful knowledge. In his classless egalitarianism he was much out of step with his times. A French dictionary in the seventeenth century deigned to note that the term *mechanic* "signifies that which is the opposite of liberal and honorable; it has the connotation of baseness and of being little worthy of an honest person."[25] To Boyle this was so much nonsense. "He deserves not the Knowledge of nature," Boyle lectured his fellows in the Royal Society, "that scorns to converse even with mean persons, that have the opportunity to be conversant with her."[26] Not only did he converse with them; he actively sought them out, in an attempt, as he put it, "to carry philosophical materials from the shops to the schools. . . ."[27]

Part of the opposition Boyle met in this endeavor stemmed from the widening breach between magic and science. As science came to be viewed, however vaguely at first, as a discriminating discipline of unique methods and standards, the would-be scientists also became aware of a discernibly different fellow-traveler: magic. In professional self-defense, they were wont to ascribe such patently unscientific nonsense to mechanics and wonder-workers. But because the line was still blurred at best, they continued throughout the seventeenth century to make mistakes in both directions—toward naive credulity on the one hand and toward narrow-minded skepticism on the other. If the members of the Royal Society detected legerdemain in the content of some proof or demonstration, they were likely to throw the baby out with the bath water. Equally often, in deference to Boyle and other neo-Baconian patrons of the crafts, they put the whole tub in the center of the meeting room floor to see if the dirty water would evaporate of its own power.

"In Boyle himself," Lynn Thorndike has observed, "we have an example *par excellence* of one beginning to shuffle off the mystic robes of the magician and putting on some of the habiliments of modern science."[28] Like the Royal Society he so clearly mirrored, Boyle entertained a variety of notions, from modern and scientific to medieval and credulous. In one instant he opened the door to modern chemistry; in the next he recommended investigation to see if "Diggers [i.e., miners] do ever really meet with subterraneous Daemons."[29] In lieu of discriminating carefully between the credible and the wonderful, Boyle collected all manner of interesting and curious reports and filed or published them as their merit or his whim seemed to dictate. And underwater warfare was no exception. We can only conjecture about the information on this subject he might have collected from the informed visitors who sought him out on trips to London. But the published material available to him, and the known resources of some of his associates, can at least suggest the range of information on underwater warfare then circulating about the English Channel and likely to pass through his study.

As has already been seen, Boyle had discussed Drebbel with the omnipresent Dr. Kuffler and had apparently been made privy to the secret of renewing the air. So too was he apprised of the more sinister side of Kuffler's inheritance. In fact his assistance was requested in diverting the doctor's interests to more productive paths. Samuel Hartlib (d. 1670?), a social critic and reformer well received in London scientific circles, wrote to Boyle in 1658 that Kuffler was reporting to him how "you had congratulated the success of his terrible destroying invention." The following year Hartlib asked Boyle to help dissuade Kuffler from "eager pursuits about his dreadful and destroying engine"; and he told at least one friend that Boyle had done this. We know that the Kufflers, including Johannes, continued their efforts in the 1660s, so this evidence seems somewhat contradictory.[30] What is clear is that Boyle knew about the "way to sink ships."

Another source of information on underwater warfare was John Wilkins (1614–1672), Bishop of Chester, organizer of the Royal Society, and a close friend of Boyle—who termed him "that Great and Learned Promoter of Experimental Philosophy."[31] In a volume revealingly entitled *Mathematical Magick* . . . (1648), Wilkins presented a chapter "Concerning the Possibility of Framing an Ark for Submarine Navigation. . . . "[32] In addition to some fanciful suggestions of his own, he displayed a familiarity with the current names and ideas in the field. He cited Drebbel as having proven the possibility of submarine navigation and included in his discussion some of Drebbel's contributions, such as compass, oars, etc. On air supply he cited Mersenne's references to "one Barriens, a Diver," who apparently used compressed air.[33] And in typical

Royal Society fashion he listed the useful purposes to which a submarine might be put, among which was the most common: "It may be of very great Advantage against a Navy of Enemies, who by this means may be undermined in the Water, and blown up."

Yet another source of information on underwater warfare available to Boyle was the writings of Gaspar Schott (1608–1666), whom Boyle styled "the industrious Jesuit."[34] A professor of physics and mathematics at Wurzburg, Schott was the author of widely circulated scientific popularizations which served to apprise Boyle of the important work on air pumps being done by Otto von Guericke.[35] Like Mersenne before him, Schott was a communicator and catalyst, and, like so many of his contemporaries, he mixed valuable science quite indiscriminately with curious magic. In this latter vein, Book IV of his *Technica Curiosa* . . . (1664), entitled "Mechanical Wonders, or New and Rare Machines," is a mine of information on underwater warfare and just the thing to attract Boyle's attention.[36]

Schott first of all gave a full description, with fold-out diagram, of the so-called Rotterdam Boat. This vessel was offered to the Belgian government in 1654 by a French engineer named DeSon. More than coincidentally similar to the craft proposed by Mer-

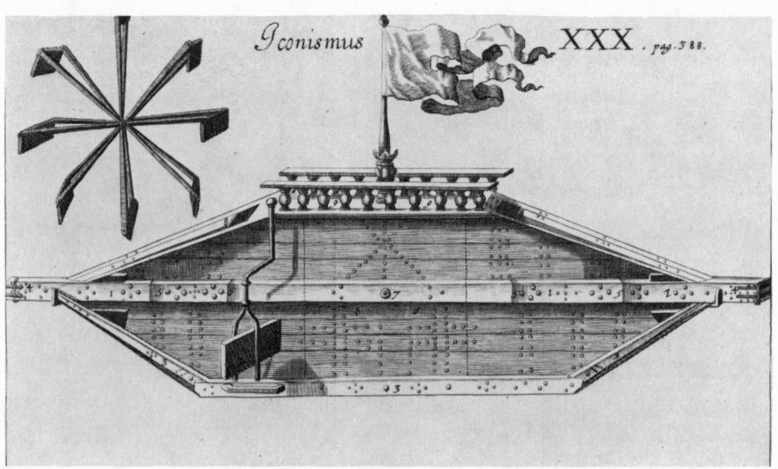

Figure 5. DeSon's "Rotterdam Boat" (1654) as it appeared in Gaspar Schott's *Technica Curiosa* . . . (1664).

senne, it was a double-ended, semisubmersible, paddle-wheeled warship, powered by a "*ressort*," or spring, which was said to be capable of running the vessel for eight hours. DeSon was reportedly "encouraged by the State" to build this machine, but when the day of demonstration arrived his boastful claims came to naught. The exhibition was canceled and nothing more was heard of the boat or its inventor.[37]

Schott also included a section on Drebbel which was a considerable improvement over earlier accounts. Not only did he cite Mersenne as a source, but he also cited George Philip Harsdorffer's *Delitiae Philosophicae et Mathematicae*. Harsdorffer was a contemporary of Drebbel and one of the first to get the submarine story into print. Furthermore, he had read Mersenne, Fournier, and even Drebbel's *Natur des Elementen* (1608 ed.), and he indulged the commendable habit of listing all his obligations.[38]

In his quest for the curious, Schott even resurrected Gianibelli's exploits at Antwerp.[39] His source in this case was P. Famianus Strada, whose account in *De Bello Belgico* has been a standard source on the events at Antwerp since it first appeared in 1632. Schott went on to mention still other dabblers in underwater warfare, but the examples given here will suffice to show the range of information likely to come within Boyle's ken.

Closer to home, the *Century of . . . Inventions . . .* (1655) by Edward Somerset, Second Marquis of Worcester, was sure to be known to Boyle. Item "ix" in this collection of curiosities was a clockwork "engine, portable in one's pocket," which could be fastened inside a ship and effect the vessel's destruction. Item "x" was "A way from a mile off to dive and fasten a like engine to any ship."[40] Worcester's biographer has researched the background of these "Inventions" carefully, and among the list of possible sources, he cites William Bourne's *Inuentions or Deuices* as one likely to appeal to the Marquis's taste for the curious.[41] Thus, in the late seventeenth century, not even the likes of William Bourne need be lost to the scientific community.

Even the submarine proposed by so remote a scientist as Giovanni-Alfonso Borelli (1608–1679) was not outside Boyle's purview. The Italian's *De Motu Animalum*, published posthumously in 1680, contained a proposal for a submarine to be raised or lowered by the simple expedient of filling or evacuating leather bags inside the craft. When filled with water they reduced the displacement of the vessel; when emptied through valves in the

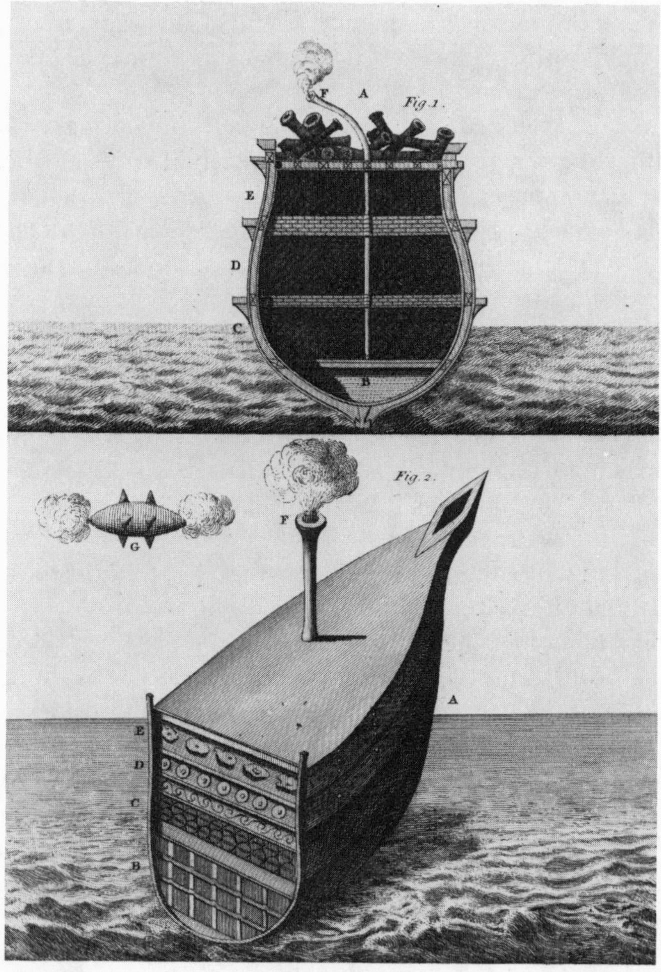

Figure 6. A century after Gianibelli's "hell-burners of Antwerp" blew up the Duke of Parma's bridge across the Scheldt River, the British were using the same principles in an attack on the fortified French seaport, St. Malo. This illustration from Francis Grose's *Military Antiquities* (1788) shows that the British too weighted down the explosive charge to direct its force horizontally. Compare with the exploding ship used at Fort Fisher in the U.S. Civil War (see figure 22). By then the lesson had been forgotten.

side of the craft they increased displacement.[42] Of the countless ways this proposal might have come to Boyle's attention, three examples will suffice to show how information traveled. Marcello Malpighi (1628–1694) was a countryman and close friend and associate of Borelli, whose enormous stream of correspondence with the Royal Society won him election as a fellow in 1668—one of the first foreigners to be so honored.[43] News of Borelli's inven-

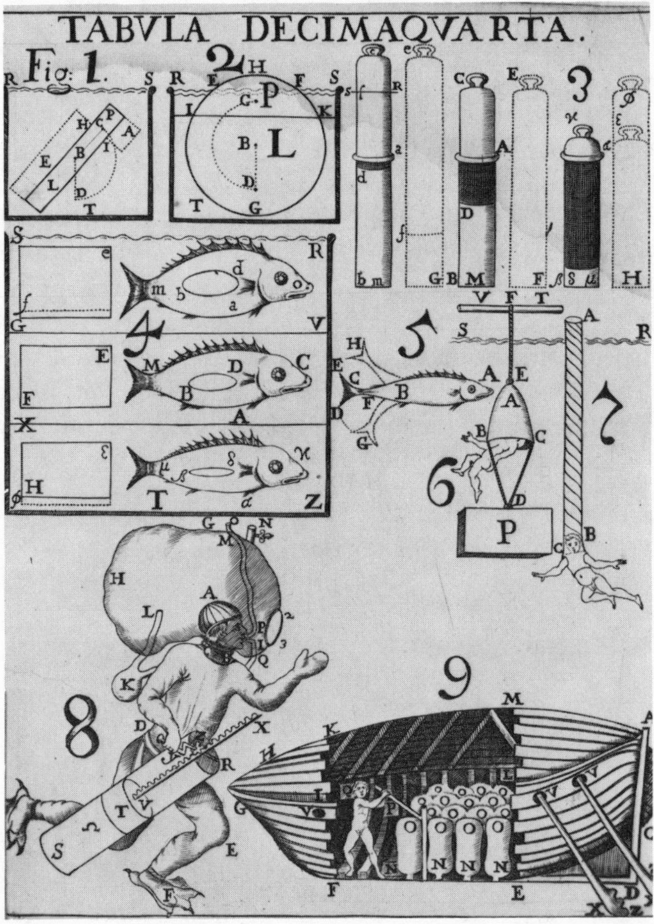

Figure 7. Giovanni Borelli's submarine and diving apparatus as they appeared in his *De Motu Animalum* (1680). Compare the submarine with the one that appeared in *Gentleman's Magazine* in 1749 (see figure 10).

tion might well have traveled in one of his missives to London. Or Boyle might have learned of it through his laboratory partner, Robert Hooke, who knew about Borelli's submarine in 1679 (a year before publication) and even conjectured that "it may be much like that which Mersenne long since published."[44] And if by some mischance notice of Borelli's work still escaped him, he could have read about it in the July 6, 1682 number of the *Journal des sçavans*, or even again in the August 6, 1683 number.[45]

To add more examples to this catalogue would only belabor the point. Robert Boyle—and, like him the Royal Society—sought out and attracted a vast array of "useful knowledge." Among this was most of the extant record of Europe's modern experience in underwater warfare. While Boyle and his colleagues had no military use for this information—living as they did in comparatively peaceful times—still they shared with William Bourne the belief that such knowledge should be used "to profit the common wealth." They published their information, not only in books and journals, but also in the meetings, conversations, and correspondence that kept them in touch with each other and with the rest of the scientific fraternity in Europe. Soon the record of underwater warfare would pass out of this select community to an even wider audience through a new and different medium.

IV

Denis Papin and Popularization

ROBERT BOYLE lifted knowledge "from the shops to the schools." The Enlightenment, following fast upon his death, returned science, in Alfred Cobban's words, "from the study to the market-place."[1] From the hands of scholars and aristocratic amateurs it was delivered to tinkerers and artisans and wonder-workers of every stripe. Having passed the barriers of language and politics, it now crossed the barriers of class and occupation. Swept up in this general diffusion of knowledge in the first half of the eighteenth century, the lore of underwater warfare collected and analyzed in Boyle's time was distributed to a new audience.

To understand how and why this happened, several tributaries of the mainstream of European history must be explored. A new kind of scientist emerged at the end of the seventeenth century. He enjoyed greater prestige and influence, and he entertained more liberal notions of the role of science in warfare. The public generally shared these views, but the military did not. Consequently, new weapons left the halls of academe by simple diffusion, but perforce entered the halls of government and the lists of battle by the back door. These changes are worth examining at some length, for they introduce the atmosphere in which underwater warfare would ultimately flourish.

Science dominated the early Enlightenment, and scientists were its early heroes. Isaac Newton (1642–1727), perhaps the premier scientist of all time, was honored and venerated in his own day as have been few men before or since. For generations to come, his magisterial analysis of the universe sent entranced converts in search of other such mechanisms—in nature, in society, and in man himself. More than just lending his name and his thought to the era which opened the eighteenth century, Newton helped to stamp the Enlightenment with a new confidence in man in general and science in particular.

But that was all the public Newton, and the public *Principia*. The private Newton was, in Lord Keynes wonderful phrase, "the last of the magicians." Cautious and secretive about his intuitions and suspicions, he closeted voluminous writings on alchemy, mysticism, numerology, and astrology. For every demonstrable law of nature he discovered, he harbored a marvelous set of metaphysical fancies and magical superstitions. As Keynes said:

> he looked on the whole universe and all that is in it as a riddle, as a secret which could be read by applying pure thought to certain evidence, certain mystic clues which God had laid about the world to allow a sort of philosopher's treasure hunt to the esoteric brotherhood. . . . He regarded the universe as a cryptogram set by the Almighty. . . . By pure thought, by concentration of mind, the riddle, he believed, would be revealed to the initiate.[2]

The public never knew this side of the man. Instead it fashioned an image to fit his published work and called that model a modern scientist. From this time on, Western man indulged the conceit that he could distinguish a scientist from a magician. While this has occasionally done injustice to both callings, it has nevertheless helped to foster measurable standards of scientific conduct and achievement. This in turn has further widened the gulf between science and magic.

This change in public thinking was not brought about by Newton himself, but by his popularizers. Few men in Newton's time were either willing or able to read and comprehend the *Principia*, so a band of generally competent scholars, perhaps two or three rungs below Newton in mental powers, translated his work into terms the educated layman could understand.[3] Not only did these popularizers perform great service by propagating Newton's explanation of the universe; they also in large measure molded the public image of the man behind the scholarship.

Aiding the popularizers in the spread of useful knowledge were the encyclopedias and the academies. The seventeenth century had been marked by what G. N. Clark called an "encyclopedia tendency"—a basic curiosity refined by a desire to interpret through classification.[4] Begun with Bacon's dream of a natural history of the world, impelled by the outlines of men like Boyle and Hooke, essayed in such early efforts as Bayle's *Dictionnaire* (1687) and Chambers's *Cyclopedia* (1728), and culminated in the epochal French *Encyclopédie* (1751–1772), this tendency led to a standardization and diffusion of knowledge never before achieved. So too did the academies continue to contribute to the same ends. "Scientific academies," said Peter Gay, "served as a model for the eighteenth century. The age of the Enlightenment was an age of academies . . . [when] intelligence, liberated from the bonds of tradition, or heedless of aesthetic scruples or religious restraints, devoted itself to practical results; it kept in touch with scientists and contributed to technological refinements."[5]

When this process led to the development of weapons, a new set of social norms faced the scientist.[6] The classical notion that scientific inquiry should not be demeaned by practical application, let alone destructive application, was giving way to the belief that improved weaponry could deter or at least shorten war. As the post-Newtonian, post-magician scientist emerged in the Enlightenment, he experienced few misgivings about using his talents to create or perfect the engines of war.

Of course, this new persuasion did not appear full-blown with the birth of the Enlightenment. Its origins extended well back into the seventeenth century. On Christmas Day in 1621 John Donne was already spreading the new gospel from the pulpit of Saint Paul's in London. By the "light of natural reason," he proclaimed, men "have found out artillery by which wars come to quicker ends than heretofore, and the great expense of blood is avoided: for the numbers of men slain now since the invention of artillery, are much less than before, when the sword was the executioner."[7] The logic here is of the *post hoc, ergo* . . . variety, but the thought itself appealed to the popular imagination.

Later in the century, the notion was applied not only to artillery, which had long since been dissociated from the devil's work, but to most other gunpowder engines as well. In a letter to Robert Boyle in 1680, John Beal congratulated the chemist on his efforts to deter Kuffler from selling "his destroying artifice." But then he changed tack abruptly and argued in the opposite direction:

> All antiquaries agree in it, that our wars have been less destructive, since our thundering artillery, than in former ages. . . . I know not what the French bombs were; but the sooner they forced a surrender, the more lives were saved on both sides. . . . If England should be in distress, I should pray for such terrifying engines, as would soon rout all our enemies. . . . Therefore I pray do not suffer your best inventions of defence or offence to die in your hands, but preserve them for our own day of need.[8]

Spawned in the seventeenth century, nurtured haphazardly through the scientific revolution, and brought into full bloom in the optimistic self-confidence of the Enlightenment, this same argument has since been rolled out and exercised to rationalize every conceivable instrument of war from the bayonet to the atomic bomb. Voiced by militarists and pacifists alike, it has been particularly popular among practitioners and historians of underwater warfare—has in fact been their most unflagging argument for new advances in the field. Commander Murray F. Sueter, himself a practitioner and historian, presented the reasoning at its paradoxical best when he said:

> War. . . .must be given her full attributes and painted in her most deadly colours in order that the misery which undoubtedly she brings to the majority of the population may extend over as short a period as possible. Let us make her as deadly as we can in the name of humanity and every good feeling.[9]

The argument flew in the face of man's dismal record of settling his disputes with other men, but when "all antiquaries agree," the scientist could hardly be expected to question their reading of the entrails.

Added to this most important rationalization, several other assumptions about weaponry emerged in the Enlightenment to counter prevailing notions of mild and restrained warfare. First, if war was a valid policy of government, as most agreed it was, then improvement of weapons was so much oil for the machine of state, and therefore a proper activity for the scientist. Furthermore, advanced civilizations were the most likely to produce the best weapons, and these were the very societies most likely to eschew warfare as an arbiter of foreign relations. Ergo, better weapons would go hand in glove with less war. Finally, Western man's sense of guilt was diminishing as the philosophers' attack on the superstitions of Christianity brought original sin and man's responsibility to God into serious question. All these influences were at work in society at large and on scientists in particular, leading them toward greater and greater contributions to weaponry.[10]

Not even international law protested this trend of thought, for its dominant contribution at this time was to raise necessity and "reasons of state" to new heights of importance. In 1737 Cornelius Bynkershock went so far as to assert that "every force is lawful in war. So true is this," he continued, "that we may destroy an enemy though he be unarmed, and for this purpose we may employ poison, an assassin, or incendiary bombs, though he is not provided with such things: in short everything is legitimate against an enemy."[11]

Other jurists tempered their readings with varying measures of humanitarianism, but could hardly escape the same final conclusion. Christian Wolff proclaimed that "we ought to love and cherish an enemy as ourselves," even going so far as to assert that "it is not allowable to have hostile feeling toward a public enemy." He advocated generosity and the use of only the force "sufficient" to achieve the ends of state. Unfortunately, "sufficient" is the operational version of "necessity"—a banner under which most any expedient can be justified. Upon that shifting foundation, Wolff erected the entirely logical conclusion that "it is just the same whether you kill [the enemy] with a sword or with poison, as is self-evident, since forsooth in either case he is removed from our midst."[12]

Wolff's inexorable logic settled poorly with another distinguished international jurist, Emer de Vattel, who observed in 1758:

> Certain writers have said if we have the right to deprive a person of life, the manner of doing so is a matter of indifference. Strange principles, fortunately condemned by even the vaguest ideas of honor![13]

Now honor was something to reckon with, surely an improvement over Wolff's suggestion of generosity. Beneath this pennant Vattel went so far as to recommend that "nations should mutually conform to certain rules," should decide outside the heat of battle what acts were beyond the pale of civilized warfare. This all sounds very civil and modern, but the "Catch 22" is that in the final analysis the sovereign in pursuit of a just end had "a right to make use of all means necessary to attain it." Vattel advocated "principles of humanity, forbearance, truthfulness, and honor"—all reminiscent of the chivalric tradition—but in no case could any of these be given absolute precedence over the ultimate arbiter: "necessity."[14]

So the scientist was servant to the prince and the prince was the sole judge of the needs of state. In this atmosphere no reason existed for the prince not to call on the scientist, and the scientist's professional and moral ethics were no longer a bar to his free participation.

What did block the scientist's contribution to war was the soldier. Content with the weapons at hand, suspicious of outside interference in his profession, and addicted still to chivalric apprehensions about infernal machines, the soldier erected a barrier to innovation behind such blanket epigrams as John Paul Jones's "Men mean more than guns in the fighting of a ship."

This peculiar intransigence is the more incongruous amidst the rise of the professional military engineer.[15] Though institutionally an outgrowth of the sappers and miners of siege warfare, these new specialists in the profession of arms were also lineal descendants of the *ingeniators* of the Leonardo mold. During the Enlightenment the term *engineer* came to encompass two separate subspecialties, as the new civil engineer became distinguishable from the older military engineer. Men like John Smeaton (1724–1792) combined scientific study with a wide range of technical and mechanical skills to set a pattern for the modern civil engineer, while men like Sébastien le Prestre de Vauban (1633–1707) combined the same scientific study with experience in siegecraft and fortress design and construction. Military writers in the late seventeenth and early eighteenth centuries were wont to catalogue in overly generous lists the skills a good engineer was expected to master. La Chesnaye-Desbois provided a modest example in his *Dictionnaire militaire*, citing geometry, fortification, architecture, mechanics, geography, physics, and history among the intellectual baggage of a good military engineer.[16] This not only demonstrates the growing compartmentalization of knowledge taking place in the eighteenth century, but also shows the high standards expected of those who would presume to take Vauban's place.

From all this one might assume that these new engineers would be the ideal conduits through which the new weaponry would pass from the academy to the battlefield. But this was not the case. La Chesnaye-Desbois observed

> that it is not easy for the *Engineers* to persuade men in favor of novelties; one does not rid himself easily of old habits, established by an error of long standing; and one does not surrender these habits readily for a truth only about to be born and having for its whole foundation only some promises of proven benefit.[17]

Just how difficult this task could be was discovered by Thomas Savery (c. 1650–1716) in England. A military engineer of wide interests and achievements and a minor figure in the development of the steam engine, Savery invented, patented, and demonstrated a paddle wheel turned by a man-powered capstan. An early version of the auxiliary engine, this simple device was intended to move ships in calm weather. But when he tried to sell it to the Navy Board, one of the members of that august body asked of him: "What have interloping people, that have no concern with us, to do to pretend to contrive or invent things for us?"[18]

This same arrogant, disdainful, clubbish self-satisfaction was also at work in Enlightenment armies, but it was particularly powerful in naval circles. Bred primarily of the continuing infatuation with the ship of the line, this view reflected the act of idolization at its worst.[19] In the seventeenth century an elaborate doctrine of naval warfare had grown up around the sailing and fighting characteristics of the ship of the line. Hard experience after the Armada had indicated that the column, or line ahead, was the most advantageous battle formation, but this generalization unfortunately became locked in dogma—as epitomized by the various editions of the English *Fighting Instructions*. The choreography of engagement was minutely planned and endlessly rehearsed. Textbook battles were hypothesized and chalked. Naval warfare came to be conducted by the numbers. Because the ship of the line was virtually unsinkable and because its utilization in these rituals was most conducive to stalemate, the ship in effect became a guarantor if not of success at least of survival. Battles might come and go, but the ship of the line sailed on, and so long as one had raised the proper pennants at the proper time, even defeat was tolerated. The unfortunate Admiral Sir John Byng was the exception that proved the rule. Court-martialed for his failure to relieve Minorca in 1756, Byng rightly claimed that he adhered scrupulously to the *Fighting Instructions*. The Navy could not well admit that such adherence resulted in failure, so they shot him for not doing "his utmost." Men might err, but never the infallible doctrine.

In this stale atmosphere of musty regulations and moldy tradition, talk of a different kind of warfare was absolute heresy. Naval officers had been trained to master one kind of ship and one method of fighting her. Twenty or thirty years might have been spent learning how to act out one programmed role, and the senior officer was reluctant to see the script changed when he was waiting in the wings for his moment upon the stage. Having spent the better part of one's life preparing for one role, it was unbearable to contemplate the role becoming obsolete. Because service life preselected people who subscribed to this view of reality, the senior ranks were virtually devoid of serious advocates of change.

Blocked by this self-satisfied conservatism, inventions from the study had to find new routes to acceptance. The answer—in addition to the books, correspondence, journals, travels, and conversation that continued to flourish throughout the age of sail—was the popular magazine. In England such familiar periodicals as *Tatler*, *Guardian*, *Spectator*, and *Examiner* heralded a new era in the history of the printed word, an era just today succumbing to radio and television. These magazines reflected the growing literacy and curiosity of the people of Western Europe, and the efforts of men like Mersenne and Robert Boyle to encourage wider use of the vernacular in print. All manner of entertainment and information filled these new periodicals, not the least of it being scientific. As Addison put it in the tenth number of the *Spectator*:

> It was said of *Socrates*, that he brought Philosophy down from Heaven, to inhabit among Men; and I shall be ambitious to have it said of me, that I have brought Philosophy out of Closets and Libraries, Schools and Colleges, to dwell in Clubs and Assemblies, at Tea-Tables, and in Coffee-Houses.[20]

This, then, completed the cycle. The scientist, liberated from moral apprehensions about contributing to the works of war, enlisted freely in the service of the state. The weapons he produced were blocked from useful application by military reluctance to change the rules or tools of the game. So news of the weapons was distributed by other media—particularly the new popular magazines—to be sown in other fields, harvested by other workers, and marketed by other vendors.

In the case of underwater warfare, the cycle was picked up in the study of Robert Boyle and in the halls of the Royal Society by Denis Papin (1647–1712). As John U. Nef has observed, Papin "illustrates the new freedom of international communications that brought the leading scientific minds of Europe into direct personal relations"[21] From the very outset he was surrounded by the people and institutions that were maintaining the record of underwater warfare. He began his scientific career as a laboratory assistant to Christian Huygens (1629–1695) at the *Académie des Sciences*. Huygens, the younger and more famous son of Drebbel's close friend Constantyn, had displayed an early penchant for science and engineering, prompting Mersenne to call him "*le petit Archimede*."[22] In 1663 he became one of the first foreign members of the Royal Society of London, and three years later he became the only foreigner among the original membership of the *Académie des Sciences* and one of the first to enjoy membership in both of these premier institutions.

In 1675 Papin left Huygens's laboratory and went to London where he worked some years with Robert Boyle. In 1679 he was employed by Robert Hooke at the Royal Society (just when

Hooke was commenting on Borelli's *De Motu Animalum*), and in 1680 he won election to the Royal Society in his own right. That same year he went back to Paris for more work with Huygens, and from 1681 to 1684 he served as curator of a scientific society in Venice. After yet another sojourn in England, Papin accepted the chair of mathematics at Marburg in Germany and settled there for some years.

With this background and exposure he was just the man to execute a project for his local prince, the Landgrave Charles of Hesse-Cassel. As Papin explained the proposition: "Drebbel's submarine had made such a noise in the world, so many Authors had spoken of it, and it seemed that one ought to expect from it so many uses of such great consequence, that S. A. S. Charles Landgrave of Hesse has not disdained to have the Invention perfected."[23] Papin not only perfected a design for the Landgrave, he actually built two of the submarines, the second being an improved version of the first, which was destroyed in an accident. In 1695, Papin published descriptions and diagrams of the two machines in a little volume entitled *Recueil de diverse Pieces. . .* ,[24] much as Bourne had published his plans more than a century earlier.

The first machine was a metal box measuring five and three-fourths by five and one-half by two and one-half feet. Made of tin reinforced with iron bars, it featured oars, a "Barometer," detachable ballast, and holes through which one could "touch enemy vessels and ruin them in sundry ways." A tube reached from the surface into the boat and ultimately to a pump with intake and exhaust valves. Through this mechanism the operator could simultaneously pressurize the craft and refresh the air. The latter function is precisely what the abbé de Haute-Feuille had suggested in his critique of Drebbel and what Mersenne proposed as his solution of the problem. The pressurization feature allowed seacocks to be opened and water to be admitted to match the interal pressure. The pressure controlled the amount of water that entered, and this in turn controlled the displacement. When running on the surface, a mast and sail were raised and the vessel plowed along awash.

The second submarine was a wooden craft, ellipsoidal in shape, six feet high with a radius varying from three to six feet. Intended for operation by two or more men, this vessel was considered by Papin to be "easier to make, and also to put into use." The major difference from the earlier model was that the entire vessel was sealed for diving, and only a large cylinder attached horizontally to

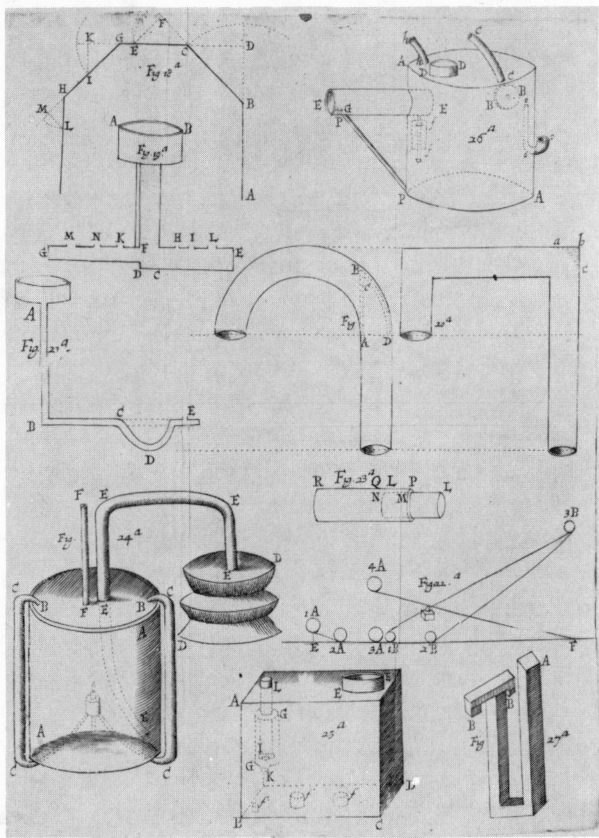

Figure 8. Denis Papin's submarines as they appeared in his *Recueil des diverses Pieces . . .* (1695). Compare his second submarine (upper right) with the illustration in *Gentleman's Magazine* of December 1747 (see figure 9). Also note the similarities of his two designs with Bushnell's *Turtle* (see figure 11). Papin's first, metallic submarine (lower center) had in common with Bushnell's craft a hatch (E) on top, holes in the bottom (f) for admitting and discharging water and for passing oars through the hull, and an air pump (GG) for pressurizing the cabin and renewing the air. Papin's second, wooden craft (upper right) had in common with the *Turtle* a barometer (O), a bellows (B) for drawing air into the craft, intake (c) and exhaust (h) tubes, and an air pump (f) for pressurizing the cylinder (E).

the side of the craft was used to vary displacement. One pump connected with tubes to the surface now refreshed the air in the cabin, while another flooded or pumped out the attached cylinder—really an early version of the modern ballast tank. It was also through this appendage that attacks were to be made on enemy vessels.

A true representative of the scientists of his day, Papin was most intrigued with the question of air supply, which he described at the outset as "a great problem." He considered Drebbel's "liquor" to have been so much wishful thinking, and he took some pains to convince Gottfried von Liebnitz (1646–1716) of his persuasion. Liebnitz wrote to Papin saying he had talked to Boyle, to one of Drebbel's daughters, and to her husband, all of whom attested to Drebbel's accomplishments but were unable (or unwilling) to tell him how Drebbel refreshed the air. Liebnitz posited that Drebbel had burned "spirits of wine," and he solicited Papin's opinion. Papin relieved him of this fancy, and cited his own experiments as proof of his position.[25] From this it would appear that even if Papin had read Haute-Feuille or Mersenne—as seems likely—he still did his own tests to be sure.

When the second machine was ready, Papin made a successful demonstration for the Landgrave, and though it had some weaknesses it nevertheless met with the prince's approval. Papin wanted to improve the machine still further and correct the defects discovered in the demonstration, but "it was then the season to take the field . . . and [the Landgrave] needed his workers for other, more pressing affairs." So the Enlightenment scientist with a nearly perfected weapon fell short of having his device adopted by the military arm of government. Like other such weapons in the eighteenth century, underwater warfare was not to pass directly from the scientist to the soldier, but would follow instead a different course.

As has been intimated, the popular magazine was the medium through which these ideas were next to pass—in this case Sylvanus Urban's *Gentleman's Magazine*. Begun in 1731 and not retired until the twentieth century, *Gentleman's Magazine*'s expressed purpose at inception was "to give Monthly a View of all the Pieces of Wit, Humour, or Intelligence, daily offer'd to the Publick in the

News-papers . . . [and to] join therewith some other matters of Use or Amusement that will be communicated to us."[26] Noting that there were over two hundred papers per month in London alone, and another two hundred or so scattered around the rest of England, Scotland, and Ireland, Urban set up his magazine as a digest of the British press.

In the December 1747 number, under the heading: "Two of the Marquis of Worcesters century of inventions," there appeared Somerset's original articles nine and ten dealing with the machine for sinking ships and the way to dive and attach the engine. As a solution to the second problem, *Gentleman's Magazine* presented the reader with an English condensation—including diagram—of Papin's second submarine. Some of the peripheral material in the original article in Papin's *Recueil* had been deleted, but all the essential features of the craft were explained. Papin's name was given, but not the title of his book.[27] This clearly brought a weapon designed by a scientist before a new and wider public, and that public soon showed its interest.

Two years later, in the June 1749 number, there appeared a letter from "T. M." questioning how the water was to be pumped out of

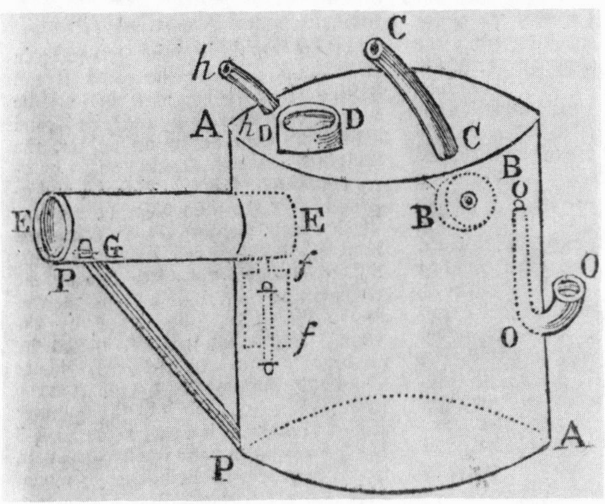

Figure 9. Diagram of Denis Papin's second submarine as it appeared in the December 1747 issue of *Gentleman's Magazine*. Compare with the original of 1695 (see figure 8).

Papin's vessel. In answer to his own question, he forwarded a solution developed by "M. Marriott." This turned out to be Borelli's collapsible bags. In fact, he even enclosed a diagram which was a reversed copy of the original diagram Borelli published in 1680.[28] Here the original source went unmentioned, an indication that Urban's standards of acknowledgment were higher than some of his readers.

The following month Samuel Ley wrote to inform the readers that the vessel described by "T. M." was inferior to one built by Nathaniel Symons, a Devon carpenter. Ley hadn't seen the submarine, but as he recalled descriptions of it, it was made with inner and outer walls joined by leather. Of course, that also describes William Bourne's essential idea, and it is quite possible that he was being plagiarized with the same anonymity as had been Borelli. In any case, Ley went on to say that Symons also invented a diving bell for salvage work, "tho' his cousin L——e, and some others, deprived him both of the honour and the profit."[29]

This closing insult brought a letter from John Lethbridge of Devon, dated 19 September 1749. In it he claimed to be the inventor of the self-contained diving bell, a machine he proceeded to describe. It was little more than a wooden, iron-reinforced cylinder six feet long and eighteen to twenty-four inches in diame-

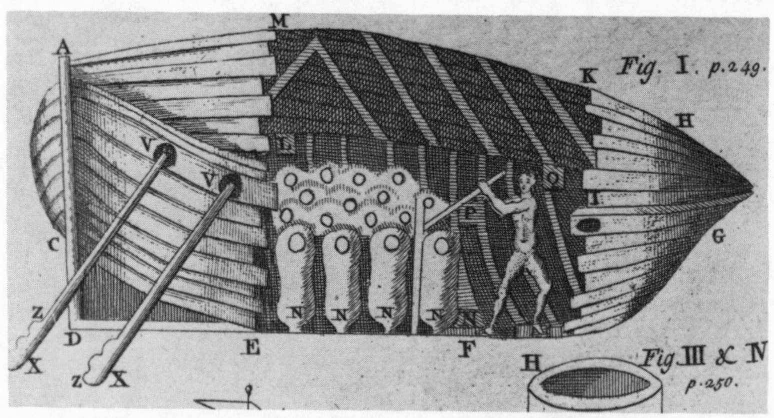

Figure 10. Giovanni Borelli's submarine as it was pictured in the June 1749 issue of *Gentleman's Magazine.* Compare this with the 1680 original (see figure 7).

ter. He hinted at having used compressed air and claimed to have stayed under water for thirty-four minutes. He credited William Phipps (1651–1695) with the original invention of the diving bell (not true, but a commendable acknowledgment nonetheless), and added that the Royal Society's famous astronomer William Halley (1656–1742)—with whom he had consulted—had made significant improvements in this field. In conclusion he avowed that Symons came to observe his work; Symons was the thief, not he.[30]

Whoever the thief was, the goal of men like Addison and Sylvanus Urban had been achieved. Through their magazines, science was being distributed to all kinds of shops and stands: it truly had descended "from the study to the market-place." Perhaps some credits were lost and some acknowledgments overlooked, but in that regard the magazines were hardly more culpable than the scholars they plagiarized. The ideas were the important thing, and they were moving ever faster, ever farther.

V

David Bushnell: Transplanting the European Experience

RUNNING BACK AND FORTH across the English Channel, the shuttle described by Herbert Butterfield was weaving a rich and colorful material in Western Europe.[1] Countries entangled themselves in scientific collaboration. New ideas spread quickly and widely. New fabric continued to flow smoothly from the loom, almost oblivious to affairs of state or upheavals in the European peace.

At the beginning of the eighteenth century the colonial satellites of Western civilization faced enormous obstacles in their attempts to imitate the science of Europe. Colonists who went forth from the lands about the English Channel carried with them as much of their culture as they could, but it was seldom enough to re-create the original on foreign shores. They could take books and magazines within reason, even some scientific apparatus; but they could not take the salons and coffee houses of Paris, nor the clubs and taverns of London. So what they wrought in the wilderness was a crude and irregular copy of the original's best-remembered features.

The English colonies in North America enjoyed the greatest advantages. Hugging the seacoast only twenty-five hundred miles from the Royal Society, they were most likely to make the best replica of the European model. And indeed they did, but not without their own irregularities. Any colonization was fraught with dangers peculiar to the new environment, and not even the New England colonies were an exception. A case in point is the ordeal of Governor Gurdon Saltonstall of the crown colony of Connecticut, who was forced to rush to the coastal town of Saybrook on 4 December 1718 to head off a crisis. Upon his arrival he issued an order to the militia Major of New London County. It read in part:

> there is a very great danger of the Peace being broken, by great & Notorious acts of Violence.
>
> You are hereby Commanded in his Majesties name, to cause your Drums to be beaten forthwith, and give order to all the officers and souldiers in the Train band, in your Town, to appear immediately in their Arms, who are hereby required to obey your Command, and have them ready to attend you in the execution of such orders as you shall receive from me, for the preventing of all such riotous doings & mutinous proceedings. And hereof fail not, at your Peril.[2]

The nub of this crisis was not Indians nor taxes nor witches, nor any such familiar disrupters of colonial tranquility. It was books. The Collegiate School of Connecticut had been located in Saybrook since its founding in 1701. But this site was unacceptable to some early faculty members, and by 1716 classes were being held in several different communities.[3] In that year the trustees elected to establish the college permanently in New Haven, partly because of a land grant from that town, and partly because of the wishes of some of the college's benefactors (the most generous of whom was Elihu Yale, a figure almost as obscure as John Harvard). Two years later the new library was ready and the custodian of the college's books was directed to deliver his charge. With most of Saybrook behind him, he refused, thus precipitating Governor Saltonstall's crisis of 4 December.

The books in question, about thirteen hundred volumes, were primarily gifts received by the college during its first fifteen years. The most important donation had been collected by Jeremiah Dummer, Connecticut's colonial agent in London, and presented to the college in 1714. Solicited largely from luminaries of the Royal Society, this seven-hundred-volume collection was a great source of pride to the college and to the townsfolk of Saybrook. When the sheriff came to remove these books to New Haven, he was asking the town to yield its most prestigious asset. He was turned away empty-handed. When he returned for a second try he still had to "break doors and call assistance."[4] And, during the night, the carts loaded with books were smashed and the horses were released. It was at this point that Governor Saltonstall called out the local militia. Even then the bridges between Saybrook and New Haven were broken up, and it finally took three days to get the precious cargo just thirty miles down the coast. An inventory in New Haven revealed that about a fifth of the volumes were missing.

In the history of underwater warfare this episode would have little relevance were it not that half a century later a native of this little seacoast town that cherished its books would travel those same thirty miles to that same Yale College and there take up the heritage of Gianibelli and Bourne, Drebbel and Papin. That he came from the seaport town of Saybrook and went to Yale is more than just coincidence.

As a field in which science might take root, Connecticut differed perhaps in degree but not in kind from the other English colonies clutching the coast of North America.[5] All to a greater or lesser extent experimented in transplanting the European experience to the new world. As it did for Europe, the Royal Society of London provided the great model and the largest stimulant for this activity. It was in fact because of national ties to this institution that science proceeded more quickly in the North American colonies that it did in other European satellites. Before the American nation was born, no less than seventeen American colonists had been elected fellows of the Royal Society, and of course these were only the more successful among the many who poured their reports and papers into the Society hoping to garner such an honor.

Natural history provided for the colonists the easiest access to the halls and publications of the Royal Society. The New World was new indeed, and the colonists could speak authoritatively to the European fellows about the flora and fauna, as well as the local geography, geology, and climate—all subjects of interest back in London. For this reason the natural historians dominated American science well into the eighteenth century, and it was in this field that many fellowships in the Royal Society were won.[6]

But natural philosophy was not entirely ignored. The prime example is John Winthrop, Jr. (1606–1676). One of four distinguished John Winthrops in colonial America, this dean of the family was a member of the circle of London scientists that ultimately became the Royal Society. He fled England during the reign of Charles I, played a substantial role in the colonization of Massachusetts, and became the first governor of Connecticut. A distinguished physician and chemist, he did extensive work in metallurgy and became the first colonist elected to membership in the Royal Society.[7]

In his wake followed other natural philosophers intent upon expanding the colonial model of European science—especially in the eighteenth century. When the forerunner of Yale opened in 1701, only two other colleges were operating in the colonies. By the time of the Revolution there were nine.[8] Gifts like the Dummer collection helped to fill their libraries, and private collections grew at a similar pace. In addition to books by the leading figures of the scientific revolution, these libraries also contained runs or abridgments of that most comprehensive repository of Western science, the *Philosophical Transactions*. When news of the establishment of Yale at New Haven reached Dummer in London, he sent back his congratulations, conveyed Mr. Yale's satisfaction, and informed Governor Saltonstall that "he'l send . . . another parcel of books, part of which he has promis'd me shall be the Royal transactions in seventeen Volumes."[9]

Not all libraries were as complete as Benjamin Franklin's, nor were all scholars as adept at using them. But colonial America's greatest scientist at least demonstrates the standards to which others might aspire. He was asked in 1788 to pass on the originality of a proposal for stoking furnaces. As soon as he saw the drawings he said he had several books in his library which could show that the device wasn't original. Thereafter he pulled down three volumes from his shelves and traced through them the one-hundred-year history of the invention, from its origins in Italy through its transfer to France and its later dissemination to Germany and Sweden. As an extra cap on the matter he was able to recall that a Spanish visitor some forty years back had provided him with drawings of the same device and told him it was in use in Mexico.[10]

Such was the success with which useful knowledge was being propagated in the eighteenth century. What is perhaps most remarkable about this incident is that Franklin was able to cite personal conversation as a source of information. Not even that facet of European scientific collaboration was denied to the colonists. Another case of the same phenomenon is Isaac Greenwood, who was sent to London in 1723 to broaden his Harvard education by studying with J. T. Desagulier (1683–1744). This distinguished natural philosopher was one of Newton's most important popularizers and a dabbler in underwater warfare in his own right. While studying under him, Greenwood met Thomas Hollis, who appointed the young scholar to hold the first chair in science to be established in the colonies—the Hollis Chair at Harvard. Greenwood's successor in this chair was John Winthrop (1714–1779), "Colonial Harvard's finest flower in the field of science."[11] One can only conjecture on the information that flowed through channels like these.

Add to this sketch the popular magazines, and one has a fair picture of the growing similarity between European and colonial American science by the middle of the eighteenth century. In 1733 Bishop Berkeley made a large contribution of books to Yale, and included in the lot such journals as *Tatler*, *Spectator*, and *Guardian*. Similar collections graced other libraries. *Gentleman's Magazine*, the most popular and widely read periodical in the New World, helped maintain its colonial circulation by publishing an unusual number of American articles. And of course local newspapers and periodicals sprang up at population centers all over the colonies.[12]

The advance of science in America was also met with its share of false starts and failed ambitions. Numerous attempts to form scientific societies failed at birthing. Astronomical observations were few in number and generally discounted in Europe. And popular periodicals printed in the colonies enjoyed little more than local circulation.

All of that changed with the transit of Venus in 1769. If accurate observations of the transit could be made, a close value for the solar parallax could be calculated. Europeans were interested in American data and encouraged the colonists to make observations. Within the colonies a campaign was launched to incite interest and to spread information. Though the results were not as heartening as might have been expected from all this activity, the event nevertheless enhanced the reputation of American scientists, both in Europe and in the colonies.[13]

In the same year, Benjamin Franklin successfully transformed a small scientific circle in Philadelphia into the American Philosophical Society, the first permanent imitation of the Royal Society in the colonies. The members of this new body had been meeting for some years to exchange books and ideas, much as the Royal Society had a century earlier, but not until 1769 did Franklin finally manage to institutionalize their collaboration. Also in the same year there appeared Lewis Nicola's *American Magazine of 1769*, the only important intercolonial periodical to appear before the Revolution.[14]

In this most propitious of years for colonial science, underwater warfare was rescued from obscurity by David Bushnell. Born in Westbrook, Connecticut (then a subdivision of Saybrook) in 1740, Bushnell grew up in the poverty of a small, marginally profitable farm.[15] When his father died and his remaining family obligations were relieved, he sold his meager patrimony to his brother Ezra and submitted to the tutorship of John Devotion in 1769. Devotion was the local Congregational minister, a graduate of Yale (class of 1754), and the logical community figure to prepare Bushnell for admission to his alma mater.[16] After two years of study, the young man entered the Yale class of 1775 at the age of thirty-one. Before his first semester was completed he was experimenting in underwater warfare.

How he may have been attracted to such pursuits is a matter for conjecture. His biographer claims that all of his work was original, and most other authorities in the field tend to agree. Argument to the contrary would have to rely upon an examination of the books, periodicals, journals, and conversation available to Bushnell—and unfortunately this evidence is extremely fragmented where it exists at all.

The best single source of evidence is the Yale library of 1771–1775, but its history during the Revolution precludes any final judgments. Catalogues of the library for 1742, 1755, and 1790 are in existence, but during the war years the library was broken up and distributed around the colony to prevent its loss or destruction at the hands of the British. When it came to be reassembled after the war, it looked as though it had suffered as much in friendly hands as it would have in the enemy's. While there were a thousand volumes in 1718, twenty-six hundred in 1742, and four thousand in 1766, there were only twenty-seven hundred in 1790. How many of those 1790 volumes were postwar acquisitions we cannot tell. Some loyalist students had even stolen volumes outright at the opening of hostilities, and this pilferage, coupled with the negligence or avarice of the friends of the library, worked a substantial loss on the holdings. It is now impossible to reconstruct the library of 1771.[17]

In spite of this lack of evidence, some conclusions can be reached. Bushnell's biographer has noted that the Birch edition of Boyle's works then in the library would tell Bushnell very little about Drebbel's submarine. This is true enough, but it only clouds the issue. Bushnell did not start with the submarine. The underwater explosion was the foundation of all his work. He began with it, and he turned to the submarine only as a means of delivering the explosion to the vulnerable point. When forced to abandon the submarine in 1777, he turned to towed and drifting mines to deliver the explosion. He first experimented detonating two ounces of gunpowder under water. Then he moved on to "large quantities of powder," all of which, he said, "produced very violent explosions, much more than sufficient for any purpose I had in view."[18]

This bit of eighteenth-century science he most assuredly could have learned from the resources available to him in the Yale library. Robert Hooke discussed the nature of explosions in his *Posthumous Works*. Bishop Sprat presented histories of saltpeter and gunpowder in his *History of the Royal–society*. And, most importantly, Robert Boyle described burning and explosions in a vacuum and underwater in his *New Experiments Physico–Mechanicall* . . . (1660) and in *Tracts* . . . (1672). The Yale library had all these works, the latter two both individually and as part of Boyle's *Philosophical Works* (6 vols., 1772).[19] Or Bushnell might have pulled from the shelves Bacon's *New Atlantis* and discovered there the references by the Father of the House of Salomon to "wildfires burning in water" and "ships and boats for going under water."[20] This work made no specific mention of Drebbel, who was demonstrating his boat on the Thames just when Bacon was writing—but Ben Jonson did. In his "Staple of the News," he reported on "Cornelius-Son," describing his craft as "an automa . . . [that] runs under water," an "invisible eel" able

> To swim the haven at Dunkirk, and sink all
> The shipping there.[21]

A copy of this work was also available in the Yale library in Bushnell's day.

Bacon and Johnson were inspirational perhaps, but short on specifics. If Bushnell wanted to learn the mechanics of submarining, he had to return to the Royal Society and its sturdy pillar, Robert Boyle. In that 1772 edition of Boyle's *Philosophical Works* it was made explicit that Drebbel was "the inventor of submarine navigation," and it was undertaken to present "some particulars of his invention."[22] In his *New Experiments Physico-Mechanicall* . . . , Boyle discussed not only the theory of buoyancy and displacement—"the grand rule of Hydrostaticks," he called it—but also the specific achievements of Drebbel. His eye was ever on the theory, his greatest interest ever in determining the nature of air, as Drebbel claimed to have done. But information like that was also grist for Bushnell's mill.

These sources, known to have been in the Yale library in Bushnell's time, could have instructed him rather thoroughly in underwater explosions—the foundation of his work—and they could have inspired him to construct a submarine. Boyle might even have conveyed to him the underlying principles of buoyancy and the suggestion of how Drebbel built and operated his boat. But none of these works can fully account for the submarine Bushnell designed and built.

The *Turtle*, named for its peculiar shape, was seven and one-half feet long and six feet high, constructed of two, roughly ellipsoidal wooden shells covered with tar.[23] On the top was a crude conning tower with several glass windows, three sealable air vents, and a brass hatch. The structure was reinforced by an internal beam across the center and by external iron bands around the hull and hatch opening. It was powered manually—in both the vertical and horizontal planes—by sets of paired oars or vanes ("formed upon the principle of the screw"),[24] and was steered in the horizontal plane by rudder and tiller. Submersion and surfacing were accomplished by means of a foot-operated valve and water pump which allowed admission and discharge of water from inside the craft. As a safety device to facilitate emergency surfacing, two hundred of the nine hundred pounds of lead ballast could be quickly dropped to the ocean floor. Auxiliary features included two brass air pipes with an attached ventilator for snorkeling, a compass, and a "water gauge or barometer."

For this remarkable machine Bushnell had been dubbed "Father of Submarine Warfare."[25] He has been credited with all manner of achievements he never claimed for himself; his predecessors have been written off as barren dreamers. Bernard and Fawn Brodie, for example, state that Bushnell's submarine "was greatly improved over the amusing device of Cornelius Drebbel,"[26] though it is hard to say just what they find amusing in Drebbel's vessel when about all we know of it for sure is that it worked. So too does Brooke Hindle miss the mark in his *Pursuit of Science in Revolutionary America, 1735–1789*. He calls the *Turtle* "undoubtedly the greatest of the wartime inventions," but fails to explain its relationship to science.[27] More erroneous still are the claims of Bushnell's biographer, who says of the *Turtle*:

> it was the first truly practical submarine in the history of all mankind, and the first submarine ever designed for offensive warfare. In addition, Bushnell devised and put into action the first mines ever used in underwater warfare.[28]

If Drebbel, Mersenne, DeSon, and Papin would be discomforted to hear that, they would be outraged to hear John S. Barnes say: "Bushnell certainly knew nothing of them, so that his submarine boat may justly be considered an entirely original conception."[29]

The known holdings of the Yale library in Bushnell's time make that the most doubtful of assertions. Adding to that doubt is the striking similarity between Bushnell's *Turtle* and the two submarines built by Denis Papin at the end of the seventeenth century. Like both of Papin's vessels, Bushnell's had a single hatch on top, a barometer for depth measurement, and a type of oar arrangement for depth maintenance and propulsion. Also like both vessels—and the Drebbel boat they were modeled on—Bushnell's craft was intended to sink ships. Like Papin's second boat, it was made of wood, in roughly oval shape, in approximately the same six-by-six-by-three foot dimensions. Like Papin's first craft, it was a one-man affair, reinforced externally with iron bands and internally with wooden braces, and it submerged and surfaced by varying the amount of water that was allowed to enter the cabin.[30]

Even where Bushnell abandoned or modified Papin's design, the alterations were suggested by Papin. Bushnell used copper instead of leather gaskets, but Papin had suggested copper for his

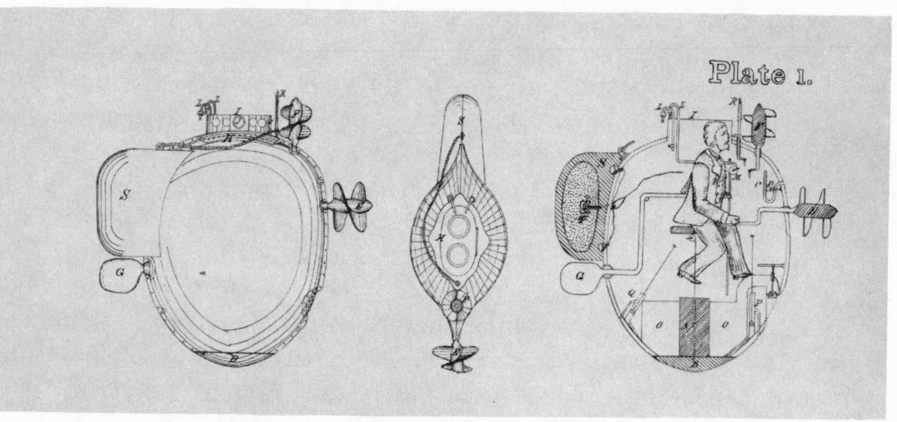

Figure 11. Lieutenant Francis M. Barber, USN, prepared this drawing of Bushnell's *Turtle* to illustrate his *Lecture on Submarine Boats* (1875). Compare it with Denis Papin's designs of 1695 (see figure 8). In common with one or both of Papin's boats, the *Turtle* had a hatch (I) on top, tubes (LL) and a pump (M) for drawing in and exhausting air, a hole in the bottom for admitting water, and forcing pumps (Q, P) for discharging water. Unfortunately, Barber also introduced some mistakes. His operator is dressed in decidedly nineteenth-century fashion, and, more importantly, Barber added a ballast tank (O) to contain the water to vary displacement. Bushnell actually let the water come directly into the cabin, as Papin had done in his first design. Barber also missed Bushnell's injunction that "every horizontal section, although elliptical, [was] yet as near to a circle, as could be admitted." This would have made Barber's drawing look much more like Papin's.

appended ballast tank and was in fact using leather gaskets only because Drebbel had. Technologically and chronologically Papin stood midway between Drebbel and Bushnell. The boats of all three were similar in principle, but Bushnell's was by far the most sophisticated because it drew upon a greatly refined technology. Papin pointed the way to these advances but clung to Drebbel's design in his own craft because that was his assignment.

The overwhelming similarity of Bushnell's ideas with Papin's suggests that he saw *Recueil des diverses Pieces . . .* or the extract in *Gentleman's Magazine* or both. But there is no record that either was in the Yale library during Bushnell's matriculation. Is it fair to assume that either or both were in the library in Bushnell's time and then lost during the war?

In the case of *Gentleman's Magazine*, no. That journal was not listed in the 1755 catalogue, and while it is possible that back issues were received in the library before 1771 and then lost before 1790, it seems highly improbable. Nor does *Gentleman's Magazine* seem to have been in the library of the Linonian Society, of which Bushnell was a member. A 1771 inventory, penned by fellow member Nathan Hale, fails to list *Gentleman's Magazine*.[31]

For Papin's *Recueil des diverses Pieces . . .*, the issue is less clear. An old book would be more likely than an old magazine to find its way in and out of the library in Bushnell's time. Yale President Thomas Clap wrote in 1766 that the library had "not many authors who have wrote within these 30 years."[32] Most of Yale's books were old books, donated by European patrons and colonial subscribers. It is not unlikely that a 1695 book could have come to the library after 1755 only to disappear in the Revolution. It borders on sacrilege, but it is even possible that Bushnell was the culprit—carrying off in 1775 the volume that was to aid him in his contribution to the war effort.

One need not assume Bushnell's guilt, however. There were other ways he might have laid his hands on either volume. Thomas Clap wrote that the course of study at Yale was designed

> so that every one educated here might have at least, a general and superficial Knowledge of every important Affair of Life; and be directed to those Books which may give him a more complete

> Knowledge of the particular Art and Science, which may be most agreeable to his own Genius or Profession.[33]

In Bushnell's case this was underwater warfare, and it is reasonable to assume that if Papin's book was available in the colonies Bushnell could manage to see it. He was, after all, in touch with Benjamin Franklin, who, in addition to his own considerable personal library, had access to the books and ideas circulating in the nascent American Philosophical Society. Franklin may even have visited Bushnell during the construction of the *Turtle*. There is no telling the books and ideas he might have brought with him.[34]

So too is there reason to believe that Bushnell saw *Gentleman's Magazine*, even if not in the Yale library.[35] Papin's article in the December 1747 number accompanied and complemented an extract from the Marquis of Worcester's *Century of Inventions*. . . . Article 9 suggested a portable engine to sink ships. Article 10, as printed in *Gentleman's Magazine*, suggested:

> A way from a mile off to dive and fasten such pocket engine to any ship, so as punctually to work the same effect, *either* for time or immediate execution.[36]

This scheme, and not anything suggested by Papin, was what Bushnell settled on to deliver his exploding device. Papin was vague about exactly how his submarine was to attack ships. The Marquis was not. Nor was Bushnell. Protruding from the top of the *Turtle* was a "wood screw." This could be turned into the hull of an enemy ship and then detached from the submarine. Through an eye in the shank of the screw passed a rope, attached at one end to the submarine and at the other to a "large powder magazine" on the back of the *Turtle*. Once the screw was implanted in the hull of a ship, the magazine would be detached from the submarine and a clockwork detonator inside the magazine would begin to run. As the *Turtle* left the scene, it would pull the rope through the eye of the screw until the floating magazine was hard up against the hull. There it would be left to go off when the clockwork released the flintlock detonator.[37] In short, the *Turtle* was a way to *dive* and *fasten* a ship-sinking engine for either timed or immediate execution. The fact that Bushnell built a machine like Papin's to perform a function like Worcester's argues strongly that he saw their ideas together in *Gentleman's Magazine*.

Lacking any firm evidence that *Gentleman's Magazine* or Papin's *Recueil des diverses Pieces . . .* were in the Yale library—or otherwise available to Bushnell—the case that he had his ideas from them must remain circumstantial and unproven. But then so too is the conventional belief that his ideas were entirely original. Given this uncertainty, the following reconstruction from an admittedly sparse record is at least as plausible as any other and has the added merit of accounting for some otherwise remarkable coincidences. Bushnell grew up in a small community with a lively interest in books and education. Through reading and the instruction available from his local clergyman, he prepared himself for Yale. Either before or during his first autumn there he came across the article in *Gentleman's Magazine*. On deciding to attempt to build a similar vessel himself, he ran down a copy of Papin's book, either one that was then in the Yale library and has subsequently disappeared or one procured from other sources, perhaps a private library like Franklin's. Relying principally on Papin, but supplementing his ideas with the collection of books and apparatus at Yale, Bushnell developed a machine that was a true product of the European heritage in underwater warfare. In the best tradition of enlightened Europe, his invention drew on a technology transferred through channels of travel, correspondence, scientific societies, and books; it marked an "advancement of knowledge" in the field of naval weaponry; and, as Benjamin Gale had observed, it was based on "principles of Natural Philosophy."[38]

That Bushnell may have drawn upon the European heritage in underwater warfare detracts nothing from his genius or his contribution. He made the best of the information available to him. He added several new refinements. And, perhaps most importantly, he executed his plans so thoroughly and well—coming so close to ultimate success—that he inspired others for more than a century.

VI

David Bushnell in Battle

BUSHNELL'S PLAN was fully developed by the spring of 1775.[1] By then the deteriorating relations between England and the colonies made it look as though a chance to use such weaponry was not far off. The students at Yale caught the revolutionary fever quickly, and did their part to stoke the flames. In December 1774, some volunteered to abstain from drinking tea until the duties were lifted. Shortly thereafter Yale's first winter recess was called, but it hardly cooled the student ardor. After classes resumed a company of troops was drawn from the student body, and serious drill and preparation began. The fracas at Lexington and Concord only served to precipitate what had long been brewing at Yale—and in David Bushnell's mind as well.

For a young college student planning to take on the British Navy early in 1775, the prospects of government support were bleak. Of the three navies raised by the colonists during the Revolutionary War, none was yet in existence. The Continental Navy would not be organized until late in 1775, and even then would busy itself primarily with outfitting ships as large as skill and resources would allow. "George Washington's Navy," an ad hoc assortment of privateers and coastal communicators, emerged willy-nilly out of the commander in chief's letters of marque and individual commissions. The various state navies consisted primarily of small coastal craft for local defense. Bushnell did try this last source once in 1775, only to find it wanting. It was reported that Connecticut "Offered him Assistance, but it was so Inconsiderable a sum, he refused it, and Says he will go through with it at his own Risque."[2]

So in his first attempt at getting government support, Bushnell took offense at the paltry assistance offered him. Two features of this initial encounter between government and inventor merit emphasis. First, Bushnell elected to have no official help at all rather than "so Inconsiderable a sum" as was offered, in spite of the fact that colonial assets were naturally dear in those early days of the war. He was in effect reversing the Gianibelli theme, for when Amsterdam offered the Mantuan less than he demanded, he simply took what he could get and made the best of it. Bushnell held out for all, or nothing at all.

Secondly, neither here nor in any other extant record of Bushnell's activities in the war is there any hint of moral misgivings among the Americans. Whether these were not felt, or were felt and not expressed, cannot be established now. In light of prevailing Enlightenment thought on weaponry, the most likely explanation is twofold. First, the advances of science were appropriate grist for the mill of state. In fact, the colonial experience had fostered just such a utilitarian view of science. Second, the state had the right to employ such means as were necessary to achieve its just ends. Men who could declare their own list of "truths" to be "self-evident" were not likely to entertain any doubts about the sanctity of their cause or the importance of its success.[3]

In any case, Bushnell set about building the *Turtle* "at his own Risque," for which read: with a little help from his friends. Evidence on how Bushnell financed and built the *Turtle* is scarce, but enough is known to sketch a suggestive outline. Benjamin Gale, a close friend and supporter, stated in August of 1775 that Bushnell and his brother Ezra did all but the iron work. That crafting seems to have been done by Phineas Pratt (1747–1813) of Saybrook. An unsigned typescript in the Connecticut Historical Society says that Pratt "served in the army near Boston till applied to by Mr. D. Bushnell to build the torpedo. He accepted and took part of the risk and expense and was promised a large reward if successful."[4] This would surely explain how the known poverty of the Bushnell brothers was circumvented without government assistance.

Whatever the financing, construction of such a craft could hardly have taken place in a more fertile environment than eighteenth-century Connecticut. The colony then contained in large measure all of the ingredients for what Lewis Mumford calls the "ancient . . . partnership between the soldier, the miner, the technician, and the scientist."[5] Bushnell provided the scientific expertise, and in 1775 Connecticut was bristling with soldiers and would-be soldiers.

Natural resources were equally abundant. The wood for the hull could be found right in Saybrook, then a minor shipbuilding center. Even Bushnell's subdivision of Westbrook had had its own shipyard since 1740. Lead for the ballast could have come from any number of nearby mines, including the Middletown lead mine, only twenty-five miles up the Connecticut River. Copper for the hatch and fittings could be procured at the Simsbury mine at Newgate—also north of Saybrook on the Connecticut River. Iron was reportedly in short supply at the time, but the "Iron Works" in northern Westbrook could be expected to help out a local inventor—not only with raw material from the mine but also with furnace and blacksmithing facilities. Gunpowder, another item in short supply, could still be gotten from the powder mills in Windham County (only a few miles from the seat of colonial government) and elsewhere around the colony.[6]

Technicians were just as plentiful as raw materials. Bushnell and his brother Ezra were reportedly knowledgeable in shipbuilding, but there were in any case numerous chandlers around Saybrook. Like Gianibelli and Drebbel before him, Bushnell called upon skilled craftsmen for specialized work. Phineas Pratt was originally a chandler himself, but had since changed to "the brass clock making and gold and silver business."[7] Gunlocks were manufactured, among other places, in Lebanon only about five miles from the gunpowder supply at Windham. The most difficult item for Bushnell to come by was probably glass. Colonial production was always low, and Connecticut was no exception. Only in the wake of the Townsend Act of 1767 did large-scale activity begin, and the records on this production are spotty. It is therefore hard to say where the glass for the *Turtle* might have come from, though the amount needed was so small a cut-up window pane would have sufficed.[8]

The clearest evidence of the use Bushnell made of Connecticut technicians is the case of "Mr. Doolittle an ingenious Mechanic of clocks." This craftsman, mentioned in the correspondence of Benjamine Gale, was probably Issac Doolittle of New Haven, whom Bushnell could have met while attending Yale. Apparently finding his skills superior to Phineas Pratt's, Bushnell awarded him the task of making the forcing pump. But he would brook no interference from a craftsman, however skillful he might be. When Doolittle delivered a pump not exactly to specification, Bushnell personally returned it for correction. There was no question here about who was the scientist and who the technician.[9]

While Bushnell was constructing his *Turtle* in the summer of 1775, his friend and neighbor Dr. Benjamin Gale was trying to drum up some support for him. An inventor in his own right, Gale wrote to Benjamin Franklin (just as Europeans before him would have written to Mersenne or Boyle) describing the vessel and advertising that "it is all Constructed with Great Simplicity, and upon Principles of Natural Philosophy."[10] He reported that Bushnell, like any good experimenter, wanted to have the craft thoroughly tested before it was actually taken into combat, adding that the intended target was the British fleet in Boston Harbor.

Bushnell continued to experiment and test as summer gave way to fall. In early November, Gale wrote to Silas Deane, a representative from Connecticut to the Continental Congress and a member of the naval affairs committee, saying he was sanguine about the submarine and that Bushnell should have, "if he succeeds, a stipend for life, and if he fails, a reasonable compensation for time and expense."[11] Gale also alluded in the same letter to what may have been an unsuccessful attempt on a British ship. He said: "I conclude by the time this reaches you the machine will be in camp."[12] Presumably he meant that it would be on the front lines, a surmise reinforced a week later by British intelligence. A report from Governor Tryon of New York stated that Bushnell had been missing for four weeks but had just reappeared. Tryon conjectured that a futile attempt may have been made on H.M.S. *Asia*, one of the few British ships then in New York.[13]

If there was such an attempt, two possible explanations for its failure present themselves. Governor Tryon noted in his report that Bushnell was in New Haven getting a new pump—an indication that Doolittle's handiwork still wasn't up to snuff. Also, the following month, Gale reported to Deane that Bushnell needed a phosphorescent material for the compass and barometer so that he could navigate at night. Furthermore, he concluded by saying Bushnell "now makes all his affairs a secret even from his best friends,"[14] a hint that the inventor may have suspected treachery.

At the opening of the new year, Bushnell was apparently out of funds. On 2 February 1776 he changed his mind on government subsidy and appeared before the Connecticut Council of Safety —albeit at their request. They reimbursed him for his travel, voiced approval of his endeavors, and advised him to continue his work "with expectation of proper public notice and reward."[15] The next day they voted him the sum of £60 to continue his experiments. At this time he changed from the Gianibelli to the Drebbel mode of using weapons. Instead of simply building the machine to demonstrate its power for whatever returns of money or prestige that might elicit, he was working now under government contract —with reasonable hopes of a bonus.

Even with financial difficulties alleviated, problems remained. Bushnell tested and retested his machine, insisting upon perfect operation before going into battle. Perhaps this excess of caution was prompted by a premature attack on the *Asia* in the fall of 1775, but in any case it delayed readiness until the summer of 1776, a full year after the *Turtle* had undergone its first trials. By then yet another problem arose. Bushnell was never hardy enough to take the craft into battle himself, so his brother was trained as operator. Just as preparations were finally completed for an attack on the British fleet—now removed from Boston to New York—Ezra took sick and had to bow out. Three soldiers who had volunteered for duty on fire ships were quickly mustered, and from amongst these Bushnell chose a replacement: Sergeant Ezra Lee.[16]

Training a new operator for the *Turtle* was an unusual phenomenon in the colonial military experience. This was no case of a career merchant sailor signing on board a privateer, or of a hunter, militia man, or veteran of the Seven Years' War picking up a long-familiar weapon. Instead this was an army sergeant unfamiliar with the construction of the *Turtle*, being asked to function in a strange and hostile environment and operate a complex machine. Before following Sergeant Lee into battle it may be well to review briefly the task he was expected to master in a few short weeks.

Assuming wind (virtually none), weather (clear but dark), and current (less than three knots) were suitable, Lee was expected to approach the enemy vessel with the conning tower of the *Turtle* awash. Then, plunging into absolute darkness, save for the phosphorescence in his compass and barometer, he had thirty minutes of air to: (1) watch the target ship through the glass in the conning tower (the Bushnell brothers could apparently do this sitting down; the diminutive Lee had to stand up), push the foot valve to admit water, turn the vertical propeller counterclockwise to descend beneath the water while watching the barometer, and pump out water to stabilize at the proper depth; (2) turn the horizontal propeller with his left hand, steer with his right, and watch the compass to close on the hull of the enemy ship; (3) estimate the distance traveled, pump more water out with his free (?) hand and turn the vertical propeller clockwise with his other (?) hand in order to bring the *Turtle* up into contact with the hull; (4) use the horizontal screw (left hand) and rudder (right elbow) to stay in position while turning the auger into the bottom of the hull; (5) detach the auger and release the magazine; (6) push the foot valve and turn the vertical screw counterclockwise to sink lower in the water while watching the barometer, and pump with his hand to stabilize; and finally (7) turn the horizontal propeller and steer with the rudder to move away from the ship in the proper direction as indicated by the compass—thereby pulling the magazine hard up against the hull of the ship. He would surface only when sufficiently distant from the enemy to avoid being spotted by the lookouts.

This heroic display of manual dexterity, physical endurance, and no small measure of courage was first undertaken in New York Harbor on 6 September 1776. As if the mission were not difficult enough in itself, Bushnell elected to attack H.M.S. *Eagle*, Lord Richard Howe's sixty-four gun flagship. Surely this was a target sufficiently massive and notorious to convince even the most thoroughly entrenched skeptic of the efficacy of underwater warfare. *Eagle* stood disdainful and unchallenged off Bedlow's Island, a symbol of England's ability to project its sea power ashore and to alter the course of battle by its very presence. Its destruction could have altered the course of the New York campaign, if not the entire war, a prospect not lost on Washington and some of his staff. Such luminaries and supporters as Israel Putnam stood watch on shore with Bushnell and a collection of soldiers and sailors as the tiny *Turtle* went forth to bring down the *Eagle*.

But such was not to be. The submarine got as far as contacting the enemy hull, but was foiled there at the last moment. As Bushnell and Lee would have it, the auger hit an iron crossbar just forward of the rudder and would not penetrate. While maneuvering to a different point on the hull, the *Turtle* slid out from under the *Eagle* and shot to the surface—"with great velocity," said Lee. He dove immediately and was about to try again when he decided that "the best generalship" was to get well clear of the area before the imminent dawn and the *Eagle's* boat combined to catch him in the open.

Ever since the event, historians have debated the reasons why this attack failed. Most have claimed the effort was foiled by the copper sheathing with which the bottoms of many British vessels were then being covered as a protection against the ravages of the teredo, or shipworm.[17] It has now been established, however, that the *Eagle* was not coppered until 1782.[18] This lends credence to the belief of Lee and Bushnell that the iron bar caused their failure, though it does not rule out the possibility that Lee was simply suffering from carbon dioxide poisoning and mismanaged the attack.

Bushnell's other ventures are not nearly as controversial, but they are nontheless equally important to the thesis presented in this study. Twice more in 1776 he tried attacks on the Hudson River—one by Lee and one by another operator (Pratt?)—but neither came as close to success as had the *Eagle* attack. Pleading bad health, Bushnell abandoned the project, noting:

> I despaired of obtaining the public attention, and assistance necessary. I was unable to support myself, and the persons I must have employed, had I proceeded. Beside, I found it absolutely necessary, that the operators should acquire more skill in the management of the vessel, before I could expect success.[19]

These twin complaints of lack of public support and the need for more training were to arise again many times before submarine warfare became an accepted naval arm.

Bushnell abandoned the *Turtle*, but not the main object with which he and others in this story were ever taken: the killing blow delivered unexpectedly to the weak, unguarded point below the waterline. His next design was a rope connecting a pair of magazines, each of which was suspended beneath a wooden float. The idea was to drop the device upwind or up-current of a moored enemy ship and let it drift onto the vessel. The connecting rope would catch on the ship's mooring line and the magazines would swing into contact with the hull—one on either side. Rubbing against the hull would turn an external wheel, thereby tripping the timed, gunlock detonators inside.[20]

To back this plan Bushnell applied to the Connecticut Council of Safety and appeared before them on 23 April 1777. Apparently impressed, the Council voted him "an order on officers, agents, commissary's, to afford him assistance of men, boats, powder, lead, &c. as he shall call."[21] In other words, they gave him a blank check. Perhaps it was not everywhere honored in those lean days of scarce resources and pressing commitments, but it was a valuable draft nonetheless. Whether the Council was impressed with his previous near misses or just sanguine about his new proposal the record fails to say. What it does say is that he still had considerable government confidence and support behind him, even if there were no mention this time of "proper public notice and reward."

But again the results were disappointing. The attack was made off New London on H.M.S. *Cerberus* on the night of 13/14 August 1777. Everything worked as planned except that one of the devices drifted astern of the *Cerberus*. There it was spotted by four sailors in a small schooner moored behind the larger vessel. They pulled the curiosity on board and were examining it when it detonated, killing three of them, blowing the fourth overboard, and demolishing the small auxiliary. In his official report of the incident, Commodore Symons of the *Cerberus* put together a detailed description of the mine, as gathered from the surviving sailor, and correctly surmised the method of attack. Surprisingly, his language and reaction were rather mild. He characterized the colonials as "villains" with "singular . . . ingenuity" for "secret modes of mischief." He referred to the magazines as "machines" and "infernals." But beyond that he made no explicitly moral condemnation, recommending only that other ships be warned to be on the lookout.[22]

Attacks against single ships having failed repeatedly now, Bushnell decided to increase the odds by launching a barrage of attacks against a whole fleet. The ships were conveniently moored in the Delaware River at Philadelphia. The barrage in this case was to be an array of paired mines similar to those used against the *Cerberus*. This time the magazines were supported by floating kegs and were to be detonated by spring-lock mechanisms as soon as they touched an enemy hull. They were constructed in Bordentown, New Jersey, utilizing the same sort of local skills and resources as had characterized the *Turtle* construction. In this case the backing seems to have come from the commander in chief himself. Washington later claimed to have given Bushnell all "the money and other aids" he needed, and it seems likely that he was referring to this effort late in 1777. Confirmation of Washington's involvement is found in a dispatch to him from Francis Hopkins dated 17 December 1777 in which the general is advised that "everything goes on with Secrecy and Dispatch to the Satisfaction of the Artist."[23]

Shortly after Christmas Bushnell set out with a guide to plant his mines in the Delaware River. Because they grossly misjudged the strength of the current and their distance from Philadelphia, the mines took more than a week to reach the anchorage. By then, some of the British ships had left; the others had been shifted from the roads to the wharves. Two curious boys lost their lives examining one of the machines and the British soldiers were reportedly alarmed by the bizarre flotsam, but there was scarcely any other result from the attack. Once more Bushnell blamed the operator—or in this case the guide[24]—but the result was nevertheless the same: he had failed the test of battle once more.

He returned to Connecticut and petitioned for still more assistance. The Council of Safety, itself in financial straits, requested its delegates in Congress to try to get funds there. The latter replied that they would, but by May of 1779 still nothing had come of it.

Then Bushnell was captured by the British in a coastal raid. They never seemed to realize (or perhaps by this time care) who they had, and they released him in a routine exchange of prisoners within two weeks of his capture. But that was apparently enough for Bushnell. Within a week of his release he asked for and obtained a position in the newly formed Engineer Corps, specifically in a company of sappers and miners, the landed counterpart of his activities at sea. In that branch of the uniformed services he served out the war in commendable if unremarkable fashion.

After his mustering out in 1783, Bushnell made a mystery of the rest of his life. It is known that he was ill for some time after the

Figure 12. One of Bushnell's floating mines, of the type used in the Battle of the Kegs in 1778. *Courtesy of the National Museum of History and Technology.*

war, that he communicated with Thomas Jefferson (the United States Minister in Paris) in 1787 about the submarine, and that he considered going to France. Whether he did in fact go, and whether, as some have claimed, he returned later to New Jersey to engage briefly in an unsuccessful business scheme, all agree that he turned up in Georgia around 1795. There he assumed the name of Dr. David Bush, lived out his life as a teacher and physician, and died in 1826, anonymous till then to all but a few close friends.[25]

The important issue in the story is whether or not he went to France, for it was there that submarine warfare was to make its next significant advance. Bushnell's biographer doubts that he went, but his argument is not entirely convincing. Nor does it address all the evidence.

First, Bushnell's service in the Company of Sappers and Miners put him in touch with numerous European engineers. Louis Lebeque de Presle Duportail, the commander of the Corps of Engineers, was one of many such French specialists imported through the efforts of Benjamin Franklin to compensate for American weakness in engineering. These men presented living

Figure 13. The inside cover of the Bushnell floating mine, showing the remnants of the flintlock detonator. *Courtesy of the National Museum of History and Technology.*

proof of the encouragement such pursuits received in France. When Franklin himself went to Paris late in 1776, he became an active link between American and European science, a link to which Bushnell had at least indirect access.[26]

A still more direct connection surfaced when Thomas Jefferson went to Paris, succeeding Franklin in 1785. In that year he saw demonstrated a crude helical device used as a propeller acting on air. It reminded Jefferson of Bushnell's *Turtle*. He began inquiries to determine who had the right to credit for invention of the propeller. He communicated with Washington, David Humphreys, and Ezra Stiles, the president of Yale. None of these could give him the specific details he required, but the latter two informed Bushnell of Jefferson's curiosity, and Bushnell in turn wrote the Minister in Paris in October 1787. He related that he had been ill and unable to reply earlier, and he enclosed a detailed description of all his underwater warfare activities. He also included a barely disguised hint that he would be grateful for any efforts Jefferson might make on his behalf. Allowing that he would entrust his plans to Jefferson's discretion, he claimed:

> I have ever carefully concealed my principles and experiments, as much as the nature of the subject allowed, from all but my chosen friends, being persuaded that it was the most prudent course, whether the event should prove fortunate or otherwise, although by the concealment, I never fostered any great expectations of profit, or even of a compensation for my time and expenses, the loss of which has been exceedingly detrimental to me.[27]

According to Bushnell's nephew, it was about this time that he "stated that he had received letters from France wishing him to go to that country. When he left Saybrook, he stated that if he went to France, he should send to [Ezra's] house for his trunk, which he did in a few days."[28] That was the last the Bushnells heard from David until they were notified of his death in 1826. The letters from France may have been from Jefferson, from engineers who served with David during the war, or from such other contacts as Joel Barlow (1754–1812), a friend from Yale days who was just then in Europe representing a rather shady land company. Barlow was soon to extricate himself from that tacky business and render distinguished public service to the United States in various diplomatic roles.[29]

Whoever lured Bushnell to France, the pattern was not an unusual one. When Thomas Paine's plan for an iron bridge across the Schuylkill River in Philadelphia was rejected after the war, he took it to Paris and presented it to the *Académie des Sciences*. It was highly praised there and ultimately adopted in England.[30] For anyone expecting to gain a substantial return on an invention, Europe was then a much more promising market than was the United States of America. Especially was this the case for Bushnell; the promise of "proper public notice and reward" was worthless in postwar Connecticut, and in the country at large the wartime navy was dissolving.[31]

Furthermore, some accounts of Bushnell's activity in France are sufficiently rich in detail to nourish the argument that more than speculation lies behind them. A case in point is the article in the New York *Herald* for 5 September 1897. It said in part:

> Fulton . . . sought out Bushnell in Paris, and by accident found him at work in an obscure part of the city under an assumed name.[32]

Bushnell has attracted as much fanciful legend as historical fact, but this type of evidence has the ring of truth to it.

Lastly, as a French historian has noted: "The experiences of Bushnell had a certain echoing in Europe. Also in France during the last quarter of the eighteenth century, numerous inventors offered the government schemes for submarine vessels."[33] Some, like the submarine proposed to the Minister of Marine by Sillon de Valmer in 1780, appeared too early to be directly affected by Bushnell. Others, like the diving machine proposed to the Academy of Rouen by P. A. L. Forfait, could be traced to French sources. But still others seem to clearly reflect Bushnell's influence. For example, Jules Fabre, a professor of chemistry and mathematics at Aix University, proposed in 1796 a submarine shaped like a peach stone. In the same year an engineer named Castera proposed to the Directory a one-man submarine for attacking British ships off the French coast.[34]

Much of this information could have been obtained secondhand, but when combined with the other evidence available, it suggests that Bushnell himself took his ideas back to their place of origin around the English Channel.

VII

Robert Fulton in France

THE PATHS of David Bushnell and Robert Fulton crossed frequently. When Bushnell was sowing his keg mines in the Delaware River to float down upon the British fleet in the harbor at Philadelphia, Fulton was a boy of twelve growing up in nearby Lancaster, Pennsylvania. He had taken an early interest in mechanics and in the major industry of his home town—gun manufacture. Bushnell's spectacular if unsuccessful assault on the British was just the thing to turn his head.[1]

At the age of seventeen Fulton set out on his own. He soon established a modest reputation in Philadelphia as a painter of portrait miniatures, and came under the wing of Benjamin Franklin when the latter returned from Paris. Franklin was fully acquainted with Bushnell's work, of course, and could well have passed his knowledge on to Fulton. In 1786, Franklin sent the young painter to England, in care of Benjamin West. There Fulton pursued his painting for a living and his mechanical and engineering penchants for a hobby. He made at least one trip to France during his decade of English residence, a three-month sojourn in 1790—about the time Bushnell was most probably in Paris.

In 1796 Fulton prepared *A Treatise on the Improvement of Canal Navigation*, in which he now styled himself "Robert Fulton, Civil Engineer."[2] He distributed copies in England and the United States, and a translation appeared in France a few years later.

Hoping to patent some of the ideas suggested in the *Treatise*, he went to France in the summer of 1797.[3] Arriving in Paris in July, he took up residence at the hotel in which Joel Barlow was living, and they soon developed a close friendship. A close friend of Bushnell's from Yale days, Barlow was one of the possible sources of letters from France which apparently prompted the young inventor to emigrate after the war. Barlow was also the brother-in-law and close friend of Abraham Baldwin, another Yale man and Linonian Society member of the Revolutionary era, in whose company Bushnell emerged in Georgia around 1795.

The evidence suggests the following: Bushnell was in France in the late 1780s or the early 1790s. Through Barlow, Jefferson, or perhaps French comrades from his days in the Engineer Corps, or more circuitously through one of the scientific academies, Bushnell tried to sell his invention to the French government. While in France, or while traveling to or from France, he met and compared notes with Fulton. Failing to sell his ideas, Bushnell returned to the United States and contacted his old schoolmate Baldwin, whose whereabouts he could well have learned from Barlow.

Whether or not this reconstruction is entirely accurate, and whether or not the two men actually met, Fulton clearly knew of Bushnell's work. He conceded as much in 1806, but dwelt rather ingraciously on what he pictured as the shortcomings of Bushnell's devices.[4] Fulton's initial projects bore an unmistakable similarity to Bushnell's, and all of his contrivances for underwater warfare were drawn from the same conceptual well.[5]

His obligations to Bushnell, however, do not detract from the original contributions he himself made. Nor do they preclude the possibility that he discovered for himself in Europe many of the same sources Bushnell used at Yale. It has been reported that while in Paris he studied hydraulics, "higher mathematics, the sciences, physicks, chymistry & perspective,"[6] and that he achieved competence if not fluency in several languages. In a 1799 letter he said: "I am not claiming any merit for having invented [underwater warfare] first. The idea could have come to any other engineer who searched with as much ardor as I."[7] No doubt Fulton was heavily indebted to Bushnell for inspiration and a considerable amount of specific information, but on the other hand there is no reason to believe that he didn't complement this knowledge with goodly amounts of European material.

What is more bothersome than how and how much Fulton knew about Bushnell's work is the question of what he did with these ideas in France. The record of Fulton's activities there was first dug out of the *Archives nationales* by Navy Lieutenant Emile Duboc in 1896. Exploiting these finds, Maurice Delpeuch and G.-L. Pesce produced their landmark histories, *Les sous-marins à travers les siècles* (1902, 1907) and *La Navigation sous-marine* (2d. ed., 1906) respectively. The latter work, by Pesce, is still the most comprehensive single volume on the subject and has been the basic reference source for most subsequent histories. Unfortunately, both of these volumes are seriously flawed in their treatments of Robert Fulton. Apparently through errors inherited from Duboc's pioneer entry into the *Archives nationales*, both authors improperly translated dates from the Revolutionary calendar,[8] leading to serious misinterpretations of Fulton's activities in France, his motives in dealing with the French government, and the French motives in treating him as they did.

Henry W. Dickinson went to the same archival sources to research his 1913 biography, *Robert Fulton, Engineer and Artist: His Life and Work*. He corrected almost all of the errors of translation made by Delpeuch and Pesce, but his adjustments went virtually unnoticed. Even historians who cited his volume have continued to perpetuate the same old errors, and the pattern of repeated mistakes is still very much alive.[9]

To untangle the fairly complex story of what actually did take place in France between 1797 and 1804, a new approach is necessary. Three primary questions must be addressed. First, how did the committees of government scientists appointed to examine Fulton's propositions perform in comparison to earlier bodies reviewing underwater warfare weaponry? Second, why were Fulton's proposals ultimately rejected? And third, who rejected them? A skeleton outline of the sequence of events may be found in Dickinson. A simplified treatment will be sufficient here, dividing

Fulton's activities into three negotiating periods. The last period can itself be divided into three segments to reveal more clearly the interaction between government and inventor.[10]

The story begins in July 1797 when Fulton arrived in France on his way (ultimately) to the United States. He took up with Joel Barlow and apparently decided rather quickly that there was opportunity in France for such as he. In the same month, he wrote back to Edmund Cartwright in England saying: "I have reason to believe there will be good encouragement to men of genius."[11] When Barlow and his wife moved into permanent lodgings, Fulton moved in with them for what turned out to be a stay of seven years.

His optimistic opinion of revolutionary France was perhaps more justified at this time than Bushnell's had been five or ten years earlier. Successive leaders of the Revolution were for years undecided about the position of scientists and intellectuals in the new order of things. In the early years they beheaded Lavoisier and closed down the *Académie des Sciences*. But as passions cooled later in the 1790s men like Carnot, Chaptal, Monge, Laplace, and Lagrange rose to high positions in government; and the *Institut de France*, *Ecole polytechnique*, and *Conservatoire des arts et métiers* resumed the institutionalization of science. The practice of government subsidy of inventions survived the turmoil, as did the habit of commissioning scientists to evaluate these inventions. And an association between science and war, reminiscent of the Enlightenment, reemerged in the late 1790s. Fulton had probably assessed his prospects in the France of 1797 correctly.[12]

His opening effort in underwater warfare occurred when he and Joel Barlow built and operated a self-propelled torpedo. Beyond the fact that they both nearly lost their lives, little is known of the incident.[13] The first really clear evidence of Fulton's activities appears on 12 December 1797.[14]

On that date Fulton entered his first period of negotiation with the French government by sending the Executive Directory a proposal. He advised them that he had a "Mechanical Nautilus" for destroying enemy ships, and a private company to manufacture it. He didn't explain what the *Nautilus* was, but simply requested a government subsidy to be paid to his company for all enemy ships the *Nautilus* might destroy. He asked for commissions for the operators of the *Nautilus*, because, he said, "fire Ships or other unusual means of destroying Navies are Considered Contrary to the Laws of war, And persons taken in Such enterprise are Liable to Suffer death."[15] Two days later he gave a copy of the same proposal to La Réveillièr-Lépaux with a covering letter stating that the *Nautilus* was too complex for laymen to understand. That, he said, was why he was financing it through private means. He added that he would be happy to have his plan submitted to the Minister of Marine, but intimated that the navy was not likely to understand it. He allowed that he would gladly explain the details to a competent engineer—like "général Bonaparte."[16]

On 2 January the Directory did exactly what Fulton didn't want: they sent his plan to the Ministry of Marine. The minister at this time was Georges-René Pleville le Pelley (1726–1805), just the sort of salty veteran who would look askance at such wave-making innovation.[17] But contrary to expectation, *"les services compétents,"* who were apparently consulted, reported back favorably to the minister, and on 13 January Fulton was informed that his proposal was tentatively accepted. There followed some negotiation between Fulton and the minister in which the requested prize money was halved, and Fulton's claim for remuneration in the event of peace with England was tied to a clear proof that the peace resulted from fear of his weapons. The most important change, however, was that the minister refused to grant commissions to the operators of the *Nautilus*. On top of a certain repugnance for the whole scheme, he noted that threats of reprisals in case the *Nautilus* crew were mistreated as prisoners of war would have little effect on the English and could well prove counterproductive.

Fulton submitted a second set of proposals on 18 January. Next to the demand for commissions in this version Pleville wrote *"ne se peut,"* indicating that it was perhaps not an entirely personal view he was maintaining. Yet a third set of proposals followed on 20 January, and with these it appeared that substantial agreement had been reached. On 4 February 1798, a draft contract was drawn up. It began propitiously enough with an affirmation of policy: "The Executive Directory considering that it ought to give encouragement to all inventions which have a useful object conducive to national prosperity. . . . "[18] This was just the persuasion Fulton had been banking on, but even this progressive philosophy could not bridge the stumbling block that was present still. The contract made no mention of commissions, and it was probably for Fulton's stubbornness on this point that he was informed on 5 February that the whole project was refused by the Directory. Whether or not his perception was correct, Fulton left this first round of negotiations with the impression that the civilian arm of government had turned down his scheme on moral grounds.

In spite of this initial defeat, Fulton remained sanguine about the efficacy of underwater warfare and about his chances of selling the idea in France. In the ensuing months he worked not only on his underwater warfare, but also on other schemes and inventions. In a letter to Edmund Cartwright on 16 February 1798 he talked of steam engines, propellers, canals, and the recently displayed hydraulic ram of the Montgolfier brothers.[19] In a letter to Bonaparte on 1 May he discoursed on the advantages of internal improvements (that is, canals) and got in a few politically correct digs at the British.[20] During the spring he was also at work on a new approach to selling the submarine, perhaps in response to Pleville le Pelley's replacement on 28 April by Eustache Bruix (1759–1805).[21] A considerably younger and possibly less hidebound admiral, Bruix gave Fulton reason to hope for a better reception at the naval ministry.

That optimism seems to have been well founded. Fulton wrote to Bruix on 23 July 1798 informing him "citizens Monge, Dufalga, Montgolfier, Perrier and other distinguished savants" had examined and approved his invention. He asked that the *Institut de France* be directed to examine and pass on the worth of his device, though he was still offering to construct and operate the craft through private financing. As he was accustomed to do, he tactlessly added: "A project of this nature will undoubtedly appear, at first glance, extraordinary, especially to a Minister of Marine . . . ,"[22] as if that post somehow disqualified its incumbent from thinking and imagination. In spite (or perhaps because) of that bit of condescension, Bruix forwarded the proposal to the Directory the next day, stating that he was "relying on the opinions of enlightened citizens."[23] A week later, apparently at the Directory's request, he appointed a commission to evaluate Fulton's invention.

This eight-man commission was a first in underwater warfare, for it was made up of men truly qualified to pass on the merits of Fulton's device. Two of the men were naval officers, one an expert on ship stowage, the other a member of the *Académie des Sciences*. One member was a distinguished chemist, one an engineer and mathematician, one a noted mechanician, and one a civil engineer specializing in harbors and canals. The naval architect of the group was P. A. L. Forfait, who had proposed a submarine of his own to the Academy of Rouen back in 1783. Only one member of the commission seems to have been a purely political appointee without special technical qualifications, but politics too had its place in such enterprises.[24] Instead of the senate of Antwerp passing on Gianibelli's scheme, or the "master Gunner" passing on Drebbel's, or the Landgrave of Hesse-Cassel entertaining himself between campaigns with Papin's, or the Connecticut Council of Safety listening to Bushnell's petition amidst the crush of war business —now a commission jointly composed of professional scientists and professional sailors was to study, evaluate, and report on the efficacy of a new weapon.

After more than a month of deliberation the commission issued its report on 5 September 1798. From it we gain our clearest picture of Fulton's early proposal—and find that it was essentially a modified *Turtle*. The central cabin of the craft had the same elliptical shape; only the tail of the vessel was greatly extended to make the overall shape more fishlike. Conning tower, glass windows, hand-turned propellers, pumps, hatch, ballast—all were the same as the *Turtle*'s. True, some additions had been made: an anchor, a vertical rudder, and a mast and sail for surface propulsion; but these hardly made it an original design. The most convincing proof of Fulton's debt to Bushnell is what the commissioners called the "horn of the *Nautilus*." This was the same detachable screw with an eye through which passed a line to the explosive charge. The only change Fulton made in the arrangement was to provide a barbed head for the screw. With this version the screw could first be pounded into the hull of a ship, then turned the rest of the way after it had the initial bite.[25] There would be no bouncing off copper sheathing or iron bars for his "Mechanical Nautilus."

The commissioners reacted positively and enthusiastically. Their report tended to be technical and detailed, but generally they concluded that the theory was sound and deserving of a trial. They recommended that a prototype be constructed and that experiments then be performed to iron out the bugs and to test the practicality of the craft in action. They were not without some misgivings, especially about the effectiveness of an underwater explosion, but they were so impressed with Fulton that they willingly deferred to his judgment. "The author," they reported, "easily pierced all the difficulties with which the commission confronted him."[26] Fulton failed to advise them that he met some of their questions with Bushnell's answers, but perhaps that is a little much to expect of him.[27]

Confident about his chances now, Fulton sent yet a fourth set of proposals to the Minister of Marine on 18 October 1798 in which he raised the ante considerably, making his largest demand yet for prize money—half a million francs for the first English vessel sunk and twenty francs per pound of cannon-shot sunk thereafter. But this exhorbitant proposal came to nought. In spite of the commission's report, the scheme went no further. Without any recorded refusal, it seems just to have died somewhere in the cavernous halls of government.

Two reasons for this failure present themselves. First, the commissioners, notwithstanding the two naval members, were as impolitic as Fulton in the wording of their report: "[This weapon] is particularly suitable to the French," they noted, "because, having a weaker navy (we should say necessarily) than their adversary, the entire destruction of both navies is of advantage to them."[28] This compounded the sin of proclaiming French naval inferiority by recommending the elimination of navies altogether. Such a panacea as that—one continually advanced by Fulton under the banner of "freedom of the seas"—was not likely to win many friends at the naval ministry.

The main obstacle, however, seems still to have been moral apprehension. Writing to Citizen Barras at the end of October asking him to intercede, Fulton argued against the moral objections:

> If at first glance, the means I propose seem revolting, it is only because they are extraordinary. They are anything but inhuman; it is certainly the most peaceful and least bloody mode that the philosopher could imagine to overturn the system of plunder and of perpetual war, which has always vexed the maritime nations.[29]

Although this was the same Fulton who earlier wanted a guaranty of payment in case his weapon so terrorized the British that they sued for peace before he could collect any prize money, this later argument, nevertheless has a certain logic to it: eliminate a monstrous evil with a frightening weapon; make war so ugly it is intolerable.

He argued in vain. His second period of negotiation ended here.

Hopefull still, Fulton wrote to a friend in England defending his plans and revealing his expectations:

> The plan of my *Nautilus* you say is not liked. This must be because its consequences are not understood. The idea is yet an Infant, but I think I see in it all the nerve and muscle of an Infant hercules which at one grasp will strangle the Serpents which poison and Convulse the American Constitution.[30]

The symbolism is colorful and romantic, but hardly Davidic; the abstraction here is once removed from his immediate goal. When he gets to that further on in the letter, his purposes become more clear. "I would ask anyone," he continued,

> if all the American difficulties during this war is [sic] not owing to the Naval systems of Europe and a Licensed Robbery on the ocean? How then is America to prevent this? Certainly not by attempting to build a fleet to cope with the fleets of Europe but if possible by rendering the European fleets useless.[31]

Here, then, are Davidic ambitions of enormous proportions. The conceit involved is at once more grand and more abstract than that of a Bushnell, for Fulton intended to undermine not only the ships of the European navies but the very navies themselves. With Goliath laid low, he assumed, the Philistines would abandon the field forever. It never occurred to him that after the first casualty they might awake from the "act of idolization" and successfully defend themselves against his slings and stones. His inflated opinion of his own powers opened to him vistas that men of lesser stature just could not imagine. For whatever private gain he planned to derive from his efforts, and this was considerable, he always wrapped himself publicly in a grand and flowing flag labeled "Freedom of the Seas."[32]

With this messianism to support him Fulton stoically endured his second rebuff by the French government. He busied himself with sundry other projects to earn some money, won a couple of French patents, built a five-foot model of the *Nautilus*, and possibly even tried to sell his idea in Holland, though the evidence on this last point is sketchy.[33] Then on 1 July 1799 came the next break in affairs. Admiral Bruix was replaced as Minister of Marine by Marc-Antoine Bourdon de Vatry (1761–1828). A civilian appointed by Director Sieyès, he represented a still more propitious change than Bruix had.[34] Sixteen days after Bourdon's appointment, Fulton had a new proposal before the government. Phase one of his third period of negotiation was under way.

This time he wrote to the military committee of the Executive Directory. He recorded for them the sorry story of the past year and a half, laying special stress on the favorable recommendation of the commission of scientists. He cited "compassionate considerations of humanity" as the apparent reason for his rebuff, and added sourly that to his mind "some particular interests believed they ought to thwart the execution of the project, in which they saw the annihilation next of all navies."[35] By this time he seems to have believed that failure resulted from obstructionism in naval circles. The military committee reported favorably, noting that only the test of battle could finally decide the issue. As for the moral objections, their opinion was that "philosophy would not reprove a means of destroying the destroyers of the liberty of the seas of the entire world."[36] They sounded more like Fulton than Fulton himself.

The committee's sympathetic report indicates that he had gained some political support during the preceding six months. This opinion is strengthened by a letter to the Minister of Marine on 5 October in which Fulton noted that "that excellent *philosophe* and good friend of humanity, the director Says [i.e., Sieyès]" had referred the *Nautilus* to the minister two months before, and as yet no action had been taken. Fulton said he was led to conclude that "there are some people in the Navy and below the Directory who are not friends of the *Nautilus* expedition." After answering to his own satisfaction the "vulgar" and "unscientific" objections that he attributed to "narrow minds" and "petty intrigues," he closed with his first recorded threat to sell his invention elsewhere if he were not treated more equitably.[37]

Self-righteousness and browbeating were not likely to move the French navy, but political muscle was. On 10 October Monsieur Bourdon, Sieyès's appointee, ordered Fulton's model to be examined, and the inventor submitted yet another (the fifth) set of proposals to the minister. This letter suggests in several places that Fulton had inside information and was confident of getting his way. On the continuing stumbling block of commissions, for example, he posited, self-confidently: "I know . . . that things can be arranged."[38]

While waiting for a decision, Fulton's dealings with the government were overtaken by events. On 9/10 November the coup of 18 *Brumaire* placed Bonaparte in power and cast all political deals in a new light. In Fulton's case it was a warm and pleasing light, for two weeks after the coup Bourdon was replaced as Minister of Marine by Pierre Alexandre Laurent Forfait.[39] This was the same engineer and architect who had proposed his own submarine to the Academy of Rouen in 1783 and who had sat on the commission that passed favorably on Fulton's plans a year before. Everything seemed to be turning in favor of the *Nautilus*.

There is no record of any correspondence between Fulton and Forfait in the first months of the Consulate—an indication perhaps that the inventor now had freer access to the Minister and didn't have to send up petitions from a reception desk. In any case Fulton finally began construction of the *Nautilus* in the winter of 1799/1800, apparently on his own initiative.[40] It may be that he had a tacit or verbal agreement with Forfait, or that he just felt the new political climate was conducive to expectations of proper reward when his machine was proven.

Phase two of Fulton's third period of negotiations opened on 10 April 1800 with a letter to Forfait. Fulton reported the near completion of the submarine, and brought up the subject of a government contract. He said he didn't want to make a deal until the *Nautilus* was demonstrated, but he did note that Forfait had been a constant friend of the project and he hoped that Bonaparte too would give him the encouragement so long denied him by "Directors and Ministers."[41] Forfait endorsed this letter and sent it along to the First Consul, expressing some misgivings about the legality of the enterprise. While this was not the kind of thing to particularly bother Bonaparte, it is perhaps a reflection of Forfait's interpretation of his role as Minister of Marine. He might well have felt constrained to represent, at least pro forma, the naval point of view in his dealings with the First Consul.

In June the *Nautilus* was launched and demonstrated (to Fulton's complete satisfaction) for the ministers of war and the navy. Fulton wrote forthwith to Bonaparte claiming success and requesting a generous contract, including commissions. Forfait put a cover letter on this missive confirming Fulton's claims—though with somewhat less enthusiasm—and noting again the legal knot.[42] The *Nautilus* was thereupon packed off to Rouen for some modifications, more tests, and an attempt on the British fleet. Through July and early August Fulton kept Forfait posted on his progress and inquired after a decision from Bonaparte on commissions. In the middle of August he took the craft to Le Havre, the jumping-off spot for his attack on the British, but still no commissions were forthcoming. Finally, in early September he wrote Joel Barlow asking him to go down personally and light a fire under Forfait. The first day, Barlow did not even get to see Forfait but was told by the porter that the minister had shrugged his shoulders at Barlow's note, repeating "*Je ne puis pas. Je ne puis pas.*"[43] When he returned the next day the story was entirely different. He was informed that commissions were executed and on their way to Le Havre, though no explanation for the change in policy was offered.[44]

If Israel Thrask, a Gloucester ship's captain then in Paris, is to be believed, Fulton had the rank of admiral, another crewman named Nathaniel Sargeant was commissioned a captain of a man-of-war, and a third crew member was made a lieutenant.[45] Unfortunately for Fulton, information that could reach a Gloucester captain could also reach the British Admiralty. The ships on station off Le Havre had been warned of Fulton's plans and simply sailed away from anything suspicious in their vicinity.[46] Like all his predecessors, Fulton relied on surprise to attack his enemy. Without it, the odds against success were overwhelming.

In spite of this failure, Fulton returned to Paris in November full of optimism and enthusiasm. Some time earlier Bonaparte had appointed two distinguished scientists, Gaspard Monge (1746–1818) and Pierre-Simon de Laplace (1749–1827), to report to him on Fulton's plans.[47] On 7 November the inventor gave them a detailed account of his activities during the summer. Unfortunately, the weeks of waiting for his commissions and the natural restlessness of Fulton's mind served to undermine the very goals he was pursuing. It seems that Fulton had made some modifications and had developed some new plans during the summer. These he mixed indiscriminately with his report on experiments with the original *Nautilus* plan, thus complicating the task of Monge and Laplace. After all, they were only to report on the submarine; Fulton, however, was changing horses on them in midstream. "In the course of these experiments," he said, "there has come to me a crowd of ideas infinitely more simple than the means I have employed hitherto."[48] What he was talking about was the concept of towed or drifting "carcasses of powder or torpedoes," but what he failed to appreciate was that he still had to convince Bonaparte of the efficacy of his first invention—the *Nautilus*. He seems to have entirely missed the impact that his failure against the British would have in Paris. He said:

> As to myself I look upon the most difficult part of the work as done. Navigation under water is an operation whose possiblity is proved, and it can be said that a new series of ideas have just been born as to the means for preventing naval wars or rather of hindering them in the future.[49]

On 18 November Fulton submitted to Monge and Laplace a formal list of his achievements and a new list of proposals (the sixth) to the government. The two scientists endorsed this letter favorably, having apparently managed to keep up with Fulton's latest schemes, and suggested a meeting between Fulton and Bonaparte. The First Consul sent this to Forfait for his opinion and met with Fulton while waiting for a reply.

With everything now going in Fulton's direction, it was Forfait, the constant supporter, who rose up as an obstacle. In his endorsement of the report of Monge and Laplace, he took exception to the new schemes proposed by Fulton. Historians of these events have generally misinterpreted this action. Through a misreading of the dates, most have erroneously concluded that it was Forfait's successor who raised objections here. Dickinson had the dates right, but concluded that Forfait had reversed his previous stand and betrayed Futon at the eleventh hour. Actually, it was Fulton who had changed and Forfait who was remaining true to the original plan of the *Nautilus*. As the minister wrote to Bonaparte:

> I have always been the most ardent defender of the diving-Boat, and it is with pain that I see it abandoned; because it is abandoned in the new system, since it plays only a secondary role. It is no longer that which attaches, in a manner so ingenious [the "horn of the Nautilus"] the petards under the bottoms of vessles. It fulfills no other functions than carrying some destructive machines and the men who must direct them in a manner new and independent of the boat. I think that one must not renounce the first idea. To do so is to remove the best feature of the boat that exists.[50]

In other words, while Fulton was waiting for his commission the previous summer, he hit upon the idea of using the submarine to steal into enemy harbors and sow drifting mines or tow mines into contact with enemy vessels. The advantages of this idea were no doubt reinforced by the frustrating experience of trying to put the "horn of the Nautilus" into a moving vessel in the Channel. Always true to his goal—like Bushnell before him—Fulton was far more concerned with effecting the lethal explosion than with rigidly adhering to any ingenious mechanical apparatus. Forfait, on the other hand, was so taken with the cleverness of the horn, that he couldn't stand to see it abandoned. As an old submarine devotee himself, he became enamored of one facet of the *Nautilus*, and thus missed the main point altogether.

Beset now by conflicting reports from advisors who were formerly in general agreement, Bonaparte told Forfait to "mediate the dispute with Fulton, Volney, and others."[51] Effectively this added Constantin-François Volney (1757–1820), the scholar and author, to the group of government scientists already investigating the matter. Volney was a friend of Joel Barlow and probably sympathetic to Fulton. With his voice added to the chorus against Forfait, a compromise was apparently worked out. Fulton was informed in March that Bonaparte had approved funds for him to repair and use the *Nautilus* and that he would receive prize money on a very liberal schedule not much less than the terms he had proposed.

During the spring, Fulton repaired the *Nautilus*, and in July he took it to Brest for tests and an attack on the British. By this time his feelings of self-confidence and independence were leading him in several directions at once. He decided upon a major modification of the submarine: the addition of compressed air. Simultaneously he planned and had constructed a pinnace that utilized a crude screw propeller and twenty-four men to power the craft by turning hand-cranks. The purpose of this craft is unclear, but it surely wasn't to Forfait's liking. He ordered Fulton to attack the British in early July, but it was not until 8 August that the inventor finally got around to complying. He failed again this year for the same reasons as last: he was unable to get close enough to a British vessel to do any harm. And, as if the failure were not bad enough in itself, it appears that he did not even use the submarine at all, but rather the pinnace. Then he had the audacity to write to Bonaparte, claiming that he had failed to sink any British ships because he didn't have a good submarine.

When he returned to Paris on 8 September a note from Monge, Laplace, and Volney awaited him, asking that he account for his activities. He recorded his achievements in glowing terms, pronounced submarine navigation a proven accomplishment, and recommended that submarines be used essentially as modern minelayers—sowing drifting, contact "Submarine bombs" in enemy harbors and rivers. In response the scientists put to him a series of specific questions. He replied on 20 September in his haughtiest, most self-confident tone yet. He expressed regret at the news that Bonaparte wished to see the submarine, for he had broken it up and sold it for scrap on his own initiative after the tests had "proved" its capabilities. Furthermore, he informed them that he was no longer willing to reveal his plans. He said he was afraid that his ideas might be incautiously spread about, and he added:

> I consider this invention as my private property the Perfectionment of which will give to France incalculable advantages over her most Powerful and Active enemy. And which invention I conceive ought to Secure to me an ample Independence, that consequently the Government Should Stipulate certain terms with me before I proceed to further explination.[52]

Even his friends and supporters must have cringed some at this arrogance, but he perceived himself to be at the peak of his influence now and he was not about to mince words. His experiments had convinced him of the power of his machines, and he assumed everyone else was convinced as well. Confident that a lucrative government contract was in his pocket, he rebelled with a vengeance against the demeaning petitioning he had been forced to pursue over the last four years.

But his strutting was short-lived, for within two weeks the whole deal melted and ran through his fingers. On 1 October 1801, the date on which preliminaries of peace were signed with England, Forfait was replaced as Minister of Marine by Admiral Denis Decrès (1761–1820), a rough, crude, uneducated professional sailor who was to retain the post for the duration of the Consulate and Empire.[53] Forfait may have been hesitant about commissions, and he may have disagreed with Fulton on how best to use the inventions, but he was always sympathetic. The depth of Decrès's sympathy for Fulton and his schemes was summed up in his oft-quoted remark to the inventor: "Go, Sir, your invention is fine for the Algerians or corsairs, but be advised that France has not yet abandoned the Ocean."[54] That was the final scene of the final act. Fulton's efforts to sell underwater warfare in France ended just when he thought he had the whole deal all sewn up. Fulton's chances rose and fell with the tide of professional naval control of the Ministry of Marine, and with an admiral back at the helm, the crest of civilian support that Fulton was riding crashed precipitously, leaving him stranded on a reef of might-have-beens.

Perhaps Fulton had missed the main chance because his projects were not suited to what the First Consul wanted of the navy. During 1800 and 1801, when Fulton had his best opportunity, Bonaparte's two main goals at sea were the rescue of the army he had left stranded in Egypt and the invasion of England.[55] Underwater warfare couldn't be of much immediate help in either effort. So in 1802 Fulton changed course. After hedging his bet by writing to a friend in England to see if he might sell underwater warfare there, he directed his efforts in France to building a steamboat. The military objective in this project was to tow barges loaded with French troops across the English Channel during a calm.[56]

The scheme was perfected in 1803, and though he had earlier rejected the whole proposal, Bonaparte now waxed enthusiastic and ordered a speedy investigation—again by competent scientists. In August a prototype was demonstrated on the Seine before representatives of the *Institut National des Sciences et des Arts*, including such familiar figures from submarine days as Perrier, Prony, and Volney—all members of committees that had examined Fulton's plans. The report of the *Institut* has never been found, but the press spoke favorably enough of the demonstration to suggest general approval. Forfait, then serving as Counsellor of State, was directed to confer with Fulton. On 2 September he advised the First Consul that the inventor "imposes one condition without which he will not set to work, it is to have a very short conference with you. He has, he says, some political views of the very highest importance to share with you."[57]

There is no record of the meeting having taken place. The next month Fulton was in Amsterdam, openly communicating with contacts in England trying to get a Watt engine, and secretly negotiating with a British agent.[58] Playing both ends against the middle, he returned to Paris early in 1804. Apparently finding prospects there less appealing than an offer from England, he left Paris on 29 April and arrived in London on 19 May 1804.

VIII

Robert Fulton in England and America

ROBERT FULTON was a mercenary. That he finally got around to peddling his weapons and services in the United States does not alter the fact that he originally attempted to sell them to any promising bidder. His protestations that he only wanted to effect the "freedom of the seas" by institutionalizing underwater warfare also ring a little hollow. More than two centuries earlier, William Bourne had shown how "to profit the common wealth" with new ideas: simply publish them. Fulton's motives, however, were not nearly so altruistic as this. His activities in England and the United States during the last eleven years of his life reveal just how complex and self-centered his motives were.

In the Joel Barlow Papers in the Pequot Collection at Yale University is a thirty-one page draft of a letter from Fulton to William Pitt.[1] Though undated, it was apparently prepared in the spring or summer of 1804, and was corrected in Joel Barlow's hand. There is no evidence that it was ever sent to Pitt, but it nonetheless offers a clear glimpse into the inventor's mind as he began negotiations with the British. In it are exercised all the themes Fulton was to parade before the British government in the course of the next two and a half years.

"Science," begins the draft, "in its progress towards the improvement of Society has now begun the destruction of military navies." This noble goal, continues the letter, will be achieved with the *Nautilus*, an invention which will put "an end to maritime wars with all the dreadful catalogue of crimes which they entrain." Because two submarines cannot fight each other, maintained Fulton, his plan was built upon the "principle of equality among nations," making him a sort of democratic David slaying aristocratic giants. So confident was he of achieving these lofty consequences that he called upon the English aristocracy to "capitulate on terms honorable to humanity," give up their "unnecessary titles and exclusive distinctions," and open the door to free, egalitarian elections. Only these momentous ends, declared Fulton, "have induced me to put my hand to a work which I should otherwise abhor." The familiar make-war-horrible-in-the-name-of-humanity argument was the only apology to English sensibilities that he could muster.

As this amazing document suggests, Fulton was as easily flattered as offended. The Britsh overtures that had tempted him across the Channel had obviously gone to his head.[2] In contrast to the history of his French negotiations, he *began* the English adventure by pontificating and demanding. He seems to have had access to inside information throughout most of his negotiations with the British government,[3] but his initial reading of his position was well off the mark. Through their excellent intelligence system, the British were well informed of Fulton's activities in France. Their motives for luring him away seem to have been purely precautionary, simply to ensure that if he did perfect a new breed of weapon it would not be used to upset their naval supremacy. They had no interest in, nor intention of, institutionalizing his system, let alone allowing it to upset their form of government.

Pitt came to power while Fulton was in transit between Paris and London. Having made his original deal with the Addington ministry, Fulton was faced at the outset with the same kind of bureaucratic musical chairs that had marked his dealings with the French Ministry of Marine. The draft letter to Pitt shows that he adjusted rather smoothly, as does his meeting on 21 May with George Hammond, the Undersecretary of State for the Foreign Department.[4] Fulton drew up a set of proposals on 22 May 1804 and submitted them to Hammond with the plans for his weaponry and the suggestion of a demonstration attack on the French flotilla at Boulogne. Shortly thereafter a committee of distinguished experts was assigned to pass on Fulton's inventions. The committee consisted of two scientists—Sir Joseph Banks, President of the Royal Society, and Henry Cavendish, the famous chemist; two military representatives—William Congreve, the inventor of military rockets, and Captain Sir Home Popham, the agent of the Royal Navy; and John Rennie, the civil engineer.[5]

From the very start this arrangement of examination by committee—the same as Fulton had enjoyed in France—went not to his liking. First, the committee members didn't work fast enough to suit him. Then he took exception to the fact that their examination was limited to his written plans; he wanted to argue his own case in person as he had done so successfully in 1798. He even wanted to be able to name as many members to the committee as the government named, "conformable," he claimed, "to Mr. Addington's proposal."[6] When the committee did report late in June, Fulton was even more displeased, for they had rejected his proposal. While allowing that submarine navigation might be possible, they could not see any advantage from it accruing to England. Fulton responded quickly that there was more to the whole system than just the submarine and that England would be well advised in any case to prevent such a system from reaching other hands.

After some confusing negotiations and a succession of letters to Pitt and Hammond, a compromise was finally worked out between Fulton and Popham. On 20 July 1804, in an interview with Pitt, a government contract was signed. It provided Fulton with a monthly salary, an expense account for construction of his weapons, a liberal allowance of prize money, and compulsory arbitration in the event of disagreement with the government. Though precise evidence is scarce, it appears that most senior naval officers, along with some civilians like Banks and Rennie, were hostile to Fulton's plans, while Pitt and some individual naval officers like Popham and the First Lord of the Admiralty, Lord Melville, and some outsiders like Major Congreve and Cavendish were favorably disposed.[7] In the first round of negotiations, the latter coalition seems to have carried the day, though the submarine was permanently removed from consideration in favor of various plans for drifting, towed, and anchored mines.

On 2 October 1804, Fulton's plans were put to the test in the "Catamaran Expedition," a combined fireship and underwater warfare attack against the threat that bothered Pitt and his countrymen most—the invasion flotilla at Boulogne, then commanded by the same Admiral Bruix who was Minister of Marine during Fulton's second period of negotiations in France.[8] Named for the catamaran floats on which Fulton's "submarine Bombs" were hung, this expedition was an almost total failure. Similar in concept and execution to Bushnell's attack on *Cerberus*, it likewise managed to sink only one small auxiliary vessel. Another attempt was made in December, this time against Fort Rouge at the entrance of Calais Harbor. It had even less effect than the Boulogne attempt.[9]

Fulton apparently took the position that his weapons were not utilized exactly as he would have desired, so in his mind at least the issue was unresolved. The spring of 1805 was a bad time for the Royal Navy, what with the scandal over Lord Melville's handling of finances and the threat of invasion still very clear and present. Fulton got little attention during this time, and on 18 July finally wrote to Pitt. He complained that Lord Barham, Melville's successor, had not answered his letters and that he was unable to conclude his business satisfactorily. He felt he had lived up to the terms of his contract with the government by demonstrating (at least in theory) the efficacy of his weapons, and he was ready to settle up and return to the United States.

In the wake of this letter, Viscount Castlereagh, the new Minister of War, entered the picture, and a second attempt on Boulogne began to materialize.[10] With Castlereagh's support, an effort utilizing Fulton's "carcasses" and Congreve's rockets was prepared for early October. Sir Sidney Smith, one of the few naval officers sympathetic to the project, was placed in charge, and Castlereagh's position was used to overcome professional hostility, from Lord Barham on down. The attack came off on 1 October, but with even less effect than had the attack of the previous year. The only casualties this time were a French midshipman and three sailors transporting one of the "infernal machines" to shore after the attack.[11]

To salvage some credibility, Fulton soon thereafter staged a demonstration in the roads below Pitt's residence at Walmer

Castle. On 15 October, before a crowd of spectators and a pride of naval officers, he succeeded in completely destroying the captured brig *Dorothea* with one of his "Torpedoes." Of course the ship was anchored in quiet waters and Fulton's men had practiced the routine thoroughly the previous day, but the display was impressive nonetheless—at least to such as Fulton and Sidney Smith. The inventor now claimed that he had solved the problem frustrating his earlier efforts. The carcasses then had been so heavy that the

Figure 14. An 1810 engraving of Robert Fulton, after a painting by Benjamin West. The scene in the background is the 1805 sinking of the *Dorothea*, one of Fulton's proudest achievements. Less informed engravers later substituted a scene depicting one of Fulton's steamboats.

current would not sweep them far enough under the hull to be effective. By adding cork to the devices, he had made them sufficiently buoyant to swing into place.[12]

Then followed another series of efforts in the Channel, and another series of failures. Fulton wrote at length to Smith and Castlereagh arguing that his scheme must be made into a "system."[13] He wanted torpedo-boat squadrons manned by men of a separate naval corps who would do this kind of work as their only job and would receive prize money for their successes. He blamed professional naval hostility and obstructionism for his failures, and, like Bushnell before him, claimed that only training and public support stood between him and success.

By the middle of December he finally recognized the futility of this argument. Nelson's victory at Trafalgar in late October gave England unchallenged command of the seas. Napoleon turned his back on the Channel and the invasion of England. Public anxiety was noticeably lessened as fear of invasion disappeared. Fulton had missed his great chance to prove his weapon in combat, and, sensing the changed status of affairs, he set out on a new tack.

In a letter to Castlereagh on 13 December, although he maintained the fiction that it was in his best interest to stay in England and try to prosecute his plans, he allowed that he wanted to return to the United States, that he had in any case proved the efficacy of his inventions, and that he was ready to settle his affairs in England according to the terms of his contract. He asked for £60,000 in lump sum, and £2,000 a month for life on condition that he not reveal his plans to anyone else. On 6 January he sent the same terms to Pitt.

From that plateau his negotiations went into a downward spiral lasting eight months and terminating in a final settlement of £1,653, 18s., 8d. The path from his claim to his settlement was strewn with intemperate letters, threats to sell his weapons all over Europe, accusations of bad faith, and delusions of grandeur. Pitt had died late in January 1806. His successor, Lord Grenville, and the new First Lord of the Admiralty, Lord Howick (Charles Grey) were noticeably cooler to Fulton than had been the previous ministers. The initial correspondence was polite enough, but when no results were forthcoming Fulton soon demanded that arbitrators be appointed, as provided in his contract. The government still delayed, and only after vituperative and threatening letters from Fulton did they finally appoint a committee.

For this commission Fulton prepared a set of papers entitled "Drawings and Descriptions. . . . " From this we learn of the modifications Fulton had made to his plans since they were first presented to the French commission in 1798. The submarine had been redesigned and considerably improved—a far more sophisticated craft now than the *Turtle* upon which it was originally modeled. Complementing the submarine were various other modes of underwater warfare in which Fulton's timed and contact "carcasses," "torpedoes," and "submarine Bombs" might be used. These called for such modern employments as patterned mine fields and drifting mines.

The arbitration committee apparently had not the scientific expertise of the bodies previously assigned to investigate Fulton's plans. At least they were considerably less impressed. Their opinion was simply that they were not as convinced as was Fulton about the efficacy of his inventions. They found his threats to sell or publish his system abroad to pose little danger to England. They found his claims of practical success less than convincing. They considered all of his arrangements to be unreliable in bad weather, and they doubted that crews could be found for such unlawful service. To all of these exceptions there was more than a germ of truth, but Fulton argued against them exhaustively, both in writing and in a personal appearance before the committee. The members heard his rebuttal, and quickly rejected it. An appeal to Lord Grenville met the same fate. Fulton finally settled for his £1,600 (raising his total government subsidy while in England to £16,000) and left for the United States.

The reason most often cited for Fulton's failure is the quotation attributed to the Earl of St. Vincent: "Pitt was the greatest fool that ever existed, to encourage a mode of war which they who commanded the seas did not want, and which, if successful, would deprive them of it."[14] Actually, that is not a quote of St. Vincent but rather Fulton's paraphrase of what the admiral allegedly said to him in an interview in October 1805.[15] It is a little too neatly phrased to have been put just that way in the course of conversation, and one is led to suspect that Fulton phrased it to suit his own purposes. The implication of the statement, as Fulton worded it, is that if successful, underwater warfare would virtually undercut British command of the seas. While Fulton surely subscribed to this persuasion, there is no reason to feel that St. Vincent did.

Still, there is a grain of truth in the remark, for professional naval hostility in England was Fulton's constant foe. Many civilian government officials, and even a few naval officers, were sympathetic, but most admirals were skeptical at best, hostile at worst. The repeated failures of Fulton's attacks on the French played right into their hands, and the single success with the *Dorothea* was not enough to turn the argument. Behind the smoke screen of practical objections, the Royal Navy really stood on grounds of principle. If Fulton's machines didn't work, then they had no business supporting them; if they did work, they could still do nothing to enhance the Royal Navy's command of the sea. They opposed him on the former terms, but they would have opposed him on the latter terms as well had it been necessary.

In this professional opposition, moral disdain also played a role. The chivalric tradition was actively nourished in the Royal Navy, and the lingering aversion to strange, gunpowder weapons and clandestine attacks lurked just behind the facade of military propriety. The scope of naval prejudices and misconceptions about Fulton was revealed in a letter from Admiral George Berkeley to an American friend in London in September 1807—when Fulton was selling his machines in the United States:

> The Author or rather projector of your Torpedoes tried his hand upon John Bulls credulity, who possess full as much as his Transatlantick Children and after a very expensive Trial The Scheme was scouted not perhaps so much from its Failure, as from the Baseness & Cowardice of this species of Warfare. All stratagems are however allowed in War, and there are certain Regulations attached to Ingenuity of this kind which I rather suspect Mr. Fulton is not acquainted with, at least in England he rather *Blinked* the Question. Every Projector ought to be the Man, who first makes trial of his own Device, and then he is entitled to the Reward of his Merit. An officer who commands a Fire Ship, has a Gold Chain put round his Neck, if he is Successful, But if he is taken, a Hempen One is the

premium he is sure to Receive, which I think Friend Fulton would rather be surprised at.[16]

Of course "Friend Fulton" wouldn't have been surprised at all. He demanded and got commissions in England just as he had in France, for he was fully aware of the treatment likely to be meted out to operators of his devices. As for personal involvement, he actually manned the *Nautilus* while in France, and he accompanied the Boulogne raids in 1804 and 1805. This misperception of Fulton and his role was outdone only by Fulton's own inability to deal tactfully and reasonably with any hierarchical structure. His rampant ego and the Royal Navy's nurtured conservatism were a bad mix.

Evidently Fulton thought that events and institutions in the United States were more conducive to his plan . After spending nearly half of his forty-one years in Europe, he was home scarcely a month before he began peddling his machines in Washington.[17] He invited Secretary of State Madison and Secretary of the Navy Smith out to Joel Barlow's nearby estate at Kalorama. A demonstration there was sufficiently impressive to win for him a chance to prove his devices. The following July he successfully blew up a small vessel in New York Harbor, much as he had done two years earlier in England. Fulton thereupon approached the government of New York with his plans, recalling perhaps the success Bushnell had had with the Connecticut Council of Safety. But before anything came of this first effort, the successful launching and operation of the *Clermont*, on which he had been working intermittently since 1802, distracted him and kept him pleasantly diverted for more than two years.

In January 1810, he turned from his now successful commercial steamship enterprise to a full-fledged campaign to have underwater warfare adopted in the United States. He opened by publishing *Torpedo War and Submarine Explosions*, a hastily written propaganda pamphlet addressed to the President and Congress. In it he revealed still more variations on the delivery of his exploding devices. The submarine had completely disappeared by now, but the schemes developed in England were still present, and spar and harpoon torpedoes had been added. The first was simply a contact mine attached to the end of a pole extending well forward of a small boat. Its use involved nothing more than ramming. The latter device entailed a small harpoon to which a time-lock torpedo was attached by a rope. The harpoon was shot from a gun mounted in a small boat. When stuck in the side of a man-of-war, it would pull the torpedo into the water to drift under the enemy hull.

In terms suited to the dominant gunboat policy of the Jefferson years, Fulton argued the cost effectiveness of his torpedoes and torpedo boats as compared to other means of harbor and coast defense. Possibly Fulton learned this approach from William Congreve, who used it to great effect in defense of his own rocket system.[18] After another demonstration at Kalorama for administration and congressional leaders, Fulton's pamphlet was introduced in Congress and an appropriation of $5,000 was awarded to defray the expense of an exhibition in New York Harbor.[19]

As in France and England a commission was appointed to evaluate Fulton's plans, but this time there were some noticeable differences. First of all, Fulton was allowed to name all—or at least most—of the seven members of the commission. Second, the members had not quite the scientific credentials of earlier commissioners. Third, two naval officers were assigned to work with the committee and report on results, but they were not formally appointed as members. And finally, Fulton had the audacity—as well, apparently, as the political leverage—to write Secretary of the Navy Hamilton and ask for "the objections and plans of defence from the officers of the navy or persons connected with the Navy or Gentlemen opposed to the system." He further requested the Secretary to "order a Circular letter to be sent to the different officers Immediately and desire such of them as may be in this city or neighborhood to state their plans of defence to me."[20] Not only did he want a stacked committee free of naval officers, he also wanted to know in advance what the navy might do to try to frustrate his demonstration! At least it was clear in his mind who the enemies of his system were.

And he was right. The senior naval officer appointed to assist the committee was Commodore John Rodgers (1773–1838), described by a biographer as "grave in demeanor, rather bluff, independent, and a stickler for the forms of his profession."[21] The patriarch of one of America's grand naval families, he was not the sort of officer to be either amused or impressed by Fulton's plans to eliminate "a useless marine" or in fact war itself, with "its consequent thousands of idlers and oppressors."[22] Writing to his wife on 13 April 1810 on the subject of Fulton's plans, Rodgers revealed the type of naval assistance to be expected at the demonstration:

> It is the most absurd visionary scheme that can be conceived to have originated in the brain of a man not actually out of his senses, & I am astonished that Congress should have suffered themselves to be so far imposed on as even to notice it. This world however is a world of experiments.[23]

That closing lament was no sign of resignation. When the committee met in New York from September through November of 1810, Rodgers worked effectively to upset Fulton's demonstration. Indeed, not much effort was needed. Rodgers had the target ship *Argus* rigged with booms and nets to prevent Fulton's torpedoists from getting close enough to attach a charge, but beyond that fair defensive measure little opposition was required. Through chance and sloppy preparation nearly all of Fulton's demonstrations that fall failed to live up to billing, and the whole performance could hardly be termed anything but a dismal failure.

One suspects that Fulton was simply overconfident. In the Robert R. Livingston Papers at the New York Historical Society is a draft in Fulton's hand of the report that the inventor apparently prepared for the committee to hand in.[24] Livingston had long been Fulton's friend and associate in his steamboat project, and he was chairman of the committee, but he would not subscribe to this sort of thing. The committee submitted its own fair and unfavorable report, concluding that underwater warfare was not an entirely adequate means of coast and harbor defense. Several of the committee members, at Fulton's behest, sent individual letters to the Secretary of the Navy noting the potential of underwater warfare, and Fulton himself wrote a defense and rebuttal along the same lines. Rodgers's report, in the form of journal records during the trials, concluded with some satisfaction that Fulton's torpedoes were "to say the least, comparatively of no importance at all."[25]

The Secretary of the Navy forwarded all of these papers to Congress in February 1811, expecting that there had been sufficient potential demonstrated to warrant further development. But there the matter died. Once again Fulton was the victim of naval opposition and his own personality. Overconfident to a fault, he had let Commodore Rodgers win the day (almost entirely), and not even the "yes, but . . . " letters from his packed committee could undo the damage.

His final chance came during the War of 1812, but here again he made the same mistake he had made in France. Just when the government needed and might have bought the project he had long been proposing, he changed to a new invention. In this case he changed from his towed, anchored, and drifting mines to the *Demologos*, a low freeboard, heavily armored, steam "blockship" intended as a floating battery for coast and harbor defense.[26]

At the beginning of the war, Fulton was active enough with his torpedoes. "I have not been idle," he informed a fellow enthusiast early in 1813, continuing to argue that underwater warfare was "an infant art which requires only support and practice."[27] Throughout 1812 and 1813 he communicated with torpedoists, supplied them with mines of his own invention, sought out information on efforts he wasn't involved in, and tried to patent his torpedo inventions. In 1814 he even exhibited two of his detonating devices to his old nemesis, John Rodgers, then the senior officer on active duty.[28] But in the midst of this activity he formed the Coast and Harbor Defense Company, a private corporation similar in form and purpose to the Nautilus Company in France, to build the *Demologos*.[29] The difference in this instance was that Congress appropriated $500,000 to defray the costs of construction. The Demologos was launched on 20 October 1814, but was not fitted out in time to see action.

Its launching and initial trials did, however, provide a last glimpse into that suspicious, mysterious world of Fulton's mind. After seventeen years of dealing with naval establishments and trying to have his ideas on naval warfare "systemitized," he could stand not one more effort at "the slow convertion of minds not occupied on or embracing the whole subject." He wrote to President Madison on 5 November 1814 and asked in complete seriousness that he be appointed to replace outgoing Secretary of the Navy William Jones. Denying that he was "ambitious for office," Fulton argued that he "should like to have the power to organize, and carry my whole System into the most useful effect, in the least possible time: for which purpose, it is better to have the power to arrange and command."[30]

Fulton was not appointed; the *Demologos* did not see combat; his underwater warfare did not become a "System." But he had a profound impact nonetheless. If on his deathbed in 1816 he looked back on twenty years' work in underwater warfare as less than satisfying, it is because he had set his sights too high. Three motives impelled him in his endeavor, and in none of them did he succeed. His protestations about securing the "freedom of the seas" failed of achievement, first because it was impossible to start with, and second because he never fully believed in it himself. Describing his own deal with the British government, he said that once he had proven the efficacy of underwater warfare he "was to receive an adequate reward, leaving government to use or bury the invention in oblivion as they might think proper."[31] This hardly sounds like the same man who said: "It has never been my intention to hide these inventions from the world on any consideration."[32] Until his return to the United States and the success of his steamship, money was always his primary consideration. However much he might have believed that the "Liberty of the seas will be the happiness of the earth," this never took precedence over his cupidity. And the money he expected for his inventions was always out of proportion to the results he could demonstrate.

The third motive, hidden throughout most of his career, came to the fore after the financial success of the *Clermont*. It was fame, *gloire*, public approbation. The exaggeration of his achievements, the boasting of the power to alter history, the indignation when he felt he was ignored or patronized—all were reflections of an enormous ego yearning to be publicly petted. His dearest ambition (at least after his fortune was assured) was to have it said of him what he said of James Watt: "here is a Virtue of the highest order here is a benefactor of mankind a proved ornament to his country the very mention of whose name fills every just and generous mind with respect for his high character."[33]

Underwater warfare failed to satisfy this desire, as it had both of his other ambitions. He looked upon the steamboat as a commercial success, but he looked to underwater warfare to win him fame, almost as if by constant repetition he had come to believe his own rhetoric about "freedom of the seas" and its influence on history. If in the wake of his steamboat the world at large forgot about his Davidic jousts, he might at least have taken some solace to know that he had spread the news of underwater warfare farther than had any man before him, and that among the peculiar devotees of this arcane warfare he won the *gloire* he so coveted.

IX

In Fulton's Footsteps

FOR MORE than two centuries the movers and shakers of underwater warfare had been strewing hints and markers in the woods as they followed one another through the otherwise pathless trek of discovery. So quickly did the flora grow up around such blazes as they left that at times the route was almost lost to sight. But always some new David would come upon the path—often fortuitously—and find enough of a trail to follow in the footsteps of his predecessors. One such was Fulton; but his was a trek with a difference. He trod with such a heavy foot, cut such a wide swath, and brought such an enormous retinue in his train that after him the path was indelible and easily spotted from afar. Even a cursory survey of the men who dogged Fulton's footsteps will reveal how thoroughly he had done his work.

His American retinue alone—were their efforts in the War of 1812 ever to be fully chronicled—could fill a volume.[1] Like Fulton's own schemes, theirs ranged from the fantastic to the practical, and like him they experienced all manner of failure and success, but never quite attained institutionalization of their efforts.

An anonymous "Gentleman from the State of New York" opted for the Bourne/Papin alternative and published his ideas on underwater warfare in an essay appended to an 1815 edition of Machivelli's *Art of War*.[2] His ideas revealed a thorough and acknowledged debt to Fulton but harbored a sprinkling of original schemes as well. Some were merely fanciful, like a horse-propelled boat and a remotely controlled exploding ship. Others, such as a magnetic mine and a spar torpedo, had the germ of important innovations. There was surely more imagination than experimentation behind these proposals, but the foundation was firmly anchored in the tradition from which Fulton drew. When the gentleman advanced the entirely practical idea of a chemical fuse, he confessed he didn't know how it worked but had read it "in old books" and heard it asserted.[3]

Rather than publishing their schemes "for the good of the common wealth," most of Fulton's imitators in the War of 1812 took the Gianibelli tack: they prepared and used their machines themselves. Of these some worked directly with Fulton, while others proceeded on their own. Sailing Master Elijah Mix, U.S.N., is the best known example of the former type. Using mines provided by Fulton he made six aborted attempts in July 1813 to send paired torpedoes drifting into H.M.S. *Plantagenet* (74 guns), then moored in Lynnhaven Roads just west of Norfolk. Finally on his seventh attempt, on 24 July, he got in the proper position and set his machines adrift. They went off prematurely and accomplished little, but Mix enjoyed a good press nonetheless.[4]

Other efforts did not directly involve Fulton, but they reflected the climate he had done so much to create. Two torpedo craft are of particular importance, for their activities on Long Island Sound evoke memories of Bushnell as well as of Fulton. One boat, "resembling a turtle" and "floating just above the surface," was built in New York, where Fulton was working on his own *Demologos*. Unfortunately it grounded on Long Island while being moved up the Sound to prey on shipping off the Connecticut coast. The British attempted to capture her, but local citizens held them off while the craft was cannibalized and destroyed.[5] A submarine built by a native of Norwich, Connecticut, was reportedly taken to New London where it made several unsuccessful attempts to fasten torpedoes to the hull of H.M.S. *Ramilles*, apparently with the same auger device Bushnell and Fulton had used.[6]

Numerous other efforts were made, all of this same familiar genre. Most seem to have centered on the Chesapeake Bay and Long Island Sound, but not even the Great Lakes were immune to such essays. Fulton took part in some, collected information on others, and generally contributed to a receptive climate for all.[7] By the summer of 1813 these attacks were so frequent and familiar that *Niles Register* was able to report: "The much ridiculted torpedo is obtaining a high reputation."[8]

The British response to all of this activity was indignation. "Inhuman," "barbarous," "infamous," "knavish," "ignoble," and "cowardly" were some of the adjectives used by the English press to describe American use of underwater warfare.[9] The officers of the Royal Navy were even more outraged. Captain Hardy off New London declared that if the government sanctioned an attack on his fleet by any form of exploding ship he would sink every vessel that came within reach of his guns, be they warship or no. H.M.S. *Ramilles* was even stocked with prisoners of war as a deterrent to future attacks.[10]

The hypocrisy of this self-righteous indignation was not lost on the Americans. Newspapers and magazines were quick to remind their readers that this same Royal Navy had paid Fulton for his torpedoes, used them against the French, and freely indulged other "cruelties" in their "bloody and brutal war" on the United States.[11] *Niles Register* lashed out at the British duplicity which ridiculed underwater warfare in one instance and condemned it as unethical in the next:

> The morality of these folks is like the *religion* of a certain celebrated city, where, it was said, they *manufactured* vast quantities for *exportation* and *foreign* service—but had *none* for *home* use.—The enemy fights in the *air* with his rockets—he fights *under the earth* with his mines, and yet *he* is hugely "religious." May it not then become "a moral and religious people," like *we* are, to fight *under the water*, with torpedoes and diving-boats?[12]

This judged the British a little harshly, for they had not uniformly taken to underwater warfare when Fulton proposed it. There was considerable opposition then, and a hot debate on the subject had been going on ever since. A correspondent signing himself "F.F.F." voiced the con side of the debate in a series of letters to *Naval Chronicle* in 1809. In a general broadside against all forms of "murderous machines," he opposed adoption of torpedoes, rockets, and even shrapnel on both practical and moral gounds. On practical grounds he rehearsed the argument Fulton attributed to St. Vincent, that England ought not to encourage naval systems that could upset her control of the seas. On moral grounds he found it "base," "Horrible," and "revolting" that "*one* crafty murderous ruffian" could secretly blow up the whole stout crew of a ship of the line. Ominously he prophesied:

> Battles in future may be fought under water: our *invincible* ships of the line [italics added] may give place to horrible and unknown structures, our frigates to catamarans, our pilots to divers, our hardy, dauntless tars, to submarine *assassins*, coffers, rockets, catamarans, infernals, water worms, and fire devils. How honourable! how fascinating is such an enumeration! how glorious, how fortunate for Britain are discoveries like these! How worthy of being adopted by a people, made wanton by naval victories, by a nation whose empire are the seas.[13]

Here, then, in a paragraph was three centuries' worth of argument against the adoption of underwater warfare. The devotee of the "invincible ship of the line" opposed weapons he associated with the devil ("infernals," "fire devils") because they would tend to upset the hierarchy of power. All this summation lacked to make it a full representation of Western military thought was a clearer statement that the clandestine nature of these weapons was their other morally objectionable feature. Oddly enough, this soon appeared in a rebuttal to F.F.F.'s letter.

A correspondent signing himself "H." gave some credence to the objection that torpedoes "are understood to be employed in the darkness and silence of night, against a helpless and unsuspecting enemy,"[14] that is, that they are clandestine and, to that degree, reprehensible. Therefore he allowed that they "ought never to be resorted to, but for the accomplishment of some great and important purpose." In other words, the sovereign could use them when he perceived them to be "necessary." The argument was right out of the eighteenth-century international law books, and its sequel was out of John Donne's "Sermon CXVII." Gunpowder weapons, argued H., "so far from . . . increasing the number of slain . . . have a tendency to shorten the contest, and thus to spare the effusion of blood . . . , as history will incontestably prove." In other words, let us make war horrible in the name of humanity. With that pronouncement these two correspondents had covered the whole debate over the adoption of underwater warfare.

The argument went on in the *Naval Chronicle*, just as it did in the Western world at large, with neither side yet winning the day. F.F.F. fueled the debate with a eulogy of "*round* and *grape*" and a further condemnation of "that diabolical species of warfare."[15] Another advocate took up H.'s cause and characterized this kind of "vulgar abuse . . . the lucubrations of a writer whose principles and stile seem more calculated for the sphere of the self-created magistry, calling itself the Society for the Suppression of Vice."[16] This correspondent addressed himself to a defense of Congreve's rockets, directing his remarks to "scientific correspondents" and "*rational* readers" as opposed to the "enthusiasts and bigots" of the F.F.F. stripe. Ignoring this insult, F.F.F. responded instead to H.'s attack, claiming that to class cannon and fire ships together, as H. had done, compared "in point of honor" to classing the duelist with "the midnight incendiary."[17] F.F.F. was satisfied with dueling, but he had no use for the "diabolical warfare" in which the foe approaches surreptitiously, "like a snake."

The prejudices these men put into words were brought together cleverly in an undated watercolor produced about this time.[18] The event portrayed was a metaphorical encounter between Underwater Warfare and the Royal Navy. The artist depicts the large green head of a sea monster rising out of the waves, its mouth spewing fire, chain shot, snakes, pistol, hammer, scissors, bones, spears, a powder keg, cannon, and a skeleton, its fists clenched in boxing style. On the serpent's head stands a devil holding a pennant of stars and stripes. The object of this assault is a British sailor standing on the deck of a large ship with his hindquarters turned toward these assailants. The thousand words encompassed in that picture run the gamut from associations with the devil through clandestine warfare to the act of idolization and professional naval disdain.

Thus progressed underwater warfare in the War of 1812. Like the torpedo attacks themselves, this propaganda barrage had scarcely any effect, other than keeping Fulton and his inventions in the public eye. As F.F.F. lamented in 1809, "the construction of the famous, or rather infamous, coffers is so well understood throughout the country, that any attempt to describe them . . . would be highly superfluous."[19] Fulton was doing his own advertising as well. In 1810 he sent Earl Stanhope ten copies of *Torpedo War* with the request that he distribute them to the right people.[20] Fulton claimed that he was only warning the British of his powers, and he made no overt offer, but Stanhope was the same old friend who had initiated the first overture to Fulton in 1803, and one suspects that the inventor would at least have listened to a similar proposal now. Just as he had done in 1803, Stanhope accommodated Fulton by announcing his plans in some detail before the House of Lords.

But more than just drawing attention to himself, Fulton drew others to research in underwater warfare. Tilloch's *Philosophical*

Figure 15. "The Yankee Torpedo," by Thomas Tegg (c.1814), watercolor inside the front cover of one of John S. Barnes's two personal copies of his book, *Submarine Warfare. Courtesy of The New York Historical Society, New York City.*

Magazine in 1804 excavated and published Napier's memoir on submarines, and noted the contributions of Drebbel and Boyle.[21] A correspondent signing himself "Vulcan" advised the editor of the *Naval Chronicle* in 1808 of William Winterbotham's 1795 treatment of Bushnell and concluded that Fulton was nothing but a plagiarist.[22] At the end of the section on "Infernal Machines" in the third edition (1810) of Charles James's *Military Dictionary* a new note advised "see Turtle." Under that heading was found a somewhat confused description of a craft that was half *Turtle* and half *Nautilus*. Capping the article was the blanket pronouncement that Fulton's inventions "were direct imitations, or rather copies, of the American Turtle."[23] Similarly, the 1815 edition of *Falconer's Marine Dictionary* listed "Torpedo" as "an infernal machine" and gave the same account as appeared in James's *Military Dictionary*, plus a description of Mix's attempt on *Plantagenet*. Under the heading of "Sub-Marine *Nautilus*" appeared a reference to a published French account of the subject, and "Diving-Bladder" was identified as "a term used by Borelli."[24] Virtually the whole Western record on underwater warfare was reappearing in print.

The story in France was much the same. Here too Fulton sent copies of *Torpedo War* to the well placed and the well disposed—in this case his old friends Monge, Laplace, and Volney.[25] If this gesture were not mercenary enough to dispel any lingering notions about the purity of his motives, then the contents of his letter should be. In an otherwise blatant appeal for financial remuneration, he covered his motives with the thin and glossy protestation that he only wanted "to see commerce free, peace restored to the continent and the Genius of the Emperor relieved from the fatigues of war, directed to repair its losses, by pursuits as dear to his heart as interesting to his people by promoting the arts and converting France into a garden."[26] Egalitarians of the order Fulton claimed to be might scruple to partake of the garden Napoleon was making in 1810, but Fulton apparently felt no qualms about offering his services to the Emperor—even while his proposals were also pending before the British and American governments.

Whatever personal rewards Fulton hoped to gain from this entreaty, such advertising was hardly necessary to keep his ideas alive in France. Imitation of his work had been going on ever since he left. Proposals for submarines were drawn up and submitted to scientific academies and to government. Articles and whole treatises were published on submarine navigation and attack. Submarines were actually constructed and tested, and at least one was named *Nautile*. Fulton's life and work were described in a national journal; his *Torpedo War* was translated into French in 1812.[27]

By far the most fascinating document to emerge from this spate of activity was Jacques-Philippe Mérigon de Montgéry's *Mémoire sur les mines flottantes et les petards flottans, ou machines infernales maritimes*.[28] The title itself, in distinguishing as it did between mines and petards, yet classifying both as infernal machines, showed a keen appreciation of the history of underwater warfare. As any such history should, Montgéry's began with Gianibelli, claiming that he deserved the credit for creating the first floating mines. Citing Strada's *De bello belgico*, the same source used by Schott and all subsequent historians, Montgéry called the Italian's efforts at Antwerp the only significant use of "infernal machines" before the attack on La Rochelle in 1628. Though he didn't seem to know that Drebbel was involved in that latter use of "floating petards," he nevertheless knew of the Dutchman's submarine through a reading of Mersenne. From there he proceeded to a discussion of British efforts in the late seventeenth century and then directly to Bushnell. His source seems to have been Bushnell's article on "General Principles," an indication that not everyone took Fulton and his claim at face value. He translated Bushnell's "magazine" as a "petard"; the term "torpedo" he rightly credited to Fulton, whose invention he likened to a cross between the petards at La Rochelle and the "barrels" of Bushnell.[29]

Following this history, Montgéry settled down to an appreciative critique of Fulton's system, and a series of proposals for improving upon it. He suggested, for example, that instead of Fulton's field of anchored torpedoes, barrages of connected mines should be used to protect harbors and channels. He stressed offensive uses of torpedo boats, as opposed to the defensive posture Fulton outlined in *Torpedo War*. And he even suggested that steam might be used to propel the torpedo boats in harpoon attacks.[30] He closed by praising Fulton's genius and scoring the French government for failure to promote and encourage underwater warfare. It was in a new and innovative country like the United States, he believed, that such inventions as Fulton's had their best chance of realization.[31]

Before returning to the United States to see if that prediction was correct, it will be instructive to look to one more European country for evidence of the distances to which underwater warfare spread in Fulton's wake. Russia was a Western oriented country by this time and as likely as any other European nation to attract innovations in weaponry. Evidence is especially rare in this case, but that any at all has surfaced is indication of considerably more yet to be discovered. The principal source on early Russian efforts in underwater warfare is A. A. Samarov and F. A. Petrov, editors, *Development of Mine Material in the Russian Navy: A Collection of Documents.*[32] This cold war propaganda piece was prepared in 1951 with the express purpose of "reconstruction of the historical truth and proof of the priority of the Russians in the invention and development of naval mines."[33] These objectives are pursued through careful selection and editing of documents so as to eliminate or gloss over any reference to Western influences. This obvious manipulation only makes the references that escaped the editors all the more suggestive.

For example, the first major figure introduced by the Russians is Ivan Ivanovitch Fitstum (c. 1765–1829), an army engineer who made various proposals and experiments in underwater warfare between 1807 and 1810. He was reportedly described by his contemporaries as one of the most educated officers of his time, and in Russia that meant a familiarity with Western knowledge. In his writing on mines, for example, he twice referred to "petards," and specifically mentioned "an incendiary English rocket."[34] What other references may have been deleted from his writings one can only guess, but it seems safe to assume that some information had reached him from Europe. This doesn't negate his original contributions—particularly in electrical detonation and the use of floating mines for harbor defense—but it does suggest that his efforts reflected similar activity in Europe.

A more original contribution, one in which the Russians hold a firmer but less appreciated claim to importance, was the Committee on Underwater Experiments, formed in October 1839 within the Engineering Section of the Army.[35] This seems to have been the first permanently organized underwater warfare institution to enjoy official status within a military hierarchy. Originally formed to investigate the feasibility of using mines in harbor defense, the committee conducted its principal researches between 1840 and 1843. It then reported favorably on the efficacy of mines and continued thereafter to work on perfecting them.

The committee was composed of four army officers, one naval officer, and one scientist—identified in the Russian documents as Boris Semyonovich Jakobi (1801–1874). (Actually, this was Mortiz-Hermann Jacobi, a German physicist whose national origin was apparently something of an embarrassment to the Soviet historians.[36]) Jacobi was the jewel of the committee; it was he who generated most of the reports and who planned most of the experiments, and it was he who contributed—in addition to his own original inventions—the most likely source of contact with Europe. Again, the documents offer little positive evidence, but the fact that the committee reported testing "a fuse, invented in England" suggests that there was no absolute bar to European influence.[37] When Jacobi reported late in 1857 that "the torpedo has not been taken seriously in the past fifty years either as a means of offense or defense,[38] he could have been referring to the Russian experience in particular or to the experience of the Western world in general. It seems safe to assume that he was acquainted with both.

With the expertise gained in the 1840s, the Russians were able to avail themselves of underwater warfare in the Crimean War. They laid various chemical, contact-detonated and electrical, command-detonated mines in both the Black and Baltic seas. These were intended as harbor and river defenses, and were also integrated with the defenses of major ports like Sebastopol, Cronstadt, and Sweaborg. Generally speaking, the mines themselves were sophisticated and comparatively reliable, but they were mismanaged and achieved little. In one instance off Sweaborg in 1855, a barrage of electrical mines was poorly prepared and hastily planted, and all of the preparations were accomplished in the face of matériel shortages. When the detonators were hooked up in the presence of advancing British ships, the mines went off prematurely and harmed nothing besides the harbor marine life. An effort at Cronstadt with contact mines enjoyed hardly more success. The mines detonated correctly when run upon by British ships, but they contained such small charges that they did virtually no damage to the vessels.[39]

The Russians recognized the failings of their mining program, and after the war various proposals were made to improve the record. As a result, a Committee on Mines was established within the navy. This committee met from 1857 to 1869, but because its members were assigned to it as an additional duty, it was never entirely effective. It seldom met in full and was restricted mostly to the examination of reports.[40] With the failure to make this committee a strong, productive body, the Russians missed an excellent chance to be the real originators of modern underwater warfare. By the mid-1860s the chance had passed them by.

What this brief survey, culled from the Russian documents, fails to mention are the numerous inputs to Russia provided by Europeans. For example, the documents do not even mention Wilhelm Bauer (1822–1875), described by one authority as "the most persistent inventor to be found in the whole history of submarine navigation."[41] A native of Bavaria, Bauer built his first submarine at Kiel in 1850. It sank the following year. He then took his ideas to Austria, where a committee appointed to examine his proposal reported favorably. He was awarded £4,240 for the construction of a new submarine, but opposition to the project soon arose within the government and construction was canceled. He then went to England, where he attracted the support of Prince Albert. Again he received financing, but the project ended in disaster when the boat went down with considerable loss of life. After an unsuccessful appeal to the United States, Bauer took his project to Russia.

There he built a fifty-two-foot, iron-hulled, hand-powered submarine with which he planned to attach a five-hundred-pound mine to enemy ships. In contrast to his earlier efforts, this craft was a complete success, and with it he reportedly made 134 dives between 1856 and 1858. The vessel was officially presented to a commission representing the Russian Navy. Jacobi was a member of that commission, but apparently he was unwilling or unable to overcome professional military hostility to the German. Officers put obstacles in Bauer's path at every turn and finally succeeded in driving him out of Russia in 1858, just as their historians would succeed in driving him from their records nearly a century later. His submarine and his ideas stayed in Russia, but he received scant appreciation or recognition for either of them.[42]

Nor do the Russian documents give proper credit to the contributions of Immanuel Nobel. This Swedish chemist, father of the more famous munitions manufacturer, Alfred, is described in a footnote in the documents as "a foreigner who owned a factory for the manufacture of mines." However, the footnote's closing judgment that "these mines were of poor quality" seems hardly borne out by the evidence. Alfred Nobel's biographers state that Immanuel was well received in Russia early in the 1840s, that he produced a "magnificent work" on his own *Systeme de défense maritime pour passages et ports sans fortifications dispendieuses et avec épargne d'hommes*, and that the Russian authorities considered his mines superior to those of native production.[43]

Even Fulton's ideas were available to the Russians in the early nineteenth century. One possible source of this information was Immanuel Nobel himself. He was active in Swedish engineering and invention before his departure for Russia in the late 1830s. It is entirely possible that he was familiar with the replica of one of Fulton's mines which was constructed at the dockyard in Karlskrona in 1831 by the yard ordnance officer, C. D. Osterman. The plans for this model were provided by a Swedish officer who visited the United States in the 1820s and reportedly made his sketches from one of the original Fulton mines.[44]

Still another source of Fulton's ideas was a set of plans he himself sent to Russia in 1798. An 1856 letter from Taliaferro P. Shaffner to George Moore, now in the Robert Fulton Papers at the New York Historical Society, reveals the strange history of these plans.[45] Fulton originally entrusted them, along with a set of his plans for canal improvement, to Augustin de Betancourt in Paris on 7 October 1798.[46] The general was requested to present them to Catherine the Great, but she died before he could complete his mission. How Betancourt disposed of the plans is not known, but apparently they remained in Russia. Later, during the Crimean

War, the allied bombardment of Sweaborg necessitated the removal of the files from the fortress there. In the archives were found Fulton's plans. They were turned over to Betancourt's nephew, who in turn presented them to Shaffner. Shaffner sent them back to the New York Historical Society and reported that the mine defenses then being used by the Russians were proof that "Fulton's ideas of the application of the sciences to the arts are realised."

To what extent the Russians drew upon these papers it is now impossible to determine. But one fact is apparent: Fulton's ideas had spread over much of the Western world. It is known that he personally visited four countries trying to sell his weapons, that he sent his plans to a fifth, and that yet another nation prepared a model of his torpedo from firsthand observation. Even where a country like Russia now tries to erase its contacts with Fulton, and with Western ideas in general, evidence of the ties still seeps through. After Fulton, underwater warfare was part of the common knowledge of the Western world, and attention must now shift from where the idea originated to where it would be consummated. As Montgéry correctly prophesied, this would be in the United States.

Figures 16 and 17. Replica of a Fulton anchored torpedo constructed in Sweden in 1831 after plans made by Axel Klinckowstrom, a Swedish officer who visited the United States in the 1820s. Immanuel Nobel may have carried the ideas of this mine to Russia when he went there in the late 1830s. *Courtesy of Marinmuseum, Karlskrona, Sweden.*

X

Samuel Colt and the Electrical Connection

SAMUEL COLT (1814–1862) took up where Fulton left off. In an undated letter to William Brents, apparently written early in 1811, Fulton revealed that he had investigated electrical detonation of mines but had discovered two serious obstacles. The first problem was the necessity of protecting the wires from damage by the elements or the enemy, and second was the difficulty of determining when an enemy vessel was over the mine.[1] Colt's years in underwater warfare were spent wrestling with these same two problems.

One of his biographers maintains that Colt first learned of Fulton and of galvanic batteries in 1825 from the same source—a book entitled the *Compendium of Knowledge*, one of three volumes owned by the family to which Colt was then indentured.[2] By his own claim, he set off his first underwater detonation in 1829 and continued to refine his procedures during the next twelve years.[3] At the same time, of course, he was also perfecting and marketing his more famous revolver, and this experience introduced him not only to the world of patents, industry, and finance, but also to the frustrating business of peddling weapons in Washington. So when he came to offer his inventions in underwater warfare, he had considerable experience in such business—most of it thoroughly unpleasant.

His principal strategy in opening negotiations with the government was to eschew all contact with the military, especially the army. He began in the spring of 1841 by approaching Samuel L. Southard, the president *pro tempore* of the Senate. He showed Southard the plans of what he called his submarine battery, enlisted his support, and on the senator's advice did the same with Major General William G. McNeil, late of the Corps of Topographical Engineers. With the endorsement of these two men, Colt then wrote to President Tyler on 19 June 1841.[4] He referred the president to reports in the *American State Papers, Naval Affairs* on Fulton's inventions and advised him that advances since then, combined with an invention of his own making, had allowed him to achieve the objectives Fulton was pursuing. He offered, as Fulton had done in France and the United States, to prepare a demonstration at his own expense on condition that if successful he would be reimbursed for his expenditures and granted an annual stipend.

The advances he referred to were refinements in underwater cables, achieved largely through the efforts of Professor Robert Hare of the University of Pennsylvania, and then being pursued most actively in the field of underwater telegraphy by Samuel F. B. Morse. Another American, Moses Shaw, had used cables to detonate underwater charges in demolition and salvage work in 1831, as had Sir Charles Pasley in 1839. Colt's claim to originality was that he successfully combined these generally known procedures with his own method of determining when a ship was located exactly above one of his charges, thus solving both of the problems earlier posed by Fulton. This second feat was accomplished either through two operators on shore making simultaneous cross-sightings, or through one operator utilizing a mirror in a camera obscura arrangment.[5]

But Colt insisted on secrecy, and these details were then known only to Southard and McNeil. From the president he was referred to the secretary of the navy, George E. Badger. To him also he revealed the plans of his battery, requesting now that the government provide some money at the outset to help defray the $20,000 he estimated a demonstration would cost. Under pressure from

Southard, himself a former secretary of the navy, Badger declared himself favorably disposed, but protested that he needed congressional approval. Thereupon Colt approached Representative Henry A. Wise, the chairman of the House Committee on Naval Affairs, and he, too, was let in on the secret.

This behind-the-scenes politicking led to an unwritten deal between Colt and the navy. Part of a $50,000 navy appropriation passed by Congress on 11 September 1841 was unofficially earmarked for Colt's experiments. To satisfy the inventor's mania for secrecy, this provision was not spelled out in the legislation, nor is it even clear how many congressmen were aware of the arrangement. A single letter from Badger to Southard confirming the agreement is in fact the only proof of its reality—except for Colt's own assertions.[6] The legality, to say nothing of the propriety, of such a deal was questionable at best, and it returned to haunt Colt for many years thereafter. Nor was this the only shady business involved, for, at the same time, Colt was selling shares in his invention, and Senator Southard was among the earliest subscribers—a clear case of what one would now call conflict of interest.[7]

Like Fulton in France and England, Colt was to have considerable difficulty with rotating naval administrations. Two days after the appropriation was passed, Badger was replaced as secretary of the navy by Abel P. Upshur, the second of six different secretaries of the navy with whom Colt would have to deal.[8] This first and most important rotation stymied Colt's efforts almost immediately. By mid-October, John D. Simms, the chief clerk at the Navy Department, balked at disbursing money to Colt without written authorization. Badger had apparently left him none and Upshur was not yet privy to the agreement. Colt asked Badger to confirm the arrangement in writing, but the retired secretary replied that his letter to Southard should suffice, though he did agree to talk to Upshur the next time he was in town.[9]

There followed a courting of the new secretary by the same forces that won over his predecessor. Upshur was apprised of Colt's system, visited by McNeil, and graced with a long letter from Colt describing the transactions to date. As he was wont to do in such entreaties, Colt enclosed some Fulton documentation to demonstrate the importance of underwater warfare—in this case an undated letter from Jefferson to Fulton commending torpedoes as a means of harbor defense. Colt asked for the secretary's discretion and support, for modest financial assistance, and for freedom from "the interference of any subordinate officers of Government," claiming that "the want of means, together with the whims of old officers, checked by fears, prejudices, or motives equally adverse to improvements, too often smother inventions in the births, which if properly fostered would prove incalculably useful."[10]

Following a personal interview, Colt and Upshur came to an understanding. Its exact conditions are unknown, but some hints do exist. In a letter to the secretary on 24 November, Colt said he would proceed with his demonstration as Upshur had requested and would "trust to the justice & future good faith of the Government for a reward adequate to my invention."[11] In January he wrote to Southard, explaining the agreement in somewhat more detail:

> Mr. Upshur seemed to understand and appreciate my plans perfectly & it is the understanding between us that if I can prove to the President & other members the cabinet that I can with positive certainty destroy a ship at pleasure by means of my submarine battery at a distance greater then the range of any known projectile he will recommend to Congress that immediate meens shall be appropriated to imploy my Engines for the general protection of our Coast & reward me for my secret.[12]

Whatever the details of the agreement, Upshur made an authorization for Colt to prepare a demonstration and even provided goverment funds for that purpose, beginning on 16 December 1841.[13] With these in hand, Colt set about catching up on the rhetoric of his own salesmanship. It appears that he was overly optimistic about the time required to transfer his plans from paper to hardware, and he stalled an increasingly impatient Upshur through the spring of 1842.[14] Finally in June he set off his first successful explosion in New York Harbor, and the following month he destroyed a small gunboat below Castle Garden—all amidst a whirl of publicity which belied his demands for secrecy. Then he went to Washington for what he believed would be the clinching demonstration. Before the president and other government dignitaries, he succeeded in sinking a schooner in the Potomac River on 20 August 1842.

Over the objections of John Quincy Adams, who considered Colt's schemes "cowardly, and no fair or honest warfare," Congress granted an appropriation of $15,000 for continued experiments.[15] By joint resolution, the secretary of the navy was directed on 31 August to assist Colt in a demonstration to determine if his system could destroy moving vessels while its operators were beyond the range of their guns. It was also to be shown that the mines could be replaced in the presence of enemy ships and that they could successfully defend harbors without endangering friendly traffic. The $15,000 was to be taken from the $50,000 appropriation of the previous September. So in addition to authorizing further expenditures, this resolution also gave retroactive sanction to the money already spent. The secretary was directed to report to the next session of Congress, that is, to the first session of the Twenty-eighth Congress.[16]

With this public legislative endorsement of his activities, Colt now waxed independent, just as Fulton had so disastrously in France and the United States. First, he showed himself to be hardly more enamored of the navy's bureaucracy than he was of the army's. Writing to the chief clerk of the Navy Department in September, he said: "If I am permitted to conduct my experiments in my own way without being bothered by Navy Yard regulations, I will guarantee to accomplish all that is required of me by Congress for less expence & in less time than can otherwise be expected." With a tactlessness reminiscent of Fulton he went on to observe that "The cost of *hack hire* (to say nothing of the personal anoyance & wast of time) was far greater than the advantages I derived from the Washington Navy Yard while making my late exhibition on the Potomac."[17] Obviously he wanted to keep uniformed interference to a minimum and his own independence at a maximum.

He established himself at New York University, and after a gratuitous display of his weapons in the harbor, he began serious work on his final demonstration. This was to be destruction of a moving vessel in the Potomac River, effected by operators beyond gun range. He kept the secretary informed of his progress by mail, but otherwise acted on his own.

One of the most interesting features of Colt's whole career in underwater warfare is the extensive research he did into earlier efforts. His citation of the *State Papers* concerning Fulton has already been mentioned, as has the letter from Jefferson. Colt also got a copy of Fulton's 1804 contract with the British government[18] and later used it to prove the importance of underwater warfare. In fact, all the Fulton material he gathered served two purposes: first, to instruct him on Fulton's torpedoes, and second, to show government officials the importance such men as Jefferson and Pitt attached to underwater warfare.

But Fulton was only the most public of his researches. Privately Colt carried on a still more intensive investigation into past exploits. In the undated section of his papers in the Connecticut Historical Society are numerous scribbled notes which suggest the depth of his researches. One refers to "mr Bushnells Submarine Boate & Torpedo" and to a Professor Park at Washington College in Hartford, Connecticut, who had information on "Halsey's Submarine exploits in New London" in 1814. Another lists various military figures and closes with the note: "John the Sizer helped to make Torpedo for Halsey." This item also includes a sketch of a craft roughly similar to the *Turtle*, labeled "J. Sizer maker of Torpedo." Yet another shows a sketch of a one-man submarine with many of the features of the *Turtle*, though it is labeled as Halsey's invention.

There is also evidence in Colt's correspondence that he ran down many of these leads. He wrote to a Captain Partridge, late of the U.S. Army, who was reportedly informed on the efforts in underwater warfare made by Uriah Brown in the War of 1812. He corresponded with a Luther Sargent, who directed him with letters of introduction to New London, Stonington, Saybrook, and New Haven. Sargent, possibly a relative of Fulton's crewmate in France, "Captain Nath'l Sargent," told Colt about Bushnell, but wasn't sure what war he had fought in. As Sargent recommended, Colt himself went to Connecticut "for the purpose of [getting]

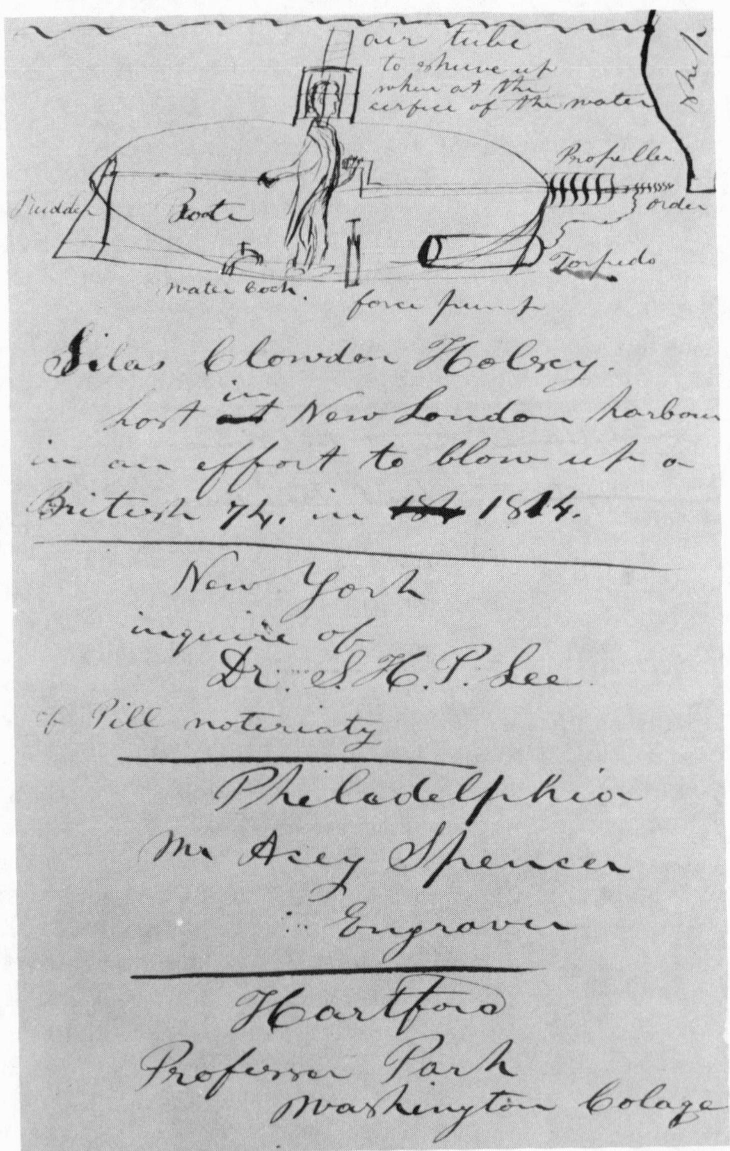

Figure 18. Samuel Colt's sketch of the submarine reportedly used by Silas Halsey in New London Harbor in 1814. It has many features in common with Bushnell's *Turtle*, including forcing pump, screw propeller, auger and detachable torpedo, and conning tower. *Samuel Colt Papers, The Connecticut Historical Society.*

what information I can in relation to the efforts that were made during the last war to blow up the British fleet while blockading those pourts."[19]

In addition to these researches, Colt made use of the facilities of New York University. Professor John W. Draper personally instructed him in Robert Hare's method of generating electricity, and a letter Colt sent to the *Army and Navy Chronicle* in May 1843 showed him to be quite familiar with the literature in the field. Arguing for the precedence of Americans in underwater demolition, he traced the work of Hare and Moses Shaw through articles in the *American Journal of Sciences and Arts.*[20] It is impossible to say how much other material on the history of underwater warfare Colt might have come across in these investigations, but it seems safe to say that he availed himself of—in fact actively sought out—a rather rich heritage.

Colt spent most of the first half of 1843 looking for a suitable vessel to blow up, one that would not consume too much of the appropriation but yet be sufficiently large and sturdy to blow apart impressively. During this time he also endured another change in secretaries of the navy, as Upshur was elevated to secretary of state and replaced by David Henshaw on 24 July 1843. Two months later, perhaps in an effort to warm up their comparatively cool relationship, Colt prematurely advised the new secretary that his preparations were complete.[21] But it was not until well into 1844 and the tenure of yet two more secretaries of the navy, Thomas Gilmer and Lewis Warrington, that Colt finally returned to Washington to put on his exhibition. After more than a month of further preparation, and the appointment of yet another secretary of the navy, John Y. Mason, Colt was finally ready.

The exhibition came off on 13 April 1844. Invitations were sent out. Public interest was stirred up. Congress even adjourned to watch. And the event lived up to billing. A five-hundred-ton vessel being towed at a speed of five knots in the Anacostia River between the Washington Navy Yard and the Arsenal was blown up and sunk by one of Colt's mines.[22] The success was complete, and at least to Colt's mind all the conditions set by Congress had been met. "I have got through with all my experiments & come of[f] with flying collors," he reported in a letter to McNeil on 22 April, "everything has succeeded to a charm so far."

But they were not home yet. His letter went on:

> You must come on here immediately & help me in my efforts to get a "quid pro quo." Movements are making to kill me of[f] without seremony. A resolution was offered the other day in the House of Representatives I presume at the instance of some officer of the Army hostile to my new mode of fortification, calling on the Secretarys of War & of the Navy for information as to the plans of my invention the claims which I have if any to originality &c. &c. The Navy department I think will treat the subject fairly but the Sec'y of War has refered the resolution to the Ordnance Department & the Engineer beauroughs. people of all others the least calculated to give a just repourt in a matter directly hostile to their own profession. Col. Tolcot & infact nearly every officer of the ordnance department has been hostile to every invention I ever made & I can't hope for any other result in my present case.
>
> Neither the ordnance or injinere Departments have a right to report on this matter for they have no knowledge of my plans of fortification & under the secret arrangements between me & the Late Sec'y. of the Navy [Upshur] they can never be enlitiened on the subject without my permission.
>
> You have influance with the injenear beaurough & I beg you to use it & [getting] them to repourt simply that Mr. Colts plans of submarine fortification have never been made know to him & that they have no more knowledge of it than any other persons who have witnessed his publick exhibitions.[23]

The resolution he referred to did have a slightly hostile ring to it, requiring the two secretaries "to communicate the fact, whether the combustible agent used by Mr. Colt was a secret before he made the same known at the seat of government, and whether the mode of its application to harbor defense be new; and, if new, what objections there are to its adoption, if objections do exist."[24] This may or may not have represented the conspiracy Colt imagined, but he nevertheless resolved to answer it with the strategy outlined in his letter to McNeil. First he would depend upon the Navy Department, where he had received his warmest welcome and made his most advantageous arrangements, to report favorably on his plans. Second, he would insist that the army, historically hostile to all his inventions, be kept in the dark as to the exact workings of his submarine battery. What they did not know about, he reasoned, they could not condemn.

The same day he wrote to McNeil he sent a letter to William Wilkins, the secretary of war, advising him that any communication of his plans to the army for the purposes of a report to Congress must inevitably become public. Therefore he must respectfully refuse to inform the army of the details of his submarine battery and insist that the secretary report to Congress "the simple fact that *nothing whatever is known*" to him.[25] Wilkins wrote back saying he was discouraged by Colt's stance but felt compelled to give him another chance to aid the army's investigation. Colt refused, informing the secretary that he feared any more dissemination of his secrets than was absolutely necessary and asserting that the Navy Department had all the information the goverment might require.[26]

On the other side of the aisle Colt prepared a glowing account of his achievements and sent it to the secretary of the navy. Mason acknowledged receipt and in return asked for an accounting of the monies Colt had expended. The response to this query revealed that the letter of the 1842 appropriation had been grossly violated, for not only had Colt spent $15,876.27 since that bill had been passed, but he had also spent $6,000 of government funds before that date, bringing his total drafts to $21,876.27, against a $15,000 appropriation. Not surprisingly, Mason immediately asked for an itemization, but Colt dodged the request. Instead he sent the secretary a copy of Fulton's 1804 contract with the British government, referred him to the *State Papers, Naval Affairs*, and boasted that his inventions were simpler, safer, and cheaper than those obviously monumental discoveries of Fulton.[27]

Soon Colt's strategy began to backfire. The secretary of the navy, understandably concerned about overexpenditures from his accounts, took to paying more attention to the ledgers than to Colt's proposal. His reckoning of the total bill—after he had added on still more hidden costs, including $2,353.60 that the Navy had expended directly in support of Colt's Washington demonstration—came to an imposing $24,914.28, almost two-thirds again what Congress had authorized. He advised the chairman of the House Committee on Naval Affairs of this situation and promised to make a full report on the matter in his answer to the House resolution of 19 April.[28] So instead of the support Colt was depending on from the Navy Department, he was going to get a financial report in which the new secretary would try to show: "It didn't happen on my watch." Unwritten agreements and secret understandings just could not survive the discontinuity of six secretaries of the navy.

On the army side the picture was bleaker still. Colonel Joseph G. Totten, the chief of the Corps of Engineers, and William Wilkins combined to knock down with a vengeance the straw man erected in the congressional resolution of 19 April.[29] The question should really have been whether or not Colt's invention was valuable in coast and harbor defense and whether or not he had succeeded in accomplishing what he claimed for his system. Instead, Congress had phrased the issue in terms of originality, and these are grounds upon which no underwater warrior in the age of sail was entirely secure.

In a carefully researched and admirably informed answer to Congress, Totten rehearsed the history of galvanic detonation of explosives, both in the atmosphere and under water. The essence of his argument was that such procedures were common scientific knowledge, long since available in the public domain. To buttress this claim, he collected opinions from Robert Hare, from other distinguished scientists, and from the pages of military journals. By discrediting the originality of the "combustible agent of Mr. Colt,"[30] Totten was of course attacking a claim Colt had not made. The array of evidence, however, did look impressive nonetheless. On the use of underwater explosions for harbor defense, Totten cited Fulton to prove that such an arrangement was not new. Again he was refuting a claim Colt had not made, but again the congressional resolution had invited such obfuscation. "The idea has long been before the world," said Totten, "to be availed of . . . when suitable occasions present themselves"[31]—a true, but hardly relevant, observation.

As for objections against the use of such weapons, Totten waxed philosophical—and not a little ridiculous. In spite of the great and propitious strides made by science, he argued, one should not lightly exhange old weapons for new, for even fists and arrows and other such "simple practices of early warfare" may have their place in a given battle. "Military experience," he pronounced, "has enacted, as an inflexible law, that no device, however plausible, shall be admitted to confidence as a military resource, except as it shall make its way by success in actual war, or in a long and severe experience analogous thereto."[32] Had this kind of logic been applied with any consistency in the modern world, the colonel's taste for fists and arrows might have been more than sated. But his object was to frustrate Colt's designs, not explain previous weapons procurement, and for such purposes military bombast was quite as effective as logic or consistency. From this tentative base he went on to argue that Colt's mines must be used in conjunction with other weapons, that they were subject to sabotage, and that the system might in any case be reconstructed "without any indebtedness to Mr. Colt, either as an inventor, an improver, or an applier of the process."[33]

Wilkins endorsed this argument and turned Colt's silence against him:

> If the means assumed to be those employed by Mr. Colt (and if we are in error, he has his own caution to blame) are actually those which he uses, then I affirm that any intelligent, scientific person, aided and encouraged by equal munificence and appropriations, could, without invading any patent or exclusive right of others, and by merely applying means which have been gratuitously contributed to science by distinguished men of our country, accomplish all that Mr. Colt has achieved under the bounty and generous encouragement of his government, in his peaceful experiments against a defenceless and untenanted ship.[34]

In other words the War Department had done just what Colt demanded they not do—evaluate his system without knowing the details of it. This left him with three alternatives. First he could make his system known—but he would be much less likely to get a reward for what would then be public knowledge. Second, he could get the Navy Department to vouch for the originality and importance of his invention—but Mason refused: "I have declined

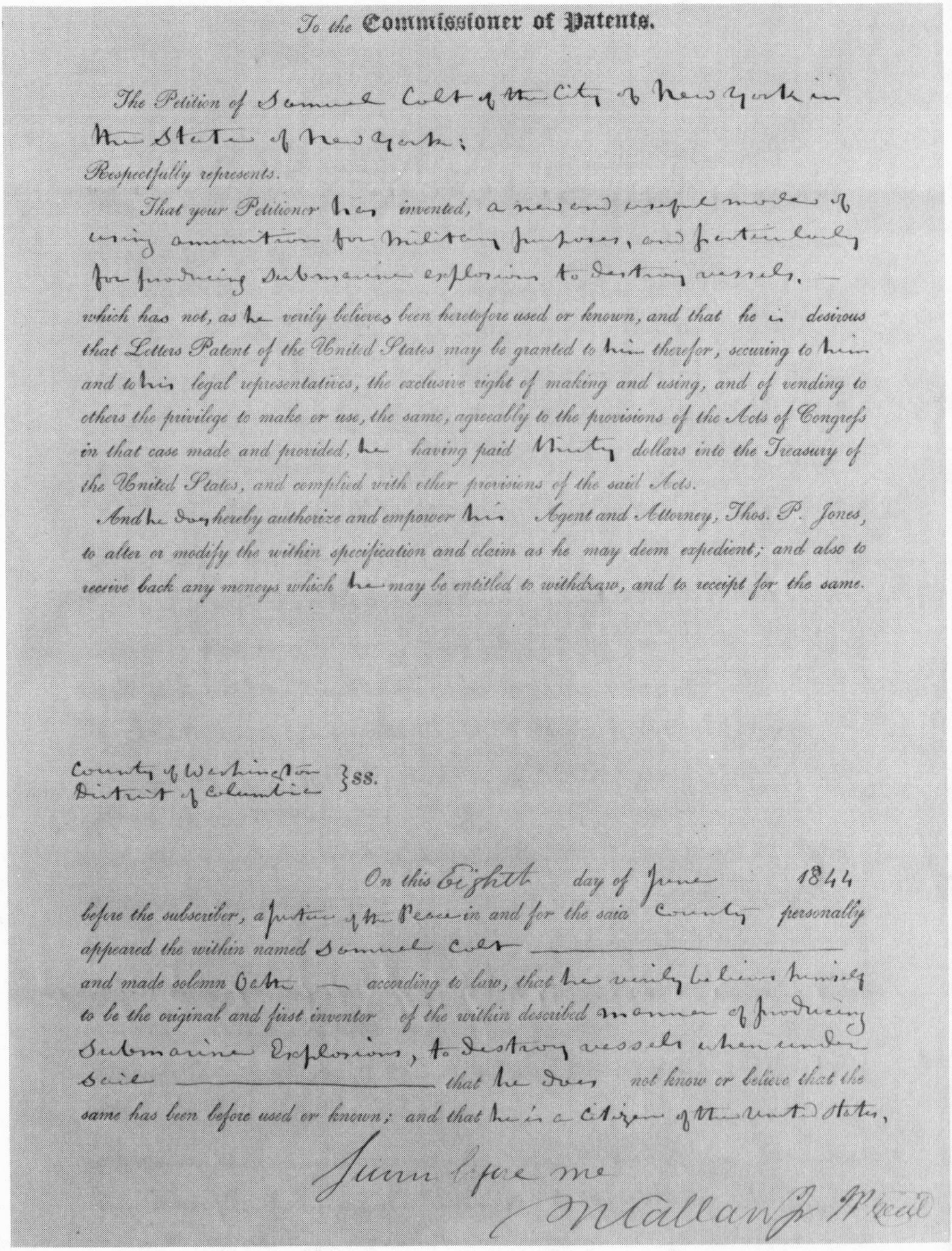

To the **Commissioner of Patents.**

The Petition of Samuel Colt of the City of New York in the State of New York;

Respectfully represents.

That your Petitioner has invented, a new and useful mode of using ammunition for military purposes, and particularly for producing submarine explosions to destroy vessels. — which has not, as he verily believes been heretofore used or known, and that he is desirous that Letters Patent of the United States may be granted to him therefor, securing to him and to his legal representatives, the exclusive right of making and using, and of vending to others the privilege to make or use, the same, agreeably to the provisions of the Acts of Congress in that case made and provided, he having paid thirty dollars into the Treasury of the United States, and complied with other provisions of the said Acts.

And he does hereby authorize and empower his Agent and Attorney, Thos. P. Jones, to alter or modify the within specification and claim as he may deem expedient; and also to receive back any moneys which he may be entitled to withdraw, and to receipt for the same.

County of Washington }
District of Columbia } SS.

On this Eighth day of June 1844

before the subscriber, a Justice of the Peace in and for the said County personally appeared the within named Samuel Colt ——— and made solemn Oath — according to law, that he verily believes himself to be the original and first inventor of the within described manner of producing Submarine Explosions, to destroy vessels when under sail ——— that he does not know or believe that the same has been before used or known; and that he is a Citizen of the United States,

Sworn before me

N Callan Jr [illegible]

Figure 19. Page one of Samuel Colt's patent application for his submarine battery. He paid his $30 fee on 8 June 1844. *Samuel Colt Papers, The Connecticut Historical Society.*

to receive a communication of Mr. Colt's secret," he advised Wilkins, "of which the knowledge could only be useful in determining the effect of experiments which had already been made [when Mason entered office], which I had not witnessed, and which there was no means at the disposal of the department to have repeated."[35] In other words, "It didn't happen on my watch."

The third alternative was suggested to Colt by the House Committee on Naval Affairs. Colt wrote to Henry C. Murphy, the chairman of that committee, on 3 June 1844. He protested his treatment and claimed that he had completely fulfilled the conditions established by Congress in the original resolution of 31 August 1842. Freely admitting that mining for harbor defense and electrical detonation of underwater charges were not original with him, he claimed that his system was still unique because of the secret manner devised by him for determining when ships had arrived over his mines. The committee thereupon required Colt to

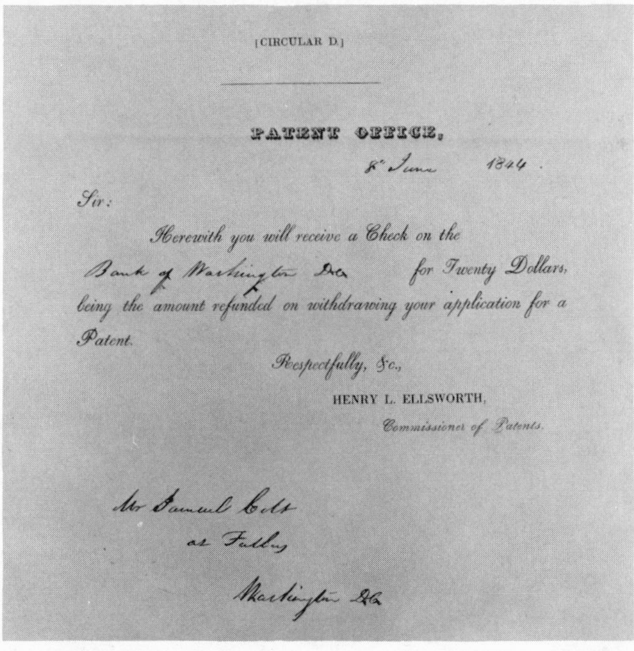

[CIRCULAR D.]

PATENT OFFICE,

8th June 1844.

Sir:

Herewith you will receive a Check on the Bank of Washington D.C. for Twenty Dollars, being the amount refunded on withdrawing your application for a Patent.

Respectfully, &c.,

HENRY L. ELLSWORTH,

Commissioner of Patents.

Mr Samuel Colt

at Fullers

Washington D.C.

Figure 20. The refund of $20 paid to Samuel Colt when he withdrew the patent application for his submarine battery. *Samuel Colt Papers, The Connecticut Historical Society.*

prepare a patent application describing his whole system. This he did, leaving it in the hands of the patent commissioner only long enough for him to pass on its originality. He then withdrew the application to prevent its publication, and the commissioner advised the committee that his plan did indeed warrant a patent. To clinch his argument Colt had his application witnessed by Thomas P. Jones, one of the scientists who had earlier told Secretary Wilkins that the plan was not original. Jones now prepared a new letter in which he confirmed that the plan "is not only novel, but is also calculated to effect the purpose with a certainty nearly unerring." He explained that he had earlier been insufficiently informed of the plan to appreciate its originality.[36]

With this Colt had successfully refuted most of the Army report. But the wheels of Congress grind exceedingly slow. The Committee on Naval Affairs digested this new information through the remainder of 1844, and not until 11 January 1845 was a report issued. This report, generally quite favorable to Colt, nevertheless hedged on the ultimate question. It allowed the originality of Colt's submarine battery, concluded that the report of the secretary of war was based on insufficient evidence, and concluded that the plan was "entitled to the favorable consideration of government."[37] Because they were not privy to the details of the plan, however, the committee members did not feel qualified to recommend its adoption. Therefore, they reported out a bill simply calling for the payment of all outstanding obligations and "compensation to Mr. Colt during the time that he was engaged in his experiments."[38]

Time and secretiveness had combined to block government adoption. By the time all the experiments and demonstrations were conducted, all the military objections overcome, all the counterclaims of originality and plagiarism settled, the machinery of government had quite lost track of what it was about. Too many secretaries of the navy, too many chairmen of the House Committee on Naval Affairs, too many new and unnecessary antagonisms, too many clouded memories of dusty reports and bygone spectaculars. During all this time only seven men besides Colt are known to have been familiar with the entire plan, and now two of them were dead, two retired, two outside the power structure, and one in Rio de Janeiro as minister to Brazil.[39] When the way was finally open to positive action, there was simply no one left on Colt's side with the will or the power to consummate the years of preparation.

Nor was Colt to salvage even a modest remuneration out of the experience. The Navy Department was admonished in the committee report for unauthorized expenditure of funds, and Secretary Mason's main objective settled on accounting for the $22,550.62 that Colt was finally charged with having spent. When one of the members of the Committee on Naval Affairs asked his advice on the possibility of the government's purchasing Colt's system outright, Mason evaded the question, noted that Colt had already received ample reward, and recommended that in the future such projects should not be subsidized by Congress without close control of the inventors by appropriate executive bureaus.[40] The debate went on and the Twenty-Eighth Congress adjourned without taking any action on Colt's case. No evidence is available that any subsequent Congress improved upon this record, and on the eve of the Civil War, Colt was still pressing a claim against the government.[41]

In many ways Colt's experience was identical to Fulton's. Both were secretive and tactless in dealing with the government; both suspected, with some cause, that military professionals were hostile to their designs; and both suffered from rapid turnover in key government offices with which they dealt. They both claimed overmuch for their weapons, though Colt had a far better performance record, and they both deserved better treatment than they received from government. It was by eliminating these and other obstacles between the inventor and the government that the Civil War was about to become the final proving ground of underwater warfare.

XI

Matthew Fontaine Maury and the Final Connection

WHEN AMERICANS chose sides for their Civil War in the spring of 1861 many found themselves torn between conflicting allegiances. So it was with Commander Matthew Fontaine Maury, U.S.N. (1806–1873), who was forced to choose between a distinguished scientific career at the Naval Observatory at Washington and the bonds of family and community which drew him to Virginia. Reluctantly he chose the latter. He resigned his commission and in April reported for duty to the governor of Virginia. In his baggage he carried thirty-six years' worth of familiarity with the men, facilities, and weapons of the United States Navy, in addition to a wide-ranging scientific background.[1]

This particular defection is significant because it brought to the Confederacy the Civil War's first important underwater warrior. No doubt the Confederates would have entered this field of naval weaponry even had Maury remained in the North. There were, in fact, so many proposals for underwater warfare during the course of the conflict that their very number occasioned a warm debate over competing claims to precedence. But Maury's position in this regard is secure. Not only was his the first recorded activity in underwater warfare, it was also the icebreaker in whose wake the others followed.[2]

Less clear than Maury's claim to priority is the source of his ideas. Dr. Phillip K. Lundeberg, Curator of Naval History at the

Smithsonian Institution, has searched Maury's papers in vain for evidence that he took serious note of Colt's experiments and demonstrations in the early 1840s.[3] However, sufficient circumstantial evidence exists to suggests that Maury had access to the essentials of Colt's plan. On the day that Maury reached Washington in July 1842 to report for duty as superintendent of the Depot of Charts and Instruments, Colt was blowing up a ship in New York Harbor preparatory to his first demonstration in Washington. The following month, Secretary of the Navy Upshur directed Maury "to allow Mr. Colt to consult such charts as he desires of the Dept.," pursuant to Colt's mining of the Potomac River.[4] If Colt went to the Depot on the date of that note—31 August 1842—he and Maury would have had more than Potomac soundings to discuss. On that day Congress was passing Colt's $15,000 appropriation and simultaneously enacting a navy reorganization bill. Maury had played a major role in this latter piece of legislation, and its abolition of the three-officer Board of Commissioners in favor of five naval bureaus was a reform for which he and Colt shared a strong liking.[5]

Besides personal contact, Maury had numerous other ties to Colt. He was associated with Robert Hare and Joseph Henry, two of the scientists who had passed on Colt's scheme in 1844. And he was deeply involved in early attempts to lay a transatlantic cable. This brought him into contact with Samuel F. B. Morse, who described himself as being "on the most friendly terms" with Colt. The two men had collaborated in 1842 on the production of waterproof cable for electrical transmission. Morse was working on an underwater telegraph, and of course Colt was perfecting underwater detonation. While Morse provided most of the expertise in electrical transmission, he was not unmindful of the innovations Colt was able to contribute.[6]

As for the torpedoes, their general currency in the middle of the nineteenth century and Maury's familiarity with them were revealed in the course of this same project for a transatlantic cable. Maury's principal contribution to the effort was locating and charting a shelf on the ocean floor of a suitable depth and topography to accommodate the cable. The soundings required to make these determinations pressed the technology of the times and led to numerous innovative schemes. One such was the use of torpedoes. In an 1855 speech Maury reported that this idea was suggested to him by a whaling captain in whose trade torpedoes were sometimes used as killing weapons. The plan proved impracticable, but the matter-of-fact manner in which Maury reported on it showed that torpedoes were common knowledge at the time, especially to such as he.[7] His familiarity with underwater warfare, as he chose sides in the spring of 1861, was perhaps more complete than his papers suggest.

When Maury reported for duty in Richmond he was assigned to the governor's advisory council. This role occupied much of his time during the early months of the war, but he was nonetheless working on underwater warfare from the very outset. When Virginia joined the Confederacy, the advisory council was disbanded and Maury was freed to devote full time to his experiments. Like Bushnell and Colt before him, he established himself in an academic environment, in this case in a laboratory at the University of Virginia. Also in similarity to Bushnell he began his experiments by setting off small charges. Because underwater cable was not to be had in the early days of the Confederacy he deferred this primary goal and worked instead on mechanically detonated drifting torpedoes.

With impressive speed he was soon ready to test his devices in combat. On the night of 7/8 July 1861 he attacked two Union flagships moored in Hampton Roads. His arrangement was the now familiar pair of floating mines connected by rope. These were planted above the enemy ships and allowed to drift down upon the mooring lines and into place alongside the vessels, just as those of Bushnell, Fulton, Mix, and others had been designed to do. The fuses proved unsatisfactory and the attempt failed, but Maury was sanguine nonetheless. In a bid for large-scale financing he prepared two models of his machines and approached Secretary of the (Confederate) Navy Stephen Mallory. Animosity between these two men, dating from strong disagreements over naval policy in the late 1850s, contributed to a first refusal. But after a simple demonstration of one of the mines in August, Mallory changed his mind and asked the Confederate Congress for a $50,000 appropriation for underwater warfare.[8]

Mallory did not, however, change his mind about Maury. On 29 September, just as a new attack was being planned, Maury was relieved from his torpedo work. In the wake of growing criticism of Mallory's handling of the Confederate navy, Maury was reinstated on 2 November, but in the meantime his subordinates had failed in two attempts to carry out the attacks he had planned. Shortly thereafer Maury was sidetracked yet again when a program to build a fleet of small gunboats—a policy he had been advocating in the U.S. Navy for years—was approved by the Confederate Congress. Maury took charge of this project, which consumed most of his time until the battle of the *Monitor* and the *Virginia* changed Southern thinking once again. The gunboat program was scrapped in March 1862, and Maury returned to torpedo work full time.

With Maury's undivided attention, the torpedo program progressed rapidly. Some insulated wire was obtained fortuitously and Maury turned to electrical mines—always his main interest—in April. The threat of Union assault up the James River loomed large at that time and mining of that waterway became a major objective. On 19 June, after less than three months' work on electrical mines, Maury was able to report to Mallory that that objective had been accomplished. Thereupon, Maury was relieved by Lieutenant Hunter Davidson, a subordinate he had been training for some months, and in August he was sent to England on a confidential mission.[9]

In a little over a year of oft-interrupted torpedo work, Maury had convinced the Confederate hierarchy of the efficacy of this form of warfare, had established a center of operations in Richmond, had trained several subordinates, and had successfully mined a critical inland waterway. In the process he had disseminated mines and instructions on their use to commands as far distant as the Mississippi River and had thus sparked activity in other parts of the Confederacy. In England he was to conduct still more experiments and send the results back to Richmond. It seems to be beyond doubt that he was the one man most responsible for introducing underwater warfare in the Confederacy.[10]

There were, however, others close upon his heels. The one most often cited as having claims to precedence over Maury is Brigadier General Gabriel J. Rains.[11] In May of 1862, Rains, a brigade commander then besieged by McClellan at Yorktown, laid out land mines and booby traps to cover his retreat. This was a tactic he claimed first to have used against Indians in Florida in the Seminole War in April 1840. In that endeavor he succeeded only in blowing up an opossum, getting himself wounded, and frightening friendly troops. In 1862, however, his devices so unnerved the Union soldiers as to delay their advance and ensure the successful withdrawal of his brigade. The following month General Lee called him to Virginia and placed him in charge of the army submarine defenses of the James and Appomattox rivers. Of course this placed him in clear conflict with Hunter Davidson, who at about the same time relieved Maury as head of naval submarine defenses in the James River. The overlapping responsibilities were divided in September when Rains turned over his James River duties to Davidson and took charge of torpedo warfare throughout the rest of the Confederacy.

Rain's claim to priority in underwater warfare stems largely from his own assertions. Maury was at work on Confederate mine warfare well before Rains, and the general's claims even to independent invention warrant close scrutiny. He freely admitted knowledge of Bushnell's use of floating mines in 1777, of the American efforts in the War if 1812, and of Russian efforts at Cronstadt—though he dismissed all as "abortions."[12] Still more instructive is a letter he wrote to a superior officer in March 1862. "That invention [the torpedo] is strictly mine," he said, "as well as the essential parts of Colt's weapons, for the use of which I have never been called to account."[13] All too many of his fellow "inventors" of underwater warfare have never been called to account for the debts they owed their predecessors, but, like them, Rains owed more than many historians have allowed.[14]

A more valid claim to priority in Confederate underwater warfare is that of Lieutenant Beverly Kennon, C.S.N. He made an attack on a Union vessel in the Potomac River at the same time that Maury was making his first attempt in July 1861. It has never been established that Kennon was working for Maury at the time, though the similarity and timing of the attacks suggests that he was. But even if he were operating independently, he had ample opportunity to avail himself of the very same sources with which Maury was in touch. Kennon's father had been commander of the Washington Navy Yard when Colt did his experiment there. Kennon himself had seen at least one of the ships destroyed in the Potomac River, and he had had the general procedure explained to him. He knew of the Russian use of mines in the Crimean War, and he was on board the U.S.S. *Niagara* during that ship's participation in the laying of the first transatlantic cables.[15]

The examples of Maury, Rains, and Kennon are but a hint of the hundreds of schemes that were presented to the Confederacy. As in the War of 1812, hostilities brought forth all manner of inventors and would-be inventors anxious to win fame, fortune, and the war with a new weapon. That these three were the first to come forth, and that they laid the most important groundwork for later efforts, may be attributed in no small measure to the shoulders on which they stood. Because of their familiarity with earlier efforts, they avoided many of the pitfalls that stymied their predecessors, and in so doing they gained a major advantage over their contemporaries. As one engineering expert observed:

> The War Department and the chief engineers of the several departments were worse than importuned by the applications of inventors, every one of whom demanded an examination of his plan or model. Such requests having to be granted for fear of possibly overlooking a perhaps really useful invention, the attention of examining committees would, naturally enough, often be called to the most absurd schemes. There were torpedo twin boats, propelled by rockets; diving apparatus by means of which torpedoes might be attached to the bottom of the enemy's ship; balloons that were to ascend, and, when arrived just above the vessel, were to drop some kind of torpedo on the deck of the ship; rotation torpedo-rockets to be fired under water; submarine boats, with torpedoes attached to their spar; in fine, any variety of plans, and yet but few, very few practicable ones.
>
> The great error which most of these inventors fell into was, that they aimed at accomplishing, all at once, too much in a field which to all of them was still an unexplored *terra incognita*. Complicatedness of the apparatus was the next consequence, out of which resulted its utter failure on being tried. Certain it is that those torpedoes by which the heaviest losses were caused to the Federal

> fleet during the American war excelled in simplicity of construction and in cheapness.[16]

Of course this wasn't really "terra incognita" to some of these men, and the simplicity and success of their machines owed much to the trials and errors of earlier inventors. But this situation had been true of other wars and it was not the prime factor in making underwater warfare a success here.

The critical innovation that made the American Civil War the final proving ground of underwater warfare was institutionalization. Before a single enemy ship was sunk, before underwater warfare was anything more than the potential naval arm it had been for centuries, the Confederacy incorporated it officially into the military hierarchy. In October 1862, the Confederate Congress passed legislation authorizing a torpedo bureau within the army and a submarine battery service within the navy.[17] These new bodies were formalized versions of the units commanded by Rains and Davidson respectively, now sanctioned by a political body claiming independent sovereignty. More than the workshop on government premises that Drebbel had enjoyed, more than the government subsidy Bushnell had been granted, more still than the ad hoc inclusion in a specific expedition that Fulton had won in England, these new units were recognized branches of a military hierarchy and had the power to initiate programs, train a permanent body of troops, establish internal doctrine and operating procedures, and integrate themselves with the overall policies of their respective branches of the service. Underwater warfare was now "systematized" as Fulton had always insisted it must be.

How and why this came to be seems fairly clear. The Confederacy was a comparatively weak naval power. Its coastline was a long, ragged invitation to invasion. Its rivers were like so many avenues to the heartland. Without the naval resources to defend the coast and rivers, it was necessary to resort to the cheapest, most promising means of defense available—underwater warfare. Furthermore, there were no entrenched military institutions to oppose introduction of new weapons. The Confederacy was a new world, and as much as some naval officers might have preferred to idolize ships of the line at the expense of cheaper, more practical substitutes, there was no opportunity to do so—there were simply no ships to speak of. Even where infatuation with mass and power held sway, it was directed toward the new ironclads and lent impetus to the growing penchant for new weapons. Rifled cannon, breech-loaders, steam warships: all were part of the modern arsenal that emerged in the Civil War, and underwater warfare seemed much less strange in their company. The government to which Maury and others presented their weapons was a plastic organization forming amidst a swirl of technological advances in weaponry. The entrenched institutions that had impeded the adoption of underwater warfare in other times and other wars were simply absent from the Confederacy in 1862.[18]

This is not to say there weren't objections, especially within the navy. Hunter Davidson said after the war:

> If anyone had to contend with the abuse and sneers, and ridicule whilst in the performance of torpedo duty day and night, that fell upon me during the war, he would realize that as late as the summer of 1863, some of the ablest men of the day did not regard torpedo warfare as worthy of consideration, and the very attempts of Fulton and of Bushnell, and of the Russians, were used by those men in argument that my attempt would also be fruitless.[19]

In addition to showing that earlier efforts were then common knowledge in military circles, this statement paints a fair picture of professional naval aversion. One enlisted member of Davidson's unit reported that "it was the common belief that summary execution would follow the capture of any person engaged in the torpedo service."[20] And one army officer expressed to his naval counterpart an appreciation of "the delicacy naval gentlemen feel in depending upon anything but their ships," let alone such unpleasant alternatives as mines.[21]

Nor was this aversion limited to the navy. General Rains aroused no little furor with his use of land mines and booby traps, as much in the Confederate as in the Union army. On 12 May 1862 his corps commander, Major General James Longstreet, forbade him to plant any more, claiming they were not "a proper or effective method of war." Rains went over his head to Secretary of

War Randolph, who allowed that they could be used on land in certain cases, but not for mere terrorism or wanton destruction of life. But he added that since "Rains and Longstreet differ in this matter, the inferior in rank should give way, or, if he prefers it, he may be assigned to the river defenses, where such things are clearly admissible."[22]

The principal army objection dated back to the sixteenth century and was closely connected to the weapon known as a fougasse. This small land mine, used for centuries in connection with field fortifications, aroused not nearly the moral uproar associated with underwater warfare because its location and time of detonation were known. It was placed in a given position in front of the fortifications—"under the glacis or dry ditches"[23] —and it would be detonated during any attempt to breach those defenses. Thus it was not a clandestine weapon in the manner of underwater charges, and it offended no one's lingering sense of chivalry.

What bothered military officers about Rain's use of land mines and booby traps in 1862 was that they were placed randomly with the intent to deceive; hence, they were being used in a clandestine mode. As General W. F. Barry said of the mines at Yorktown:

> These shells were not . . . placed on the glacis at the bottom of the ditch, etc., which, in view of an anticipated assault, might possibly be considered a legitimate use of them, but they were planted by an enemy who was secretly abandoning his post, on common roads, at springs of water, in the shade of trees, at the foot of telegraph poles, and, lastly, quite within the defenses of the place—in the very streets.[24]

In response to the same criticism from his own comrades, Rains took to laying the mines in patterned fields and actually marking them. When that gentlemanly concession to chivalry took effect, Rains was able to report that "the objection to the sub-terra shells have been met," and the officers now "gladly avail themselves of this means of defense." "These shells are now appreciated," he reported with some satisfaction, even going so far as to claim that they "now seem popular with our officers."[25]

That the weapons got this chance was due in large measure to Jefferson Davis. He had been secretary of war in 1858 when

Colonel Richard Delafield, Corps of Engineers, reported to him on Russian activities in the Crimean War. Delafield had been impressed with the underwater warfare he observed, and in his report he gave particular attention to the importance of electrical detonation of charges "as a most powerful auxiliary in harbor defenses."[26] As president of the Confederacy, Davis received a complete history of mines and torpedoes from General Rains, and thereafter he was a firm advocate of underwater warfare.[27] Confederate Secretary of War Seddon reported in May, 1863:

> The President has confidence in [Rains's] inventions, and is desirous that they should be employed both on land and river. . . . Such means of offense against the enemy are approved and recognized by the Department as legitimate weapons of warfare.[28]

In this judgment, Davis was much closer to contemporary international law then were the uniformed officers who objected. The dominant theme of the *jus in bello* continued to be necessity, tempered only by a humanitarian regard for noncombatants and a belief that the ends of war must not be jeopardized by the conduct of war. A draft code prepared for the Union secretary of war covered the ground as adequately as any in its treatment of necessity:

> Military Necessity admits of all direct destruction of life or limb of the armed enemies and of those whose destruction is incidentally unavoidable in the armed contests of the war; [and] it allows . . . of all deception which does not involve the breaking of good faith either positively pledged regarding agreements entered into during the war, or supposed by the modern law of war to exist, even in the fiercest struggle, as a basis of intercourse between honorable belligerants. Men who take up arms against one another in public war, do not cease on this account to be moral beings, responsible to one another, and to God.
>
> Military Necessity does not admit of cruelty—that is, the infliction of suffering for the sake of suffering or for revenge. . . . [29]

That is a fair reflection of international law before the Civil War. In it Davis found nothing that barred the use of mines or torpedoes on land or in water. If any Confederate officer harbored misgivings about that reading of the law, he was soon drowned out by the roar of success.

As if to mark the institutionalization of underwater warfare, U.S.S. *Cairo*, a 512-ton armored gunboat, struck two mines on the Yazoo River in Mississippi on 12 December 1862, and went to the bottom. She was the first major warship ever to succumb to underwater warfare, and ironically she carried not a single sail.[30] What had been attempted all down the centuries of the age of sail was now finally consummated in the age of steam and iron. The act of idolization was still present, but it was not as important in execution as it had been in motivation. The new infatuation with steampowered ironclads was still an emotion with no tradition, and the overconfidence which sank the *Cairo* was fostered as much by disdain for the torpedo as by reverence for the gunboat. As Acting Rear Admiral David Porter noted in his report of the incident: "These torpedoes have proved so harmless heretofore . . . that officers have not felt that respect for them to which they are entitled."[31]

This first success spurred the Confederates to still greater activity in underwater warfare. Weapons, information, and assistance spread out from Richmond to local commands all over the South. These commands in turn established their own autonomous units and weapons, some in imitation of the main bureaus, others entirely original. The Congress legislated a bounty in 1862 equal to half the value of any enemy vessel sunk, and this increased activity still more. Private companies were formed; submarines and torpedo boats were built; mines and torpedoes were towed, pushed, anchored, drifted, and otherwise forced into proximity with enemy hulls.

The operational side of this story has been ably described in Milton F. Perry's *Infernal Machines* and need not be repeated here. A brief look at the use General P.G.T. Beauregard made of these weapons in the defense of Charleston will suffice to reveal the problems and achievements of this new naval arm. Beauregard was unusually receptive to innovation, and soon after his assignment to Charleston he became a staunch advocate of underwater warfare. At times he even sounded as if he had been reading from Robert Fulton's letter book. He said, for example, that the torpedo ram proposed by one of his subordinates "is destined ere long to change the system of naval warfare," and later, on the same subject, he professed to feel "as Columbus must have felt when he maintained that there was a New World in the West across the Atlantic, but could find no one to believe him or assist him in determing the fact."[32] What was holding up prosecution of this particular device was a goodly measure of interservice rivalry, a continuing problem in Confederate underwater warfare and an unfortunate concomitant of the very institutionalization which made these weapons a success. The torpedo rams—cigar-shaped, steam-powered spar torpedo boats designed to run almost awash—were the invention of Captain Francis D. Lee, an army engineer. When he first proposed their use, the War Department and the army engineers told him it was a navy matter, and the navy refused to take action because Lee was an army officer. "There was not much accord between the army and navy in those days," one torpedoist observed after the war, and as late as mid-1864 Robert E. Lee lamented that the same problem was still hampering tor-

Figure 21. A Confederate David aground in Charleston Harbor, South Carolina, about 1865.

pedo activity. But Beauregard was equal to such obstacles, and with his help Captain Lee's craft finally did get into action. The first attack was appropriately enough against the largest ship in sight, the 3,486-ton *New Ironsides*. With like propriety, the torpedo ram was named *David*. The resulting clash on 5 October 1863 put the *New Ironsides* out of action for a year and led to production of a whole series of *Davids*.[33]

By the end of the war the toll from Confederate underwater warfare was impressive. Damage was found to have been sustained by forty-three Union vessels, twenty-nine of which were sunk.[34] This was more damage than was effected by the rest of the Confederate navy. Federal naval operations were slowed and in some cases even stopped by underwater warfare. In short, this branch of naval weaponry proved almost as effective as its advocates had predicted for three centuries. While it did not, and could not, appreciably change the outcome of the war, it accomplished far more than its detractors had predicted.

The response of the Union navy to this impressive performance can be clearly traced through the correspondence of Rear Admiral John A. Dahlgren, U.S.N., commander of the blockading squadron on the south Atlantic coast and himself an expert on naval ordnance. Initially it was the same kind of disdain that Porter noted in connection with the sinking of the *Cairo*. "So much has been said in ridicule of torpedoes," reported Dahlgren, "that very little precautions are deemed necessary."[35] For his part, the Admiral was much less taken by this contempt born of idolization, and he insisted upon the utmost vigilance: "I have attached more importance to the use of torpedoes than others have done,"[36] and sooner or later his fellow officers came to his way of thinking.

None of this is meant to imply that Dahlgren condoned this method of naval warfare. He referred to it as "this base style of rebel warfare," and said: "It savors to me of murder."[37] He even threatened (hollowly as it turned out) to hang the crew of the *David* that attacked the *New Ironsides* "for using an engine of war not recognized by civilized nations."[38] But his moral aversion did not impair his military judgment. After the *New Ironsides* affair he reported to Assistant Secretary of the Navy Gustavus Fox:

> Among the many inventions with which I have been familiar, I have seen none which have acted so perfectly at first trial.

> The secrecy, rapidity of movement, control of direction, and precise explosion indicate, I think, the introduction of the torpedo element as a means of certain warfare. It can be ignored no longer.[39]

That last sentence spoke volumes about the military response to underwater warfare in the age of sail. Officers had ignored the issue whenever possible, opposed it when necessary, always hoping that it would simply go away. But at every turn there was some new inventor to resurrect the idea yet again. Now a navy was faced with the harvest of its own neglect, and there was only one course of action available. "By all means," continued Dahlgren, "let us have a quantity of these torpedoes, and thus turn them against the enemy. We can make them faster than they can." In the face of a successful weapon, ethical restraints, infatuation with the ship of the line, concerns about the future of warfare—all were abandoned to the ultimate arbiter: necessity. In urging Admiral S. P. Lee to mine the James River, General Ben Butler counseled that "in a contest against such unchristian modes of warfare as fire rafts and torpedo boats, I think all questions of delicacy should be waved by the paramount consideration of protection for the lives of the men and the safety of the very valuable vessels of the squadron."[40] Dahlgren wrote in much the same tone to Secretary of War Gideon Welles and concluded: "It is evident . . . that the enemy intends to prosecute this mode of warfare, and I therefore urge reprisals in kind." Welles replied: "The Department concurs."[41]

With Northern will committed to the effort, means were not lacking. Schemes for underwater warfare were received by the American government throughout the nineteenth century. The opening of the Civil War increased this input enormously and flooded the Northern bureaucracy just as it had the Southern. A full description of Bauer's submarine was sent to Gideon Welles late in 1861,[42] and one of the numerous inventors of French submarines personally petitioned Lincoln and succeeded in getting a subsidy to build one of his boats here.[43] The craft was actually constructed, but its commissioning and use were forestalled by disagreements between the inventor and the government. Of course, Richard Delafield's report on the Russian uses of underwater warfare was still available in Washington, and he was now General Delafield, Chief of Engineers. Detailed intelligence reports flowed into Washington on Confederate activities and weapons.[44] Even a copy of Maury's original plans for the James River mines was in Northern hands, having been captured soon after Davidson took charge.[45] The battle between the *Monitor* and the *Virginia* touched off a particularly heavy influx of proposals to Washington. Many of these displayed a familiarity with earlier efforts in underwater warfare, especially with the work of Robert Fulton, a reflection of the heavy coverage such material was then getting in the Northern press.[46] In short, the record of underwater warfare was so readily available in Washington that the Union forces had no difficulty in answering the Confederate challenge in kind.

Federal use of underwater warfare was comparatively limited, not from lack of weapons or will, but from lack of opportunity. As the superior naval force trying to penetrate harbors and traverse rivers, the Union navy had little use for defensive mines. Offensively, the opportunities were just as scarce, because the Confederate navy could most often be subdued by the simple weight of superior firepower. The much heralded sinking of the C.S.S. *Albemarle* by torpedo ram on 28 October 1864 was an exception of more renown than importance. It evidenced Union willingness and ability to use such weapons, but it masked the general lack of opportunity.

Union forces found sufficient uses for underwater warfare at least to alarm their Southern counterparts. Flag Officer John K. Mitchell, C.S.N., warned Secretary Mallory late in 1864: "There is no doubt that the enemy has prepared and is making still futher preparations to follow our example in the use of torpedoes, and with his unlimited resources, great ingenuity, and enterprise he may make the mode of warfare very effective."[47] Similarly, Lieutenant General W. J. Hardee, C.S.A., lamenting the interservice rivalry that was still entangling underwater warfare, warned the chief of the engineer bureau: "Unless some action is taken soon by our government in this matter I fear the enemy will beat us with our own weapons."[48]

The important feature of the Federal use of underwater warfare was that it was predicated on retaliation. Legally this was a perfectly valid justification. As Henry Wheaton had said:

> The whole international code is founded on reciprocity. The rules it prescribes are observed by one nation, in confidence that they will be so by others. Where, then, the established usages of war are violated by an enemy, and there are no other means of restraining his excess, retaliation may justly be resorted to by the suffering nation.[49]

However, retaliation in military terms is nothing more than an open admission that the enemy's methods have been so effective as to demand a response in kind. When Maury and Rains used the moral argument of retaliation as a justification for their activities in 1861, they were obviously giving vent to deep-rooted frustration occasioned by their inability to deter Union naval operations.[50] When the Union in turn invoked such ethical posturing, it was likewise in response to a clear and present military necessity. Shortly before damning the torpedoes at Mobile Bay in 1864, Admiral David Farragut wrote to the Navy Department: "Torpedoes are not so agreeable when used on both sides; therefore I have reluctantly brought myself to it. I always deemed it unworthy of a chivalrous nation, but it does not do to give your enemy such a decided superiority over you."[51] Both sides claimed retaliation, but in using the weapon against each other, they had, by definition, legitimatized it: it had entered the hallowed portals emblazoned "Usages of War." Underwater warfare had arrived.

XII

David Triumphant

THE CIVIL WAR ended in 1865, but activity in underwater warfare went on apace, both in the United States and abroad. Armies and navies throughout the world recognized mines and torpedoes as part of the modern arsenal. They examined the history of these weapons and the current state of the art. They instituted programs to incorporate underwater warfare in their arms inventory. In short, they did just what the Davids had been advocating for close to three centuries.

In the United States the navy response was exemplified by John S. Barnes's *Submarine Warfare* (1869). Lieutenant Commander Barnes had been actively involved in combatting Confederate mines and torpedoes, and in his postwar billet at the Naval Academy he prepared this semiofficial history of the art. In it he traced the course of underwater warfare from Bushnell through the Civil War, giving particular attention to American contributions. There followed a detailed treatment of mines and torpedoes in the late war, culled primarily from official records and from Barnes's own experience. The evidence he presented argued strongly as to the efficacy of these new weapons. In conclusion he predicted that underwater warfare, "no longer trammelled by the humanitarian ideas which have made the system obnoxious to the sense of the warlike nations . . . must advance under the guidance of able and intelligent minds to the first position among the recognized engines of war."[1] Though far from being a statement of policy, Barnes's volume nonetheless reflected informed thought within the navy.

The response of the U.S. Army was more interesting still, for it did lead to an official history and something akin to a statement of policy. In October 1865, General Delafield sent Major W. R. King to Willets Point, New York, to conduct experiments on "the force of powder under water." These completed, King returned to the engineer department early in 1866 "to collect and prepare for publication such information as could be obtained, relative to the invention and use of Torpedoes." The result, *Torpedoes: Their Invention and Use, from the First Application to the Art of War to the Present Time* (1866), was specifically intended "for the use of the officers of the Corps of Engineers."[2]

The first part of this volume recorded the American use of underwater warfare in the Civil War. Drawn from official correspondence and reports, it previewed in many respects the better organized, more complete account prepared by Barnes three years later. This section was followed by a poorly arranged but highly informative treatment of the history of underwater warfare. In it were rehearsed the now familiar accounts of the pioneers in the field. Fulton and Colt were singled out for emphasis, but all of the important European figures from Gianibelli on received their due. As might be expected, primary sources were cited for the American activities, while recourse was had to secondary accounts of the European efforts. What is surprising is that this latter body of information was available almost *in toto* in professional military journals.

The most important part of King's treatise was his conclusion. While conceding the critical defects still plaguing land and sea mines, he attributed these exclusively to the "slight attenton which has been given to the subject by those who are competent to discover and correct them."[3] His proposed solution was a "Torpedo Corps," a permanent, institutionalized branch of the Army through which a continuous program of technical refinement and unit training could be integrated with overall military policy. His treatment of coast defense, for example, might well have been a page out of Fulton's copy book:

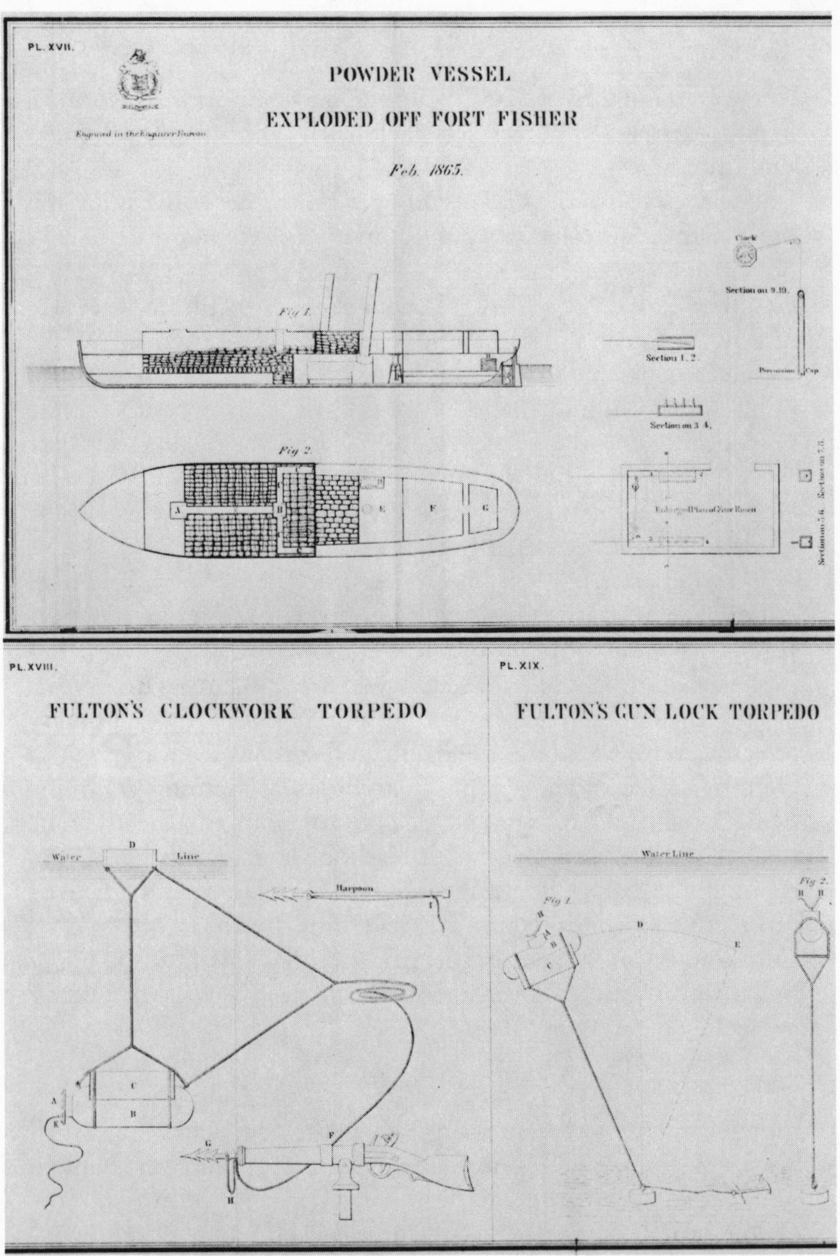

Figure 22. These plates, which appeared together on a single page of W. R. King's *Torpedoes* (1866), reveal Captain King's grasp of the history of underwater warfare. Plate XVII shows the powder vessel exploded ineffectively off Fort Fisher during the Civil War. The concept of the vessel was inferior to Gianibelli's of 1585, for the 1865 ship had no weights set up on the explosive to direct the charge horizontally. Juxtaposed with this diagram are two illustrations from Robert Fulton's *Torpedo War, and Submarine Explosions* (1810).

Whatever details may be adopted for a system of torpedoes, adequate to the defence of our principal harbors, the practical working of the system will not only require the employment of a large number of skilled and intelligent men as observers and operators, but an amount of organization, drill and practice at least equal to that required for the proper service of artillery.[4]

This is essentially what was done. In 1869 the army and navy formally institutionalized underwater warfare. The army established an experimental station and a school for engineer officers at Willets Point, New York Harbor, while the navy established its torpedo station at Newport, Rhode Island. From these two installations issued numerous important studies of underwater warfare, and while the American military establishment contracted in the postwar years, this important new facet of weaponry was kept very much alive.[5]

The European response was much the same. Particularly in England, the interest and activity aroused by the use of mines in the Crimean War was greatly increased by the Confederate experience. A "Memorandum on Floating Obstructions and Submarine Explosive Machines," written on 20 July 1863 by General Sir John F. Burgoyne, inspector general of engineers, cited the Russian and American examples as proof of the great potential of underwater warfare. His recommendation that the experiments already conducted at Chatham be expanded upon by a formal study led directly to the appointment in September 1863 of the Committee on Floating Obstructions and Submarine Explosive Machines. Its report, published in 1868, was similar in many respects to King's.[6] It too rehearsed the history of underwater warfare, and it too cited most of the leading figures in the story. Not surprisingly it showed more strength on the European than on the American facets, but this was a difference in degree, not in kind. While it fell short of recommending formation of a separate torpedo corps, it nonetheless advised continuing the instruction given to royal engineers at Chatham and to naval gunners and gunnery officers at Portsmouth and Woolwich. As the report concluded:

It is now generally acknowledged that these engines of destruction are destined to play a most important part in future operations

> of war, and there is, even now, scarcely a civilized country of importance in which attention has not been directed to the necessity of being in some way prepared for their employment.[7]

The activity in other European countries confirmed that evaluation. Matthew Fontaine Maury capitalized on and encouraged this activity by establishing a school in London at which instruction in his system of underwater warfare was given to foreign naval officers for a fee. France, Sweden, Norway, and Holland all sent officers to study at the school. Even the Russians, who had invited Maury to immigrate at the beginning of the Civl War, examined his system in London, although they alledgedly rejected it as inferior to their own. Since Maury's course included instruction in the history of underwater warfare, it may be assumed that this rich European heritage was now being even more widely promulgated.[8]

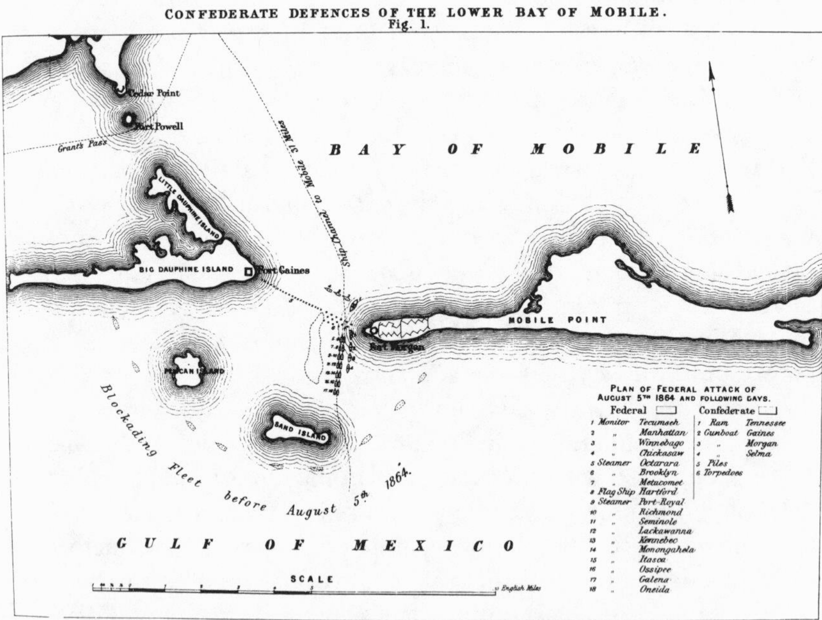

Figures 23 and 24. The torpedoes that Admiral Farragut damned at Mobile Bay in 1864 were those grouped off Fort Morgan, as shown in figure 1 from V.E.R. von Scheliha's *Treatise on Coast Defense* (1868). His figure 6 shows how many more awaited the admiral further up the bay.

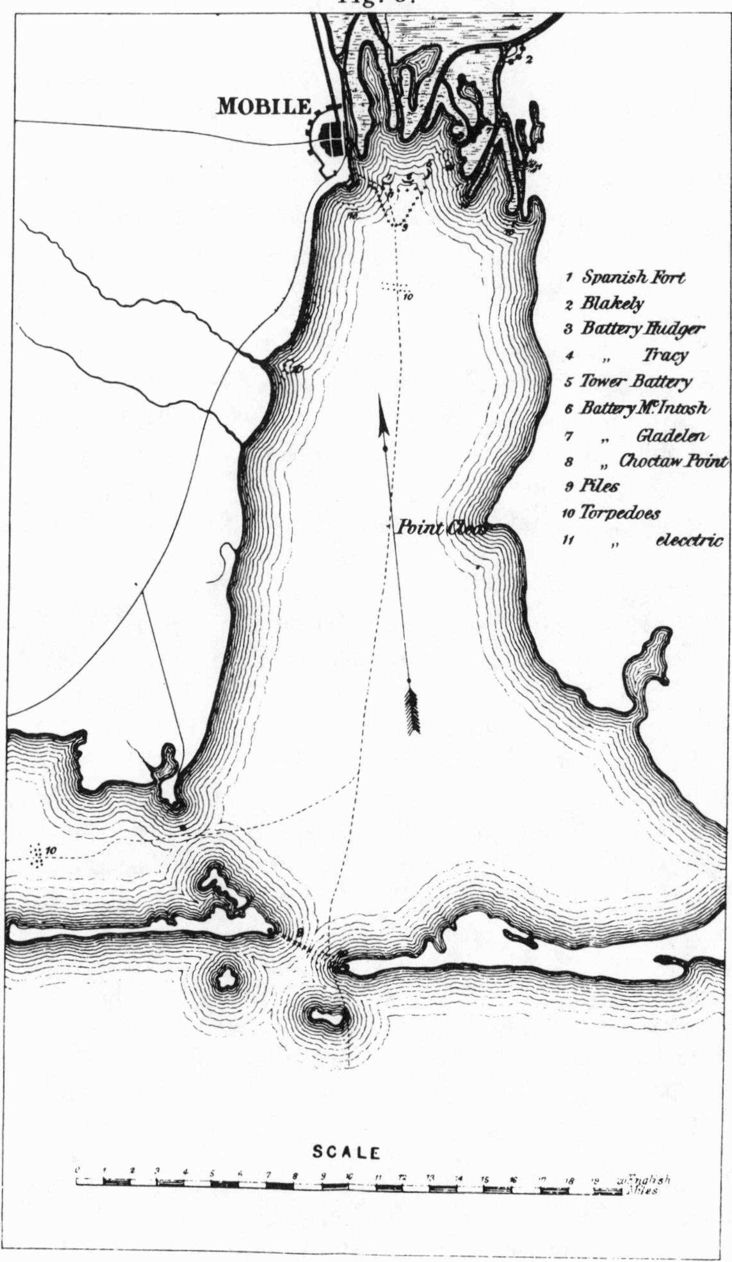

BAY OF MOBILE.
Fig. 6.

Other veterans of the Civil War also spread the news abroad. The best known example is Victor Ernest Rudolph von Scheliha's *Treatise on Coast Defense*. . . . Scheliha, a German mercenary and engineering expert, was a lieutenant colonel in the Confederate army and served as chief engineer to General Dabney H. Maury, nephew of the more famous torpedoist. During the war Scheliha observed Southern activity in underwater warfare at first hand, and in fact took part in many of the efforts along the Gulf coast. After the war he returned for a while to Germany, saw his book through the press, and then went to Russia, where he worked on development of a self-propelled torpedo. His judgment was a fair measure of professional military opinion at the time: "Although torpedoes may have been known previous to the American War, their use on a large scale and with marked success dates from that period only."[9] Being present at that creation was so much military capital to a man like Scheliha, and he was quick to exploit it.

Without publishing a volume as impressive as Scheliha's, Hunter Davidson had the same sort of impact. While Scheliha carried the message to Europe and Russia, Davidson took it to South America, where he sold his services and expertise to Venezuela and Argentina. More than a decade after the American Civil War he was able to report: "I have been almost constantly on torpedo duty ashore and afloat since our war."[10]

Further evidence of the world's appetite for underwater warfare appeared in 1866, in a new edition of Henry Wheaton's *Elements of International Law*, edited by Richard Henry Dana, Jr. The 1848 edition, which Dana had annotated, contained no specific reference to underwater warfare, but a footnote in the new edition addressed the subject under the heading of "Usages of War." Said Dana:

> As to the nature of weapons not poisoned, there is, and perhaps can be, no rule. Concealed modes of extensive destruction are allowed, as torpedoes to blow up ships, or strewed over the ground before an advancing foe, and mines; nor is the destructiveness of a weapon any objection to its use. . . . As war will avail itself of science in all departments, for offence and defence, perhaps the only test, in case of open contests between acknowledged combatants is, that the material shall not owe its efficacy, or the fear it may inspire, to a

> distinct quality of producing pain, or of causing or increasing the chances of death to individuals, or spreading death or disability, if this quality is something else than the application of direct force, and of a kind that cannot be met by countervailing force, or remedied by the usual medical and surgical applications for forcible injuries, or averted by retreat or surrender.[11]

This thoroughly modern formula pronounced two judgments relative to underwater warfare. First, no stigma of immorality any longer attached to a gunpowder weapon *per se*, no tangible association with the devil that could be translated into a reasonable objection. Second, the fact that a weapon was clandestine—or "concealed," as Dana put it—was no bar to its employment. The "secret murder" so much dreaded by Francis Bacon was now a sanctioned reality. Though not all military men subscribed willingly to this new state of affairs, most conceded the fact in the same tone as did Commander Henry A. Wise, U.S.N., chief of the Bureau of Ordnance:

> The torpedo . . . has been successfully tried in many instances during the [Civil W]ar. There seems to be, no doubt, a want of fair play and manly courage in using a concealed and destructive weapon against an enemy, while you are secure from danger and quietly waiting for the catastrophe which launches hundreds of human beings into eternity without warning; but it is nevertheless perfectly legitimate warfare, and the danger must be met, and can only be overcome by caution, skill, and the free use of similar means.[12]

This, then, is the real meaning of the usages of war. A weapon would be sanctioned if used so effectively in war that it forced the other side to retaliate in kind. When that confrontation of power occurred, law and morality would have to bend to the reality of conflict, and Clausewitz's dictum that war gravitates toward unlimited violence would be that much reinforced.

While the lawyers and soldiers were adjusting themselves to this new state of things, a young Frenchman was at work on a novel destined to immortalize the newfound popularity of underwater warfare. In the late 1860s, Jules Verne, always a stickler for technical accuracy, researched *Twenty Thousand Leagues under the Sea* in what was then the most complete repository of information on underwater warfare, the *Bibliothèque national*. He studied accounts of Drebbel, Bushnell, Fulton, and others. He consulted with Cyrus Field, a contemporary historian of the submarine. He even read Matthew Fontain Maury's classic *Physical Geography of the Sea*, though there is no evidence that he availed himself of Maury's expertise in underwater warfare.[13]

When he came to writing his great novel, Verne evidenced a thorough familiarity with the history of underwater warfare and a conviction that the American Civil War heralded its maturity. His story opens in 1866, when Captain Nemo's *Nautilus* (named for Fulton's boat) first appears in the world's sea-lanes. Believed at first to be a sea monster, *Nautilus* causes such a stir that an expedition is fitted out in the United States to find and destroy it. The expedition sails in U.S.S. *Abraham Lincoln* under "Commander Farragut," an obvious reference to the Northern admiral who had so recently damned the torpedoes at Mobile Bay. Verne stated that the *Abraham Lincoln* "might have been called the *Argus*, for a hundred reasons"—most of them related to classical mythology. But one reason that might have escapted Verne's readers then and since was that a like-named vessel in the hands of Commodore John Rodgers, U.S.N., had frustrated the ambitions of another *Nautilus* builder years before.[14]

Of course, the story goes on to sing the praises of Captain Nemo and his underwater world, however tragically flawed they may have been. But the importance of the story here is not where it ended, but where it began. It opened in 1866 with obvious allusions to the American Civil War. So too did modern underwater warfare.

The evolution of underwater warfare in the age of sail was continuous. A trunk line of information led directly from Bourne and Gianibelli to Maury and Captain Nemo. No doubt there were branchings that dead-ended in failure and obscurity, just as there were infusions that joined from unknown and perhaps original sources. But the trunk itself was unbroken. No matter how thin it may have become at times, or how devious a course it may have followed, it conveyed a growing body of information from one mind to another across three centuries of Western history.

Figure 25. An illustration from the original (1869) edition of Jules Verne's *Vingt mille lieues sous les mers*. Sitting in the library of the *Nautilus*, Captain Nemo explains where he got his ideas for the vessel.

The issue is not really whether the message got through—it clearly did—but rather how garbled and incomplete it was. Did successive inventors gain anything more from their predecessors than inspiration and incentive? When Maury came to blow up Union ships, did it really matter that Gianibelli had used a shaped charge in 1585 or that Bourne understood varied displacement in 1578? Surely Fulton, for example, took up where Bushnell left off and profited enormously from a detailed familiarity with the *Turtle*. But does this pattern hold true across the entire age of sail?

The evidence here is less conclusive, but several responses suggest themselves. First, the case for independent invention is no less circumstantial and incomplete than that for continuous evolution. Second, research for this book has consistently shown that the more that is uncovered about the work of underwater warriors, the more evidence there is of their interdependence. And finally, almost without fail, the men who attained the greatest success in underwater warfare were those familiar with the efforts of their predecessors. While no final verdict is possible, the evidence suggests that continuous evolution contributed to the ultimate adoption of underwater warfare in the American Civil War.

This continuity was maintained by a combination of individual and cultural phenomena. The personalities of the successive inventors were the most important individual factors. To a man they were taken by a Davidic impulse to overcome with cleverness and skill the mass and power of the age's dominant naval weapon, the ship of the line. While minds of more pedantic bent sought to engage the hierarchy of power by getting a bigger hammer and thus perpetuating the arms race, the Davids sought to strike at the Achilles heel and send the whole structure—ships and hierarchy alike—to the bottom. They were intensely proud of being what e. e. cummings mockingly called

> . . . that Upwardlooking
> Serene Illustrious and Beatific
> Lord of Creation, MAN:
> at a least crooking
> of Whose compassionate digit, earth's most terrific
>
> quadruped swoons into billiardBalls![15]

In short they stalked Goliath for the simple exhilaration that comes from felling a giant. That the the ship of the line played such a perfect Goliath in the age of sail was the last essential catalyst. These magnificent machines—larger and more powerful than even Don Quixote's windmills—enraptured their admirers to the point of idolization. They exposed themselves, daring David with their mass and at the same time inviting him with their arrogance.

The arrogance of the Goliaths was matched by the conceit of the Davids. Conceit, in fact, was the very heart of the Davidic impulse. It was anathema to these men to stand in the shadow of a power larger than themselves. What little we know of their personalities suggests that they were egocentric, iconoclastic, ambitious, self-confident, and independent. Goliath stirred in them dreams of power, sent them searching for engines of fulfillment. When they took the field, they sought out the largest foe: Bushnell against *Eagle*, Mix against *Plantagenet*, and finally *David* against *New Ironsides*.

From the very start David preyed upon—in fact depended upon—the act of idolization. Gianibelli profited from Parma's overweening confidence in his palisades. Sergeant Lee made contact with *Eagle* because she sat complacently in enemy waters. After *Harvest Moon* was blown out from under him, Admiral Dahlgren commented on the former "ridicule of torpedoes" and the "little precautions" that were deemed necessary. When these precautions were taken, when naval officers were awakened from the act of idolization, then David's plans were almost sure to fail. Fulton learned this twice in the English Channel, and again in New York Harbor at the hands of Commodore Rodgers and the crew of the *Argus*.

If the Davids occasionally forgot how dependent they were on the act of idolization, they never forgot the heart of their plans: the killing explosion set off in close proximity to the soft underbelly of Goliath. Bushnell, Colt, and Maury all began their work with experiments on underwater explosions. That was the stone. The sling came second. Most of the Davids tried a variety of slings—submarines; towed, drifting, and anchored mines and torpedoes; contact and command-detonated mines. Historians of underwater warfare have often focused on the slings—because they were so ingenious—and have lost sight of the explosion. This was the same mistake made by Forfait when he seized upon the "horn of the Nautilus" and forgot that the delivery system was secondary to the weapon itself. Successful Davids, however, always also kept the explosion in mind.

The means employed by the underwater warriors to dispose of their weapons also contributed to keeping their ideas alive. Those like Bourne and Mersenne openly donated their plans to the "common wealth" convinced that ideas had a worth of their own and were not private property. Those like Gianibelli and Mix, who made gratis demonstrations, sparked the popular imagination and kept their ideas alive in war stories, folktales, and histories, the reach of which no one can gauge today. Those like Fulton and Colt, who tried to keep their plans a secret in hopes of winning government subsidy, eventually saw their ideas enter the public domain. Sometimes this was due to leaks of private documents, but as often as not the inventors themselves published their plans when their hopes for government reward disappeared. In fact, most Davids deployed their weapons in more than one of these modes, and the net result was to make almost the entire record available to succeeding generations.

Science played an important role in the evolution of underwater warfare, not by providing any crucial theory or law, but by providing an impetus and a forum for such activity. Science changed enormously over the three centuries of the age of sail, but always it was a spur to further progress. For the first century or so, magic and science were hardly distinguishable, and in the nether world between them such underwater schemes as those of Drebbel and Mersenne could flourish. When Europe entered upon more peaceful times, between the Reformation and the democratic revolutions, science kept underwater warfare current by sweeping it along in the search for oxygen. Then as science became institutionalized in the late seventeenth century, it provided a forum in which just such curiosities and useful knowledge as that surrounding underwater warfare might find a hearing. From the halls of the Royal Society and her sister institutions, news was distributed to an ever wider audience through journals, periodicals, newspapers, and correspondence. Throughout these years, the small circle of men who were most responsible for the nurturing and advancement of science in the age of sail served as an intellectual clearinghouse for the Davids who advanced underwater warfare.

More complex than the reasons for the survival of underwater warfare across three centuries are the reasons why it failed of adoption in the age of sail. The record suggests that the necessary preconditions of acceptance were institutionalization in a military hierarchy and simultaneous use by two combatants. The failure of acceptance must be explained by the failure to take these two steps.

The insurmountable obstacle was always military opposition. Significant inroads were often made, particularly with the help of government scientists and powerful citizens, but they never led to institutionalization. Whether this was an impossible goal or simply an unperceived one is difficult to say, but without it all other schemes were futile. Often enough someone like Drebbel would get a workshop in the Minories or someone like Fulton would get a government dole to go build his device. But until some uniformed officer was responsible for integrating this activity with overall military operations, there was little chance of success in combat. At times the inventors seemed to be vaguely aware of the problem. Again and again they blamed military obstructionism and lack of training for the failure of their expeditions. Only Fulton, however, seems to have been fully alive to the whole solution. "Systematize," he said, repeating the message over and over again to deaf ears. Not until his advice was heeded did underwater warfare become an effective weapon in battle.

The reasons for professional military opposition may be classed under the headings of pragmatism, conservatism, and morality. The pragmatic objection stemmed from the simple fact that the weapons did not work. Trial after trial in combat found underwater warfare wanting, and the excuses and protestations of the inventors could not diminish the failure. However, the pragmatic objection was also a self-fulfilling prophecy. The military refused to adopt these weapons because they failed in combat, yet they failed in combat largely because the military refused to adopt them. There was more than a little validity to the inventors' claims that all their weapons lacked was time, subsidy, encouragement, and—most important of all—a trained corps of experts. Without these their failure was virtually assured—but failure precluded adoption.[16]

The technological ceiling was another practical factor, but not an especially important one. The near success of Bushnell's *Turtle* can be attributed in some measure to advances in technology that made his craft better than those of Drebbel and Papin: the copper gaskets, the efficient forcing pump, the screw propeller. But more often than not the Davids failed to make full use of the technology already available to them. An attack on Fort Fisher by an exploding ship in 1864 was an absolute failure because the arrangement was technically inferior to Gianibelli's. Similarly, Papin's version of Drebbel's submarine was hardly improved upon in the age of sail. The two major advances in underwater warfare made between 1588 and 1865 were the screw propeller and electrical detonation—and neither of these was indispensible to Confederate success in the Civil War.

The second facet of military resistance to underwater warfare was conservatism. In many respects this was simply a special case of the general rule that those in power tend to resist change because they are by definition successful in the current order of things and are not likely to risk their positions for an uncertain future. This behavior is especially important in military circles where tradition plays such a powerful role in the group mentality. To get men to voluntarily participate in two biologically abnormal activities—the risk of life and intraspecific killing—it is necessary to interpose between them and reality a montage of symbols and reinforcements. Often these take the form of worship for the tools of war. This act of idolization, in addition to distracting attention from what the tools are meant to do, also reinforces the pride and satisfaction derived from successful use of a powerful machine. When some interloping iconoclast solicits the aid of professional soldiers in destroying the dominant tools of their trade, he offends not only the practical opinion that these weapons have been successful and ought not lightly to be discarded but also the aesthetic persuasion that there is something intrinsically worthy in the weapons themselves. The admiral loved his ship of the line for three reasons: first because it made him an admiral, second because he and it had been through a lot together, and third because it was a pleasing buffer between him and the harsh realities of what those cannons it carried were meant to do.

The third objection of uniformed officers was one that they perceived even less clearly than their conservatism. Their moral objections—most often paraded under the banner of chivalry—were a combination of medieval aversion to clandestine weapons and a lingering association of gunpowder weapons with the devil. Underwater warfare always offended both of these prejudices, but as time went on the officers were less and less able to remember why. The association with the devil was forgotten (but not lost) in the epithet "infernal machine," and though this term came to be applied to fewer and fewer weapons, underwater warfare was always one of them. The prejudice against clandestine weapons, a persuasion derived from the medieval view of war as a judicial duel, could only be expressed in terms like "want of manly courage." To this day officers continue to wear swords at ceremonial occasions because it was the last weapon in their profession to offend neither of these prejudices. When faced with the reality of the "usages of war," officers overcame these prejudices, but never without pain and reluctance.

One last factor influenced military hostility to underwater warfare: the personality of David. Inventors who proposed these weapons were often tactless in dealing with military professionals. They claimed overmuch for their weapons, predicted the elimination of navies, circumvented military channels whenever possible, and generally treated officers with condescension and impatience. Worst of all, they undertook to instruct a professional in how to conduct his profession—a chancy business in any realm, but a particularly hazardous one in military circles. In fact, almost by definition, a David needed a Saul. By the time of the age of sail, however, the professionalization of armed force had replaced the autonomous warrior king with a civilian sovereign counselled by professional fighters. The solitary warrior could no longer go straight from the presence of Saul to the battlefield to face Goliath. He had to pass through the military hierarchy, just the sort of thing Davids were notoriously bad at doing.

But the other side of the coin is that once military professionals adopt a weapon as their own, it then gathers an independent existence. More difficult still than gaining adoption of a new weapon is forcing retirement of an old one. Once underwater warfare received official approval in military circles, there was no way of stopping it. There is none still.

Notes

CHAPTER I: UNDERWATER WARFARE AND THE AGE OF SAIL

1. Theodore Ropp, lecture delivered at Duke University, 18 February 1971.

2. On earlier efforts see G.-L. Pesce, *La Navigation sous–marine* (Paris, 1906), pp. 11–14, 21–25, 125–28; and Alan H. Burgoyne, *Submarine Navigation: Past and Present* (2 vols.; London and New York, 1903), I, 6.

3. Michael Roberts, "The Military Revolution, 1560–1660," in *Essays in Swedish History* (London, 1967), p. 218.

4. The words *technics* and *technology* are now essentially synonymous, with the former word passing out of usage. In this study, however, they will be used to describe distinct phenomena. Technics will refer to those methods or techniques which distinguish the successful practice of an art or craft, as, for example, the technique employed by early French vintners. In contrast, technology will refer to these same methods and techniques when they are treated as a science or a branch of study, as, for example, the technology employed in producing the "standardized" wines of present-day California. The distinction is that technics retains its original Greek meaning of art or craft, while technology refers to the science or study of such arts or crafts. As modern usage suggests, the technics of most arts and crafts today are succumbing to analysis and systematization within the meaning of technology. In the realm of underwater warfare, the distinction between technics and technology is reflected in the differences between the approaches of Cornelius Drebbel and Samuel Colt. See chapters two and ten below.

5. John U. Nef, *War and Human Progress: An Essay on the Rise of Industrial Civilization* (Cambridge, Mass., 1950), p. 135.

6. Bernard and Fawn Brodie, *From Crossbow to H–Bomb: The Evolution of the Weapons and Tactics of Warfare* (rev. and enl. ed.; Bloomington and London, 1973), p. 64. Other casualty estimates vary, but all agree it was a bloody affair.

7. Cervantes, *The First Part of the Life and Achievements of the Renowned Don Quixote de la Mancha* [1605], trans. by Peter Motteux (New York, 1941), p. 88.

8. Ibid., p. 182.

9. J. Huizinga, *The Waning of the Middle Ages: A Study of the Forms of Life, Thought and Art in France and the Netherlands in the XIVth and XVth Centuries* (London, 1924), pp. 91–94. Except for this one service, however, chivalry had no charms for Huizinga. In his chapter seven, on "The Political and Military Value of Chivalrous Ideas," he presented a thorough and moving catalogue of the crimes and abuses indulged in in the name of chivalry.

10. See Maurice H. Keen, *The Laws of War in the Late Middle Ages* (London, 1965).

11. Cervantes, *Don Quixote*, pp. 427–28.

12. Ibid., p. 428.

13. Ibid.

14. [Louis] de Gaya [Sieur de Treville], *Traite des armes, des machines de guerre, des feux d'artifice, des enseignes & des instrumens militaires anciens & modernes . . .* [1678], ed. by Charles Ffoulkes (London, 1911), p. 67.

15. Nef, *War and Progress*, p. 42.

16. Lewis Mumford attributes the first infernal machine to Konrad Kyeser (1366–1405) in 1405, presumably a reference to Kyeser's *Bellifortis*, published between 1396 and 1405. See *Technics and Civilization* (New York, 1934), p. 439; and compare Paolo Rossi, *Philosophy, Technology, and the Arts in the Early Modern Era* [1962], trans. by Salvator Attanasio, ed. by Benjamin Nelson (Torchbook Library ed.; New York, 1970), pp. 15–16, and A. C. Crombie, "From Rationalism to Experimentalism," in Philip R. Wiener and Aaron Noland, eds., *The Roots of Scientific Thought: A Cultural Perspective* (New York, 1957), p. 129. If correct, this would place the origins of infernals in the immediate wake of the emergence of gunpowder in the fourteenth century. On *machina*, see Lynn Thorndike, *A History of Magic and Experimental Science* (8 vols.; New York, 1929–1958), VII, 620–21. On the association of infernals with naval weapons, see Francis Grose, *Military Antiquities Respecting a History of the English Army from the Conquest to the Present Time* (2 vols.; London, 1788), II, 333–34.

17. A. Rupert Hall, "Early Modern Technology, to 1600," in Melvin Kranzberg and Carroll W. Pursell, Jr., eds., *Technology in Western Civilization*, Vol. I: *The Emergence of Modern Industrial Society, Earliest Times to 1900* (New York, 1967), p. 88.

18. Cervantes, *Don Quixote*, p. 76.

19. Pesce, *La Navigation*, p. 129.

20. William Bourne, *The Art of Shooting in Great Ordnance . . .* (London, 1587), p. Aii.

21. Lynn Montross, *War through the Ages* (New York and London, 1944), p. 179.

22. William Bourne, *A Regiment for the Sea* [1574] *and other writings on navigation*, ed. by E. G. R. Taylor, Works Issued by the Hakluyt Society, second series, no 121 (Cambridge, 1963), pp. xiii–xxxv; and E. G. R. Taylor, *Tudor Geography,*

1485–1583 (London, 1930), pp. 153 ff., and *The Mathematical Practitioners of Tudor and Stuart England* (Cambridge, 1954), p. 176. Bourne's career fits almost perfectly the hypothetical model sketched by A. R. Hall in his study of seventeenth-century ballistics: "The gunner . . . could rise to be a workaday member of one of those groups which existed on the fringe of science, nourishing himself and his studies on the crumbs from philosophic feasts. Recruited from the hard service of the seas, from the impoverished gentry or a line of martial ancestors, such men as these, with the intellectual cream of other crafts, were the aptest interpreters of science and the discoverers of its utilitarian charms." *Ballistics in the Seventeenth Century: A Study in the Relations of Science and War with Reference Principally to England* (Cambridge, 1952), p. 58.

23. Edgar Zilsel, "The Genesis of the Concept of Scientific Progress," in Wiener and Noland, *Roots of Science*, pp. 262–64.

24. William Bourne, *Inuentions or Deuices. Very necessary for all Generalles and Captains, or Leaders of men, as wel by Sea as by Land* (London, [c. 1590]), "The Preface to the Reader."

25. Quoted in Zilsel, "The Genesis of the Concept of Scientific Progress," p. 264.

26. Pesce, *La Navigation*, pp. 24–25.

27. William Bourne, *A Book Called the Treasure for Traveilers* . . . (London, 1578), p. 2.

28. J. S. Cowie, *Mines, Minelayers and Minelaying* (London, 1949), p. 7.

29. F. von Ehrenkrook, "History of Submarine Mining and Torpedoes" (trans. by Frederick Martin), No. 1 in U.S. Engineer School of Application, *Professional Papers* (Willets Point, N.Y., 1881–1882), p. 3. See also Jacques-Philippe Mérigon de Montgéry, *Mémoire sur les mines flottantes et les petards flottans, ou machines infernales maritimes* (Paris, 1819), p. 12.

30. For a discussion of the sixteenth-century Italian engineer as fortifier, see Lynn White, Jr., "Jacopo Aconcio As an Engineer," *American Historical Review*, LXXII (January 1967), 425–44.

31. Drayton, *The Battaille of Agincourt* . . . (London, 1631), p. 12; and *Hamlet*, Act III, Scene iv.

32. The definition is from Randle Cotgrave, *A dictionarie of the French and English tongues* [1611] (Columbia, S.C., 1950), S.V. "Petart." One dictionary in 1599 described the petard as "lately invented" (John Minsheu, *A Dictionarie in Spanish and English* . . . ,ed. by Ric. Percival [London, 1599], p. 189), and most writers attributed its origin to Henry of Navarre at the siege of Cahors. See, for example, François Alexandre Aubert La Chesnaye-Desboise, *Dictionnaire militaire; ou, Recueil alphabetique de tous les termes propres à l'art de la guerre* . . . (3 vols.; 2d ed., rev., corr., and aug.; Paris, 1745–1746), II, 222–27; and George Smith, *An Universal Military Dictionary* . . . [1799] (Ottawa, Ontario, 1969), p. 202. One modern author even credits Henry with the creation of a "corps de [*sic*] pertardiers." [Eugene] Hennebert, *Les Torpilles* (Paris, 1888), p. 151.

33. Information on Gianibelli is derived from John Lothrop Motley, *History of the United Netherlands from the Death of William the Silent to the Twelve Years'*

Truce—1609 (4 vols.; New York, 1867), I, 189–99; Jervis Wegg, *The Decline of Antwerp under Philip of Spain* (London, 1924), pp. 285–86, 291–92; and Archibald Montgomery Low, *Mine and Countermine* (New York, 1940), chapter two.

34. Wegg, *Antwerp under Philip*, p. 291. Motley gives the clockmaker's name as "Borg" (*United Netherlands*, I, 191), but in either case it is most likely the same Jan Bourg whose *Pyrotechnie militaire* (1591) Michael Roberts credits with presenting the first practical torpedo. "The Military Revolution," p. 212.

35. Motley, *United Netherlands*, I, 191–92.

36. Balthazar Ayala, *Three Books on the Law of War And on the Duties Connected with War And on Military Discipline* [1582], trans. by John Pawley Bate, ed. by John Westlake; No. 2, Vol. 2 of The Classics of International Law, ed. by James Brown Scott (Washington, 1912).

37. Ibid., p. 7.

38. Ibid., pp. 133, 135.

39. Friedrich Schiller, *The Revolt of the Netherlands*, trans. by E. B. Eastwick and A. J. W. Morrison, in *The Works of Friedrich Schiller*, ed. by Nathan Haskell Dole, V (New York, 1901), p. 339.

40. Motley, *United Netherlands*, I, 190.

41. Ibid., p. 191.

42. Ibid. Parma himself gave testimony to the overweening confidence the Spanish had in their bridge. Writing to Philip, he said: "It would stand though all Holland and Zeland should come to destroy our palisade . . . ; if the enemy should attempt to assail us now, they would come back with broken heads." Quoted in Low, *Mine and Countermine*, pp. 22–23.

43. Theodore Ropp, *War in the Modern World*, Collier Books (new, rev. ed.; New York, 1962), p. 64.

44. Motley, *United Netherlands*, II, 486n. Winter was at one time William Bourne's commander. Taylor, *Mathematical Practitioners*, p. 176.

45. Garrett Mattingly, *The Armada* (Boston, 1959), p. 323; and Brodie and Brodie, *Crossbow*, p. 68.

46. Mattingly, *Armada*, pp. 401–2.

47. Palmer, *The World of the French Revolution* (New and Evanston, 1971), pp. 151–52.

48. Arnold J. Toynbee, *War and Civilization*, selected by Albert V. Fowler from *A Study of History*, (New York, 1950), p. 114.

49. Ibid., p. 129.

50. Quoted in Mumford, *Technics and Civilization*, p. 208.

51. Nef, *War and Progress*, p. 129.

CHAPTER II: CORNELIUS DREBBEL AND THE USES OF MAGIC

1. "Advertissment" to *Divers traitez de la philosophie naturelle* (Paris, 1672). This work contains "Deux traitez philosophiques de Corneille Drebel," pp. 175–273.

2. Gerrit Tierie, *Cornelis Drebbel, 1572–1633* (Amsterdam, 1932), p. xi. Unless otherwise indicated biographical information on Drebbel is drawn from this

volume and from L. E. Harris, *The Two Netherlanders: Humphrey Bradlee and Cornelis Drebbel* (Leiden, 1961).

3. Drebbel to James I, c. 1613, quoted in Harris, *Two Netherlanders*, p. 147.

4. Tierie, *Drebbel*, pp. 10, 13, 17, 18, 27, 28, 54, 109; Harris, *Two Netherlanders*, pp. 126, 131: *Dicionary of National Biography* (22vols.; London, 1921–22), VI, 13.

5. *The Works of the Honourable Robert Boyle* . . . , ed. by Thomas Birch (5 vols.; London, 1744), I, 69.

6. Lynn Thorndike, *A History of Magic and Experimental Science* (8 vols.; New York, 1929–58), VII, 497; Tierie, *Drebbel*, p. 16; and G. N. Clark, *Science and Social Welfare in the Age of Newton*(Oxford, 1937), p. 7.

7. John Minsheu, *A Dictionarie in Spanish and English, First Published into the English Tongue by Ric. Percivale Gent. Now Enlarged and Amplified* . . . (London, 1599), p. 64.

8. Quoted in A. Wolf, *A History of Science, Technology, and Philosophy in the 16th & 17th Centuries* (New York, 1935), p. 132.

9. Frazer, *The Golden Bough: A Study in Magic and Religion* (1 vol.; abr. ed.; New York, 1955), p. 50.

10. Thorndike, *Magic and Science*, I, 2.

11. Ibid., VII, 492.

12. Cited in Harris, *Two Netherlanders*, p. 146.

13. Pierre Duhem, *Etudes sur Leonardo de Vinci* (Paris, 1906), quoted in John U. Nef, *War and Human Progress: An Essay on the Rise of Industrial Civilization* (Cambridge, Mass., 1950), p. 49.

14. Peter Gay, *The Enlightenment: An Interpretation*, Vol. I: *The Rise of Modern Paganism*, Vintage Books (New York, 1968), p. 313.

15. Thorndike, *Magic and Science*, VII, 65.

16. Wolf, *Science in the 16th & 17th Centuries*, p. 76. See Marjorie Nicolson, "Kepler, the *Somnium*, and John Donne," in Philip P. Wiener and Aaron Noland, eds., *The Roots of Scientific Thought: A Cultural Perspective* (New York, 1957), pp. 306–27, for another example of the speed with which ideas traveled at the opening of the seventeenth century.

17. John Francis Waller, ed., *The Imperial Dictionary of Universal Biography* . . . (14 vols.; London [c. 1863]), V, 146.

18. Cited in Thorndike, *Magic and Science*, VII, 495.

19. Harris, *Two Netherlanders*, pp. 164–65, 200–201; Nef, *War and Progress*, pp. 57–59; Tierie, *Drebbel*, pp. 63–64; and E. G. R. Taylor, *The Mathematical Practitioners of Tudor and Stuart England* (Cambridge, 1954), pp. 184, 191.

20. Murray F. Sueter, *The Evolution of the Submarine Boat Mine and Torpedo from the Sixteenth Century to the Present Time* (Portsmouth, England, 1907), p. 9; and Harris, *Two Netherlanders*, p. 165.

21. Francis R. Johnson, "Gresham College: Precursor of the Royal Society," in Wiener and Noland, *Roots of Science*, p. 343.

22. Constantyn Huygens, *Autobiography* [1631], quoted in Tierie, *Drebbel*, p. 61.

23. Harris, *Two Netherlanders*, p. 195; Tierie, *Drebbel*, p. 11: [Great Britain,

Public Record Office,] *Calendar of State Papers, Domestic Series, of the Reign of Charles I* (23 vols.; London, 1858–1897), Vol. 1625–1626, p. 367.

24. Harris, *Two Netherlanders*, p. 126.

25. Cited in ibid., p. 187.

26. See John B. Rae, "The Invention of Invention," in Melvin Kranzberg and Carroll W. Pursell, Jr., eds., *Technology in Western Civilization*, Vol. I: *The Emergence of Modern Industrial Society, Earliest Times to 1900* (New York, 1967), p. 325; and Tierie, *Drebbel*, p. 28.

27. Cited in Harris, *Two Netherlanders*, p. 194.

28. Information for this discussion is dervied from A. R. Hall, *Ballistics in the Seventeenth Century: A Study in the Relations of Science and War with Reference Principally to England* (Cambridge, England 1952), pp. 16–22; and Bernard and Fawn Brodie, *From Crossbow to H–Bomb: The Evolution of the Weapons and Tactics of Warfare* (rev. and enl. ed.; Bloomington and London, 1973), p. 53.

29. Francis Grose, *Military Antiquities Respecting a History of the English Army from the Conquest to the Present Time* (2 vols.; London, 1788), II, 326. Grose does not explain what Rotispen's innovation was.

30. *Calender of State Papers, Domestic, Charles I*, Vol. 1625–1626, p. 367.

31. Ibid., Vol. 1627–1628, p. 206.

32. Ibid., Vol. 1628–1629, p. 161; and Vol. 1629–1631, pp. 212, 215.

33. Constantyn Huygens, *Autobiography*, cited in Tierie, *Drebbel*, p. 73.

34. Ibid. Drebbel himself was an Anabaptist, even given to lecturing James I on the evils of kings who "allow themselves to be misled by blind desire, seeking by bloody war to extend their kingdoms." Ibid., p. 19.

35. *Henry V*, Act III, Scene ii.

36. Alberico Gentili, *De Iuri Belli Libri Tres*, trans. by John C. Rolfe, No 16, Vol. II of The Classics of International Law, ed. by James Brown Scott (Oxford, 1933).

37. Ibid., p. 164. While this idea is now considered medieval and is associated with such examples as the papal ban on the crossbow, it is nonetheless, as Gentili reminds us, a classical notion. Archimedes, for example, thought the catapult would end man's chance to prove his valor in battle, and such considerations weighed heavily on the minds of early international jurists, steeped as they were in classical sources.

38. Ibid., p. 165.

39. Ibid., p. 156.

40. Bacon, *Sylva Sylvarum*, quoted in Thorndike, *Magic and Science*, VII, 69.

41. Gentili, *De Iuri Belli*, pp. 160–61.

42. *The Diary of Samuel Pepys*, ed. by Henry B. Wheatley (10 vols.; London, 1923–24), II, 204, and III, 341; [Great Britain, Public Record Office,] *Calendar of State Papers, Domestic Series, of the Reign of Charles II* (28 vols.; London, 1860–1939), Vol. 1661–1662, p. 327; and Tierie, *Drebbel*, p. 75. See pp. 40–41 below.

43. Robert Lenoble, *Mersenne ou la naissance du mécanisme* (Paris, 1943), p. 35. See also H[erbert] Butterfield, *The Origins of Modern Science, 1300–1800* (2d. ed.; New York, 1957), pp. 71–76; and Thorndike, *Magic and Science*, VII, 427–30.

44. Quoted in Thorndike, *Magic and Science*, VII, 430.

45. Lenoble, *Mersenne*, pp. 489–92. See, for example, Marin Mersenne, *Cogitata Physico-mathematica . . .* (Paris, 1644), pp. 207, 251–59. The historians of underwater warfare have been at odds over the exact time and place of Mersenne's comments on the subject. See G.-L. Pesce, *La Navigation sous-marine* (Paris, 1906), pp. 136–37, and compare Farnham Bishop, *The Story of the Submarine* (rev. & enl.; New York, 1929), p. 6, and Maurice Delpeuch, *Les Sous-marins à travers les siècles* (Paris, 1907), p. 25.

46. Georges Fournier, *Hydrographie contenant le theorie et la practique de toutes les parties de la navigation* (2d. ed.; Paris, 1667), p. 606.

47. Alan H. Burgoyne, *Submarine Navigation: Past and Present* (2 vols.; London and New York, 1903), I, 8.

48. Huygens, *Autobiography*, quoted in Tierie, *Drebbel*, p. 33; "disgusting folly, this, on the part of a chemist," observed Huygens.

49. Drebbel, "Deux traitez," pp. 245–58.

50. Quoted in Harris, *Two Netherlanders*, p. 171.

51. Lewis Mumford, *Technics and Civilization* (New York, 1934), pp. 40–41.

CHAPTER III: ROBERT BOYLE AND THE OXYGEN CONNECTION

1. Quincy Wright, *A Study of War* (2d. ed.; Chicago, 1965), p. 160.

2. Cited in R. R. Palmer and Joel Colton, *A History of the Modern World* (4th ed.; New York, 1971), p. 128.

3. John U. Nef, *War and Human Progress: An Essay on the Rise of Industrial Civilization* (Cambridge, Mass., 1950), p. 135. This conclusion is not entirely justified by statistical evidence. See Wright, *A Study of War*, chap. IX and Appendixes XIX–XXIV.

4. See Paolo Rossi, *Philosophy, Technology, and the Arts in the Early Modern Era*, trans. by Salvator Attanasio, ed. by Benjamin Nelson, Torchbook Library ed. (New York, 1970), pp. 146–73, esp. p. 15 n., for a bibliography of the debate. A penetrating account of Bacon's philosophy as it relates to the Royal Society of London is Margery Purver, *The Royal Society: Concept and Creation* (Cambridge, Mass., 1967), Part I, chapters two, three.

5. H[erbert] Butterfield, *The Origins of Modern Science, 1300–1800* (2d. ed.; New York, 1957), p. 100.

6. Francis Bacon, *New Atlantis*, The Harvard Classics ([50 vols] reg. ed.; New York, 1937), [III] p. 172.

7. Ibid., pp. 179–80.

8. Ibid., pp. 178–79.

9. Ibid., p. 181.

10. Butterfield, *Origins*, 103; and Martha Ornstein, *The Rôle of Scientific Societies in the Seventeenth Century* (Chicago, 1928), p. 44.

11. Francis R. Johnson, "Gresham College: Precursor of the Royal Society," in Philip P. Wiener and Aaron Noland, eds., *The Roots of Scientific Thought: A Cultural Perspective* (New York, 1957), pp. 328–53. On the scientific academies in general, see Ornstein, *Scientific Societies*; Harcourt Brown, *Scientific Organizations*

of 17th Century France (1620–1680) (Baltimore, 1934); and A. Wolf, *A History of Science, Technology, and Philosophy in the 16th & 17th Centuries* (New York, 1935), pp. 54–70.

12. Charles Richard Weld, *A History of the Royal Society, with Memoirs of the Presidents, Compiled from Authentic Documents* (2 vols.; London, 1848), I, 146–47.

13. Actually the *Transactions* were at first published privately by the successive secretaries of the Society, but they had the Society's formal endorsement and were always, for all practical purposes, an official journal. Since 1887 the *Transactions* have been published in two series: Series A for mathematical and physical sciences and Series B for biological sciences.

14. *Philosophical Transactions* [117 vols.; London, 1665–1886] (Amsterdam, 1963–1964), I. 1.

15. Butterfield, *Origins*, p. 75.

16. G. N. Clark, *Science and Social Welfare in the Age of Newton* (Oxford, 1937), p. 56.

17. The relationship of the *Journal des sçavans* to the *Académie des Sciences* was strikingly similar to the relationship between the *Philosophical Transactions* and the Royal Society. For many years it was, in Roger Hahn's words, the "quasi-official publication of the Academy," but in neither concept nor early execution was it an organ of the institution *per se*. See Roger Hahn, *The Anatomy of a Scientific Institution: The Paris Academy of Sciences, 1666–1803* (Berkeley, Calif., 1971), pp. 63–64 and *passim*.

18. Butterfield, *Origins*, p. 180.

19. Thorndike, *A History of Magic and Experimental Science* (8 vols.; New York, 1929–1958), VIII, 261.

20. *Dictionary of National Biography*, II, 1026—31.

21. Information on oxygen and chemistry is drawn primarily from Wolf, *Science in the 16th & 17th Centuries*, chapter fifteen; and René Taton, ed., *History of Science*, trans. by A. J. Pomerans, Vol. II: *The Beginnings of Modern Science: From 1450 to 1800* (New York, 1964), pp. 119–32, 322–32, 489–510.

22. *The Works of the Honourable Robert Boyle* . . . , ed. by Thomas Birch (5 vols.; London, 1744), I, 69. This is actually a paraphrase of Paracelsus, with whom he agreed on this subject.

23. Ibid.

24. L. E. Harris, *The Two Netherlanders: Humphrey Bradlee and Cornelis Drebbel* (Leiden, 1961), pp. 171–81.

25. Richelet, *Dictionnaire français* (1680), quoted in Rossi, *Philosophy, Technology, and the Arts*, p. 12.

26. Quoted in Bernard and Fawn Brodie, *From Crossbow to H–Bomb* (rev. and enl. ed.; Bloomington and London, 1973), p. 90.

27. Quoted in Clark, *Science and Social Welfare*, p. 77. I did not find the quotation where Clark cited it, but I do not doubt its authenticity.

28. Thorndike, *Magic and Science*, VIII, 31.

29. *Philosophical Transactions*, II, 343.

30. H[enry] Dircks, *A Biographical Memoir of Samuel Hartlib* . . . (London, n.d.),

passim; and Boyle, *Works*, V, 280–81, 284, and 503–504. See also Nef, *War and Progress*, p. 197. Professor Nef seems to have overworked the evidence a bit. See Oldenburg to Boyle, 4 July 1665, in Boyle, *Works*, V. 331.

31. Boyle, *New Experiments Physico–Mechanicall, Touching The Spring of the Air* . . . (Oxford, 1660), p. 145.

32. Wilkins, *Mathematical Magick: or the Wonders That May Be Performed by Mechanical Geometry* . . . [5th ed., 1707], in *The Mathematical and Philosophical Works of the Right Reverend John Wilkins, Late Lord Bishop of Chester* (London, 1708), Bk. II, chapter four, 105–11.

33. Boyle also cited Mersenne on "BARIEUS." See *Works*, III, 174. Compare G.-L Pesce, *La Navigation sous–marine* (Paris, 1906), pp. 25–26.

34. *Works*, I, 4.

35. Wolf, *Science in the 16th & 17th Centuries*, p. 102.

36. There is no direct evidence that Boyle read *Technica Curiosa* . . . (Nuremberg, 1664), but Schott's *Mechanica Hydraulica* had been sufficiently important to him that it seems safe to assume that he would have availed himself of the 1664 treatise, especially since Book I opened with a treatment of von Guericke's experiments, in which Boyle was most interested.

37. Schott, *Technica Curiosa* . . . pp. 387–90. See also Maurice Delpeuch, *Les Sous–marins a travers les siècles* (Paris, 1907), pp. 26–29. This could well be the "monsieur de Son" mentioned in the *Philosophical Transactions* of 1665 as "one of the most Excellent Mechanicks in the World" (I, 83).

38. Schott, *Technica Curiosa* . . . , pp. 390–92. George Philip Harsdorffer, *Delitiae Philosophicae et Mathematicae* (3 vols.; Nuremberg, 1636–1692), I, "Register der Scribenten."

39. Schott, *Technica Couriosa* . . . , pp. 392–93.

40. [Edward Somerset, Second] Marquis of Worcester, *A Century of the Names and Scantlings of Such Inventions* . . . (1655) (Glasgow, 1767), pp. 10–11.

41. Henry Dircks, *The Life, Times, and Scientific Labors of the Second Marquis of Worcester* . . . (London, 1865). Dircks also suspected that Worcester knew Hartlib, Boyle's friend and correspondent. Dircks, *Hartlib*, p. vi.

42. Pesce, *La Navigation*, pp. 141–43.

43. Wolf, *Science in the 16th & 17th Centuries*, pp. 415–17.

44. Robert Hooke, *Philosophical Collections* (1679), quoted in Dircks, *Worcester*, p. 404.

45. Thorndike, *Magic and Science*, VII, 620.

CHAPTER IV: DENIS PAPIN AND POPULARIZATION

1. Cobban, *A History of Modern France*, Vol. I: *Old Regime and Revolution, 1715–1799*, Penguin Books (3d ed.; Harmondsworth, England, 1963), p. 101.

2. Lord Keynes, "Newton, the Man," in *Royal Society Newton Tercentenary Celebrations* (Cambridge, 1947), pp. 27, 29, and *passim*.

3. I. Bernard Cohen, "Some Recent Books on the History of Science," in Philip P. Wiener and Aaron Noland, eds., *The Roots of Scientific Thought: A Cultural Perspective* (New York, 1957), p. 628.

4. G. N. Clark, *Science and Social Welfare in the Age of Newton* (Oxford, 1937), pp. 128–29.

5. Gay, *The Enlightenment: An Interpretation*, Vol. II: *The Science of Freedom* (New York, 1969), pp. 9–10.

6. John U. Nef, *War and Human Progress: An Essay on the Rise of Industrial Civilization* (Cambridge, Mass., 1950), pp. 195, 302–303.

7. "Sermon CXVII," in *The Works of John Donne, D.D., Dean of St. Paul's, 1621–1631, with a Memoir of His Life*, ed. by Henry Alford (6 vols.; London, 1839), V, 58.

8. Robert Boyle, *The Works of the Honourable Robert Boyle . . .*, ed. by Thomas Birch (5 vols.; London, 1744), V, 503.

9. Sueter, *The Evolution of the Submarine Boat Mine and Torpedo from the Sixteenth Century to the Present Time* (Portsmouth, England, 1907), p. xx. Actually, Sueter was quoting an unidentified speaker at the Royal United Service Institution, but the ellipsis made the thought very much his own. He deleted a phrase describing war as "that splendid mistress for whose favours we have all longed since we reached man's estate." Quoted in full in Herbert C. Fyfe, *Submarine Warfare: Past, Present, and Future* (London, 1902), p. 63.

10. A. R. Hall, *Ballistics in the Seventeenth Century: A Study in the Relations of Science and War with Reference Principally to England* (Cambridge, 1952), pp. 5, 78–79; Nef, *War and Progress*, pp. 200–1.

11. Bynkershoek, *Quaestionum Juris Publici libri Duo*, trans. by Tenney Frank, No. 14, Vol. II of The Classics of International Law, ed. by James Brown Scott (Oxford, 1930), p. 16.

12. Wolff, *Jus Gentium Methodo Scientifica Pertractatum*, trans. by Joseph H. Drake, No. 13, Vol. II of The Classics of International Law, ed. by James Brown Scott (Oxford, 1934), pp. 383, 450.

13. Vattel, *The Law of Nations or the Principles of Natural Law Applied to the Conduct and to the Affairs of Nations and of Sovereigns*, trans. by Charles G. Fenwick, No. 4, Vol. III of The Classics of International Law, ed. by James Brown Scott (Washington, 1916), p. 287.

14. Ibid., pp. 338 and 279–90.

15. See A. Wolf, *A History of Science, Technology, and Philosophy in the 16th & 17th Centuries* (New York, 1935), pp. 551–52, and *A History of Science, Technology, and Philosophy in the Eighteenth Century* (New York, 1939), p. 635; James Kip Finch, "Transportation and Construction, 1300–1800," in Melvin Kranzberg and Carroll W. Pursell, Jr., eds., *Technology in Western Civilization*, Vol. I: *The Emergence of Modern Industrial Society, Earliest Times to 1900* (New York, 1967), 194–97; and Hall, *Ballistics in the Seventeenth Century*, pp. 7–9, 28, 57, 104.

16. Francois Alexandre Aubert La Chesnaye-Desbois, *Dictionnaire militaire; ou, Recueil alphabetique de tous les termes propres à l'art de la guerre . . .* (3 vols.; Rev., corr., and aug.; Paris, 1745–1746), II, 25–26, s.v. "*Ingenieur*."

17. Ibid., p. 27.

18. Quoted in Wolf, *Science in the 16th & 17th Centuries*, p. 551.

19. Nef, *War and Progress*, pp. 245–46. Colbert tried with only limited success

to cut down on the ornamentation of naval vessels in the late seventeenth century.

20. *Spectator,* Vol. I, 12 March 1711.

21. Nef, *War and Progress,* p. 184. Biographical information is from *Dictionary of National Biography,* XV, 192–93.

22. P. Valkhoff, "Constantin Huygens, poète et homme d'etat hollandais, et ses amities françaises," in Lanson Collection Pamphlets, Duke University Library, Vol. 153, No. 4, p. 7.

23. Papin, *Recueil de diverses Pieces touchant quelques nouvelles Machines . . .* (Cassel, 1695), pp. 127–28.

24. Ibid., pp. 127–43.

25. *Correspondence,* cited in L. E. Harris, *The Two Netherlanders: Humphrey Bradlee and Cornelis Drebbel* (Leiden, 1961), pp. 178–79.

26. *Gentleman's Magazine and Historical Chronicle,* I (January 1731), "Introduction."

27. Ibid., XVII (December 1747), 581–82.

28. Ibid., XIX (June 1749), 249.

29. Ibid., (July 1749), 312.

30. Ibid., (September 1749), 411–13.

CHAPTER V: DAVID BUSHNELL: TRANSPLANTING THE EUROPEAN EXPERIENCE

1. See above, p. 37.

2. Quoted in Gilman C. Gates, *Saybrook at the Mouth of the Connecticut: The First One Hundred Years* (Orange and New Haven, Conn., 1935), p. 190.

3. See Edwin Oviatt, *The Beginnings of Yale (1701–1726)*(New Haven, 1916), pp. 304–23.

4. "Some Historical Remarks Concerning the Collegiate School of Connecticut in New Haven Written in part Nov. 20, 1717 per S. Johnson," in Franklin Bowditch Dexter, ed., *Documentary History of Yale University Under the Original Charter of the Collegiate School of Connecticut 1701–1745* (New Haven, 1916), p. 160.

5. On colonial science see Brooke Hindle, *The Pursuit of Science in Revolutionary America, 1735–1789* (Chapel Hill, N.C., 1956); and Frederick E. Brasch, "The Newtonian Epoch in the American Colonies, 1680–1783," *Proceedings of the American Antiquarian Society,* 2d ser. 49 (October 1939), 314–32. On the influence of the Royal Society see Brasch, "The Royal Society of London and Its Influence upon Scientific Thought in the American Colonies," *Scientific Monthly,* XXXIII (1931), 337–55, 448–69; and Margaret Denny, "The Royal Society and American Scholars," *Scientific Monthly,* LXV (November 1947), 415–27.

6. Hindle, *Pursuit of Science,* pp. 58–59; and Raymond P. Stearns, *Science in the British Colonies of America* (Urbana, Ill., 1970), pp. 44–83.

7. *Dictionary of American Biography* (22 vols.; New York, 1928–1958) [hereafter cited as *DAB*], XXI, 408–16; and John W. Oliver, *History of American Technology* (New York, 1956), p. 78.

8. Henry P. Johnston, *Yale and Her Honor-Role in the American Revolution, 1775–1783: Including Original Letters, Record of Service, and Biographical Sketches* (New York, 1888), p. iv. See also Louis Shores, *Origins of the American College*

Library, 1638–1800 (Nashville, Tenn., 1934); and Theodore Hornberger, *Scientific Thought in the American Colleges, 1638–1800* (Austin, Texas, 1945).

9. Dummer to Gurdon Saltonstall, 14 April 1719, in Dexter, *Documents of Yale*, p. 193.

10. Franklin to Benjamin Chambers, 20 September 1788, in *The Writings of Benjamin Franklin*, ed. by Albert Henry Smith (10 vols.; New York, 1905–1907), IX, 664–65.

11. Hindle, *Pursuit of Science*, pp. 87–88. On Desagulier see *Dictionary of National Biography*, V 850–51; Peter Gay, *The Enlightenment: An Interpretation*, Vol. II: *The Science of Freedom* (New York, 1969), p. 164; and Charles William Sleeman, *Torpedoes and Torpedo Warfare* (2d ed.; Portsmouth, England, 1889), p. 330.

12 Andrew Keogh, "Bishop Berkeley's Gift of Books in 1733," *The Yale University Library Gazette*, VIII (July 1933), 25; and Hindle, *Pursuit of Science*, p. 62.

13. Hindle, *Pursuit of Science*, pp. 146–65.

14. Ralph S. Bates, *Scientific Societies in the United States* (2d ed.; New York, 1958), pp. 1–27; and Hindle, *Pursuit of Science*, pp. 59–79, 391.

15. Unless otherwise noted, information on Bushnell is taken from Frederick Wagner, *Submarine Fighter of the American Revolution: The Story of David Bushnell* (New York, 1963). Mr. Wagner has taken some liberty with the evidence in filling the gaps in the record on Bushnell. Only the supportable material has been extracted here.

16. Johnston, *Yale and Her Honor–Roll*, pp. 1–3; and Louis W. McKeehan, *Yale Science: The First Hundred Years, 1701–1801* (New York, 1947), pp. 17–42.

17. Edward P. Morris, "A Library of 1742," *The Yale University Library Gazette*, IX (July 1934), 3–11; T[homas] Clap, *A Catalogue of the Library of Yale–College in New–Haven* (New London, Conn., 1743); [Clap], *A Catalogue of Books in the Library of Yale–College in New–Haven* (New Haven, 1755); *A Catalogue of the Books in the Library of Yale–College in New–Haven* (n.p., 1790); and Thomas Clap, *The Annals or History of Yale–College, In New–Haven, In the Colony of Connecticut, from the First Founding thereof, in the Year 1700, to the Year 1766 . . .* (New Haven, 1766). The card catalogue of the 1742 library in the Beinecke Library, Yale University, was also consulted.

18. [David Bushnell,] "General Principles and Construction of a Sub-marine Vessel, communicated by D. Bushnell of Connecticut, the inventor, in a letter of October, 1787, to *Thomas Jefferson*, then Minister Plenipotentiary of the United States at Paris," *Transactions of the American Philosophical Society, Held at Philadelphia for Promoting Useful Knowledge*, IV (1799), 308–9.

19. *The Posthumous Works of Robert Hooke*, ed. by Richard Waller (London, 1705), pp. 169–70; Thomas Sprat, *The History of the Royal–society, for the Improving of Natural Knowledge* (London, 1667), pp. 260–83; Robert Boyle, *New Experiments Physico–Mechanicall, Touching The Spring of Air* . . . (Oxford, 1660), p. 201, *Tracts* . . . (London, 1672), pp. 71–79, and *Philosophical Works* . . . (6 vols.; London, 1772). The 1790 catalogue lists Boyle's *Philosophical Works* as an eight-volume edition. Since there never was an eight-volume edition this most probably refers to the six-volume 1772 edition. If so, and if it arrived at Yale in time for Bushnell to use

it, then he had the added advantage of a comprehensive index containing numerous citations on gunpowder and other subjects of interest to him.

20. See above, pp. 33–34.

21. *The Works of Ben Jonson with a Biographical Memoir by William Gifford* (6 vols.; New York, 1869), V, Act iii, Scene I. The six-volume edition at Yale in Bushnell's time had the same play.

22. Boyle, *Philosophical Works*, Vol. VI, Index.

23. Description taken from [Bushnell,] "General Principles," pp. 303–7.

24. Ibid., p. 305. The translation of this phrase into French gave rise to the erroneous belief that Bushnell's propeller was formed on the principle of a helix or worm gear. In fact, it was a bladed propeller, forerunner of the modern type. Sergeant Ezra Lee, the operator of the craft in its most famous attack, reported that the *Turtle* "had two oars of about 12 inches in length, and 4 or 5 in width, shaped like the arms of a windmill. . . ." Quoted in Henry P. Johnston, "Sergeant Lee's Experience with Bushnell's Submarine Torpedo in 1776," *Magazine of American History*, XXIX (March 1893), 263.

25. Henri Le Masson, *Du Nautilus (1800) au Redoutable: Histoire critique du sous–marin dans la marine française* (Paris, 1969), p. 19, scores American authors for this penchant.

26. Bernard and Fawn Brodie, *From Crossbow to H–Bomb*: *The Evolution of the Weapons and Tactics of Warfare* (rev. and enl. ed.; Bloomington and London, 1973), p. 116.

27. Hindle, *Pursuit of Science*, pp. 244–45. Dirk J. Struik makes the same omission in *Yankee Science in the Making* (Boston, 1948), pp. 52–53.

28. Wagner, *Submarine Fighter*, p. ix.

29. Barnes, *Submarine Warfare* (New York, 1869), p. 152. Only Royal Bird Bradford, *History of Torpedo Warfare* (Newport, R.I., 1882), p. 5, notes Bushnell's obligations to his predecessors. Bradford wrote: "There were writers of the seventeenth century who predicted that powder submerged would some day play an important part in coast defence. Doubtless Bushnell, who was a fine scholar, had read the works of these writers, yet he was the first to produce a practical submerged weapon." Unfortunately, Bradford did not pursue this educated guess further.

30. The comparison is based on the verbal descriptions by Papin and Bushnell. A comparison of the sketches of their craft can lead to different, and I believe erroneous, conclusions. Papin's diagrams in his *Recueil des diverses Pieces* . . . are schematic and do not accurately reflect the details brought out in the text. There is no known contemporary drawing of the *Turtle*. The one appearing most frequently in the literature was prepared by Francis M. Barber a century after the fact to illustrate his *Lecture on Submarine Boats and their Application to Torpedo Operations* (Newport, R.I., 1875). Barber rendered a far more elaborate drawing than Papin and in the process introduced some errors. He shows, for example, a ballast tank in the *Turtle*, when in fact Bushnell had varied displacement by allowing the water to rise or fall directly within the cabin, as Papin had done in his first design. Barber also missed Bushnell's injunction that "every horizontal section, although ellipti-

cal, [was] yet as near to a circle, as could be admitted." This would have made Barber's drawing look much more like Papin's.

31. See the list of Linonian books in Hale's handwriting in George Dudley Seymour, *A Documentary Life of Nathan Hale* (New Haven: Privately printed for the author, 1941), pp. 151–53. The "Records of the Linonian Society 1768–1790," containing the original three pages, are in the Historical Manuscripts and Archives collection of the Sterling Memorial Library at Yale. A photostatic copy is in the Beinecke Rare Book and Manuscript Collection under the designation: Nathan Hale. List of Books in the Linonian Library, MS Vault, Section 1, Drawer 1.

32. Clap, *Annals or History of Yale–College*, p. 86.

33. Ibid., p. 85.

34. Philip K. Lundeberg believes Franklin did visit Bushnell. *Samuel Colt's Submarine Battery: The Secret and the Enigma*, Smithsonian Studies in History and Technology, Number 29 (Washington, 1974), p. 2. I am not convinced, but regardless, Bushnell still had access to Franklin through their mutual friend, Benjamin Gale. See below, chap. 6.

35. By 1846 two of the fraternities at Yale, including the one to which Bushnell had belonged, had complete runs of *Gentleman's Magazine* going back to the first number in 1731. *Catalogue of the Library of the Linonian Society, Yale College* (New Haven, 1846); *Catalogue of the Library of the Society of the Brothers in Unity, Yale College* (New Haven, 1846). How or when they came by these sets is not known. At least two of the possible answers could put *Gentleman's Magazine* within Bushnell's reach. Perhaps the Linonian Society had the periodical all along and Nathan Hale simply failed to record it in his 1771 inventory. Or perhaps these were common journals in Connecticut and came to the societies in the estates of alumni who had held them in their private libraries.

36. *Gentleman's Magazine*, XVII (December 1747), 581.

37. This account is drawn from Bushnell's "General Principles," pp. 307–8.

38. In earlier versions of this chapter I attributed to Bushnell the introduction of the term *torpedo*. I based that conclusion on the appearance of the term in James Thacher, *A Military Journal during the American Revolutionary War . . .* (Boston, 1823), in which Thacher reports on 10 February 1778 that he had seen the "American Torpedo," invented by Bushnell. It has since been brought to my attention that this journal was most probably edited in the forty years between the war and its publication. Barring any conclusive evidence that Thacher used *torpedo* in 1778, the credit for introducing that term must remain with Robert Fulton. The 1928 Supplement to the *Oxford English Dictionary* makes the same mistake as I did.

CHAPTER VI: DAVID BUSHNELL IN BATTLE

1. Here, as in the previous chapter, biographical information on Bushnell is derived from Frederick Wagner, *Submarine Fighter of the American Revolution: The Story of David Bushnell* (New York, 1963).

2. Banjamin Gale to Banjamin Franklin, 7 August 1775, in William Bell

Clark, ed., *Naval Documents of the American Revolution* (5 vols. to date; Washington, 1964–1970), I, 1089. On the three navies see Harold and Margaret Sprout, *The Rise of American Naval Power: 1776–1918* (rev. ed.; Princeton, 1942), chap. 2; William Bell Clark, *George Washington's Navy: Being an Account of His Excellency's Fleet in New England Waters* (Baton Rouge, La., 1960); Charles Oscar Paullin, *The Navy of the American Revolution: Its Administration, Its Policy, and Its Achievements* (Cleveland, 1906); and Louis F. Middlebrook, *History of Maritime Connecticut during the American Revolution, 1775–1783* (2 vols.; Salem, Mass., 1925).

3. The sniping tactics of American marksmen surely revealed no great sympathy for the rules of the game. Bernard and Fawn Brodie, *From Crossbow to H–Bomb* (rev. and enl. ed.; Bloomington and London, 1973), p. 105.

4. "Such of the History of Deacon Phineas Pratt/Son of Mr. Azariah and Mrs. Agnis Pratt of Saybrook, Conn.," an unsigned, undated typescript in "Source Material relating to David Bushnell," Connecticut Historical Society MS. 65910.

5. Mumford, *Technics and Civilization* (New York, 1934), p. 87.

6. See Gilman C. Gates, *Saybrook at the Mouth of the Connecticut: The First One Hundred Years* (Orange and New Haven, Conn., 1935), pp. 161–62, 238–39; John Warner Barber, *Connecticut Historical Society Collections . . .* (New Haven, 1838), pp. 533–35; Middlebrook, *Maritime Connecticut*, I, 3, 10–12, 204, 218–21; and *History of Middlesex County, Connecticut: With Biographical Sketches of Its Prominent Men* (New York, 1884), pp. 76, 78–79, 424–25, 479–84, 550.

7. Typescript of letter from Phineas Pratt (son of the deacon) to "H.W.K." dated June 1870, in "Source Material relating to David Bushnell."

8. Middlebrook, *Maritime Connecticut*, I, 201–4; J. Leander Bishop, *A History of American Manufactures from 1608 to 1860 . . .* (2 vols.; Philadelphia, 1864), I, 232–43.

9. See Gale to Franklin, 7 August 1775, in Clark, *Naval Documents*, I, 1089; and Gale to Silas Deane, 22 November 1775, ibid., II, 1099–1100. See also Rollin G. Osterweis, *Three Centuries of New Haven, 1638–1938* (New Haven, 1953), pp. 133, 252.

10. 7 August 1775, in Clark, *Naval Documents*, I, 1089.

11. 9 November 1775, *Collections of the Connecticut Historical Society* (31 vols.; Hartford, 1860–1967), II, 317.

12. Ibid.

13. Middlebrook, *Maritime Connecticut*, I, 160–61; and Clark, *Naval Documents*, I, 542, and II, 1050, 1230. If Bushnell did attack *Asia*, Gale seems to have been unaware of it. See his letter to Deane, 11 November 1775, Clark, *Naval Documents*, II, 1099.

14. 7 December 1775, *Collections of the Connecticut Historical Society*, II, 334.

15. Royal R. Hinman, *A Historical Collection, from Official Records, Files, &c., of the Part Sustained by Connecticut, during the War of the Revolution* (Hartford, 1842), p. 343. See also Clark, *Naval Documents*, III, 1101, 1111.

16. This and other information regarding Sergeant Lee's association with Bushnell is derived from Lee's account in a letter to David Humphreys dated 20 February 1815. Yale MSS., Miscellaneous B, David Bushnell Folder. This letter

was printed in *Magazine of American History,* XXIX (January–June 1893), 262–66.

17. See, for example, Gardner Weld Allen, *A Naval History of the American Revolution* (2 vols.; Boston and New York, 1913), I, 155.

18. Letter, N. E. Upham, Assistant Keeper I, Curator of Models, Department of Ships, National Maritime Museum, London, to D. Shaw, 28 October 1976, citing the museum's Progress Books.

19. [David Bushnell,] "General Principles and Construction of a Sub-marine Vessel, communicated by D. Bushnell of Connecticut, the inventor, in a letter of October, 1787, to *Thomas Jefferson,* then Minister Plenipotentiary of the United States at Paris," *Transactions of the American Philosophical Society, Held at Philadelphia for Promoting Useful Knowledge,* IV (1799), 311.

20. Description is derived from ibid., and the report of Commodore Symons aboard H.M.S. *Cerberus* dated 15 August 1777, as quoted in Henry L. Abbot, "The Beginning of Modern Submarine Warfare, Under Captain-Lieutenant David Bushnell, Sappers and Miners, Army of the Revolution," No. III in U.S. Engineer School of Application, *Professional Papers* (Willets Point, N. Y., 1881–1882), pp. 192–93.

21. *Public Records of the State of Connecticut* (9 vols.; Hartford, 1894–1953), I, 212. See also Hinman, *Historical Collection,* p. 437.

22. Report dated 15 August 1777, quoted in Abbot, "Beginning of Submarine Warfare," pp. 192–93.

23. Quoted in Wagner, *Submarine Fighter,* p. 86. See p. 85 on construction of the kegs. Washington's claim appeared in a letter to Thomas Jefferson dated 26 September 1785. *The Papers of Thomas Jefferson,* ed. by Julian P. Boyd (20 vols. to date; Princeton, 1950–1974), VIII, 557. Washington added that Bushnell "wanted nothing that I could furnish to secure the success of it."

24. [Bushnell,] "General Principles," p. 311.

25. The essential story is in Wagner, *Submarine Fighter,* pp. 114–21. For examples of the more speculative brand of Bushnell biography, see the sketch in *History of Middlesex County,* pp. 575–77; and *DAB,* III, 248–49.

26. Brooke Hindle, *The Pursuit of Science in Revolutionary America, 1735–1789* (Chapel Hill, N.C., 1956), pp. 219–20, 241–42.

27. Bushnell to Jefferson, October 1787, in *Papers of Thomas Jefferson,* XII, 303–5. On Jefferson's inquiries, see ibid., VII, 641–43; VIII, 298–301, 555–58; and IX, 150–52.

28. Letter from Ezra Bushnell to Charles Griswold dated 15 April 1826, quoted in full in letter from James H. Manning to Anson Phelps Stokes in Yale MSS (Stokes), Group 402, Series I, Box 2, Folder 93.

29. See chapter seven below.

30. Hindle, *Pursuit of Science,* p. 373.

31. Sprout and Sprout, *American Naval Power,* chap. 3.

32. Typescript copy in Connecticut Historical Society, MSS 65910.

33. Maurice Delpeuch, *Les Sous–marins á travers les siécles* (Paris, 1907), p. 63.

34. Ibid., p. 45; Alan H. Burgoyne, *Submarine Navigation: Past and Present* (2 vols; London and New York, 1903), I, 13–15; and G.-L. Pesce, *La Navigation sous–marine* (Paris, 1906), pp. 36–37.

CHAPTER VII: ROBERT FULTON IN FRANCE

1. Alice Cracy Sutcliffe, "The Early Life of Robert Fulton," *Century*, LXXVI (September 1908), 780–94; and *Dictionary of American Biography* VII, 68–72. Hereafter, unless otherwise noted, biographical information on Fulton is derived from Alice Crary Sutcliffe, *Robert Fulton and the "Clermont"* (New York, 1909); and H. W. Dickinson, *Robert Fulton, Engineer and Artist: His Life and Work* (London, 1913; reprint ed., Freeport, N.Y., 1971).

2. Robert Fulton, *A Treatise on the Improvement of Canal Navagation* (London, 1796), title page.

3. Wallace S. Hutcheon, Jr., "Robert Fulton and Naval Warfare" (Ph.D. Dissertation, George Washington University, 1975), pp. 27–28.

4. *Letters Principally to the Right Honourable Lord Grenville on Sub–Marine Navigation and Attack* . . . (London, 1806), quoted in Frederick Wagner, *Submarine Fighter of the American Revolution: The Story of David Bushnell* (New York, 1963), p. 116.

5. Fulton may have gotten some information on Bushnell from W. Winterbotham's *An Historical Geographical, Commercial and Philosophical View of the American United States* . . . (4 vols.; London, 1795), II, 274; but there was not really enough detail there to account for Fulton's thorough familiarity with the *Turtle.*

6. Ruth Barlow to Cadwallader D. Colden, 24 July 1815, at Yale University, Beinecke Library, Pequot Library Collection, Joel Barlow Papers, M943.

7. Fulton to French Minister of Marine, quoted in G.-L. Pesce, *La Navigation sous–marine* (Paris, 1906), p. 193.

8. The calendar of the first French republic, adopted in 1793, dated from 22 September 1792. It divided the year into twelve months of thirty days each. At the end of the year there were five or six complementary days. The Revolutionary calendar remained in effect until 1806.

9. See, for example, Henri Le Masson, *Du Nautilus (1800) au Redoutable: Histoire critique du sous–marin dans la marine française* (Paris, 1969), p. 32; and Claude Chambard, *Les Sous–marins* (Paris, 1968), pp. 21–23.

10. Because not even Dickinson has all his causes and effects or all his dates in proper order, the following procedure was used to piece together the chronology presented here. Four main sources were used: (1) Pesce, *La Navigation,* (2) Dickinson, *Fulton,* (3) William Barclay Parsons, *Robert Fulton and the Submarine* (New York, 1922), and (4) Maurice Delpeuch, *Les Sous–marins à travers les siècles* (Paris, 1907). Some primary, and occasional secondary, sources were used to augment these when necessary. For each event, best evidence of the actual date was sought, either through primary sources, internal evidence in quoted documents, or the most reasonable interpretation of the evidence available. When critical issues are involved, sources will be noted; otherwise it may be assumed that chronology can be derived from close scrutiny of the four volumes cited.

11. Quoted in Dickinson, *Fulton*, p. 65.

12. Henry Guerlac, "Some Aspects of Science during the French Revolution," *Scientific Monthly*, LXXX (February 1955), 93–101; Lewis S. Feuer, *The Scientific Intellectual: The Psychological and Sociological Origins of Modern Science* (New York

and London, 1963), chap. 9; René Taton, ed., *History of Science*, Vol. II: *The Beginnings of Modern Science: From 1450 to 1800*, trans. by A. J. Pomerans (New York, 1964), p. 498; Harold T. Parker, "French Administrators and French Scientists during the Old Regime and the Early Years of the Revolution," in Richard Herr and Harold T. Parker, eds., *Ideas in History: Essays Presented to Louis Gottschalk by His Former Students* (Durham, N.C., 1965), pp. 85–109; and L. Pearce Williams, "Science, Education and the French Revolution," *Isis*, XLIV (December 1953), 317.

13. See Charles Burr Todd, *Life and Letters of Joel Barlow, LL.D.: Poet, Statesman, Philosopher* (New York and London, 1886), p. 177.

14. This first date may be used to demonstrate how correct dates were determd. The authors consulted give the following versions:

	Revolutionary	*Gregorian*
Pesce (p. 168)	22 *frimaire an* VI	13 *décembre* 1797
Dickinson (p. 74)	22 *Frimaire an* VI	13 Dec. 1797
Parsons (p. 24)	24 *Frimaire an* VI	13 December, 1797
Delpeuch (p. 74)	22 *frimaire an* VI	13 *décembre* 1797

Pesce, Dickinson, and Delpeuch all quote this letter at some length. Their quotations confirm that 22 *frimaire an* VI is the correct Revolutionary date. Translation from *Concordance des calendriers grégorien et républicain* (Paris, 1963), reveals that 12 December 1797 is the correct Gregorian date. Other cases were far more difficult, but this same general procedure was followed in all.

15. Dickinson, *Fulton*, p. 75.

16. Pesce, *La Navigation*, p. 170.

17. Dickinson, *Fulton*, p. 76n.; and Georges Six, *Dictionnaire biographique des généraux & amiraux français de la Révolution et de l'Empire (1792–1814)* (2 vols.; Paris, 1934), II, 319. The terms of the successive Ministers of Marine are of some importance, as it is confusion on this subject that has led to misunderstanding of Fulton's dealings with the government. The terms of the five ministers with whom Fulton dealt may be found in François de Veillechéze de la Mardiére, *L'Evolution historique du controle de la marine* (Poitiers, 1912), pp. 103n., 124n.

18. Pesce, *La Navigation*, p. 177.

19. Though most famous for the hot air balloon they first flew in Paris in 1783, Joseph Michel (1740–1810) and Jacques Étienne (1745–1799) Montgolfier were successful inventors in numerous fields, including the water-raising device referred to by Fulton.

20. Sutcliffe, *Fulton*, pp. 313–16.

21. Six, *Dictionnaire*, I, 164–65; and Dickinson, *Fulton*, p. 79n.

22. Pesce, *La Navigation*, p. 179.

23. Dickinson, *Fulton*, p. 80.

24. Ibid., p. 81n.; Delpeuch, *Les Sous–marins*, pp. 83n., 84n; and Six, *Dictionnaire*, II, 390–91.

25. Dickinson, *Fulton*, pp. 82–88; and Pesce, *La Navigation*, pp. 180–88.

26. Pesce, *La Navigation*, p. 185.

27. For example, the commission observed that the horizontal rudder might not be adequate to raise and lower the submarine, so Fulton immediately proposed adding a vertical propeller—the same arrangement the *Turtle* had to begin with. Dickinson, *Fulton*, p. 86.

28. Ibid., p. 87.

29. Sutcliffe, *Fulton*, pp. 319–20.

30. Dickinson, *Fulton*, p. 92.

31. Ibid.

32. The motto on the title page of Fulton's book *Torpedo War, and Submarine Explosions* (1810) was "The Liberty of the seas will be the happiness of the earth." See Hutcheon, "Robert Fulton and Naval Warfare," for evidence that he had these ideas from Joel Barlow and Thomas Paine.

33. It is known that he took his Nautilus proposal to Holland, but it is not clear when. The eight months between his second and third periods of negotiation would have given him the most free time.

34. *Nouvelle biographe générale* . . . (46 vols.; Paris, 1853–1866), VII, 69–70.

35. In Edouard Desbriére, *Projets et tentatives de débarquement aux Iles Britaniques: 1793–1805* (5 vols.; Paris, 1900–1902), II, 256–57.

36. Ibid., p. 257.

37. Pesce, *La Navigation*, pp. 190–94. Dickinson is the only author to get this date right. All others read it as 6 October 1800 and interpret it as meaning that Fulton made his fourth appeal to the government because Bonaparte had become First Consul. Actually this is only the continuation of the appeal begun on 17 July 1799 in response to the appointment of a new Minister of Marine.

38. Pesce, *La Navigation*, p. 194.

39. An example of the confusion created by this succession of ministers appears in Delpeuch, *Les Sous-marins*, p. 98. The author cites the memo authorizing examination of Fulton's submarine in October 1799, attributing it to Forfait. But on the same page he says that Forfait became Minister on 24 November 1799, and he fails to explain why the memo is signed "M. A. B." [Marc-Antoine Bourdon]. This kind of confusion permeates all treatments of Fulton in France, to a greater or lesser degree.

40. Desbriére, *Projets*, II, 258.

41. Pesce, *La Navigation*, p. 196.

42. See Holden Furber, "Fulton and Napoleon in 1800: New Light on the Submarine Nautilus," *American Historical Review*, XXXIX (April 1934), 489–94. It was previously believed that the *Nautilus* was first launched in July at Rouen.

43. Barlow to his wife and Fulton, 6 September 1800, Harvard University, Houghton Library, Joel Barlow Papers, #351. This letter is printed in Todd, *Barlow*, p. 182, but its date there is left uncertain.

44. Hutcheon, "Robert Fulton and Naval Warfare," p. 59, states that Fulton never did receive the commissions.

45. Thrask to his wife, 12 October 1800, National Archives, Record Group 45, Subject File AD, Box 3½. [Hereafter this record group will be cited as NA, RG 45.]

46. Dickinson, *Fulton*, p. 108.

47. Monge was a particularly close and trusted advisor. See Paul V. Aubry, *Monge: Le savant ami de Napoléon Bonaparte, 1746–1818* (Paris, 1954).

48. Dickinson, *Fulton*, p. 108.

49. Ibid., p. 109.

50. Pesce, *La Navigation*, p. 207.

51. *Correspendance de Napoléon Ier* (32 vols.; Paris, 1858–1870), VI, 522.

52. Fulton to Monge, Laplace, and Volney, 20 September 1801, Parsons, *Fulton and the Submarine*, p. 46.

53. Jean Savant, *Les ministres de Napoléon* ([Paris,] 1959), pp. 101–8; Six, *Dictionnaire*, I, 305–6; and Philippe Masson and José Muracciole, *Napoléon et la marine* (Paris, 1968), pp. 221–24.

54. Quoted in Pesce, *La Navigation*, p. 208.

55. Masson and Muracciole, *Napoléon*, p. 119.

56. See David Whittet Thomson, "Robert Fulton and the French Invasion of England," *Military Affairs*, XVIII (July 1954), 57–63; and Desbriére, *Projets*, III, 307–15.

57. Desbriére, *Projects*, III, 308.

58. See Fulton to Daniel Parker, 27 October 1803, New York Historical Society, Robert Fulton Papers, Box 1; and various letters from Fulton between November 1803 and March 1804 in New York Public Library, James Monroe Papers.

CHAPTER VIII: ROBERT FULTON IN ENGLAND AND AMERICA

1. Joel Barlow Papers, Pequot Collection Yale University, #M915.

2. The principal sources of information on Fulton in England are H. W. Dickinson, *Robert Fulton, Engineer and Artist: His Life and Work* (London, 1913; reprint ed., Freeport, N.Y., 1971), pp. 167–205; William Barclay Parsons, *Robert Fulton and the Submarine* (New York, 1922), pp. 54–138; the somewhat fuller Parsons Collection at the New York Public Library [Hereafter cited as "Parsons Collection"], containing Fulton's version of his stay; and E. Taylor Parks, "Robert Fulton and Submarine Warfare," *Military Affairs*, XXV (February 1962), 177–82.

3. Parks, "Fulton," p. 177.

4. Since the appearance of Parsons, *Fulton and the Submarine*, it has been believed that Hammond was an alias for Lord Hawkesbury (1770–1878), the Secretary for Foreign Affairs in the Addington ministry and the Home Secretary in the new Pitt ministry. Wallace Hutcheon established his correct identity in his "Robert Fulton and Naval Warfare" (Ph.D. dissertation, George Washington University, 1975), p. 89.

5. Dickinson, *Fulton*, p. 185. This committee was not appointed in July, as Dickinson maintains, but rather in late May or early June. See Fulton to Hammond, 12 June 1804, in "Parsons Collection."

6. See Fulton to Hammond, 21 June 1804, in "Parsons Collection." This contradicts Dickinson's suspicion that Fulton had been able to name two of the commission's five members.

7. See Fulton's memoranda of 28 June and 20 July 1804, "Parsons Collection."

8. *The Keith Papers III (1803–1815)*, ed. by Christopher Lloyd, Vol. XCVI of Publications of the Navy Records Society, ([London,] 1955), pp. 7–8.

9. See the account in *Naval Chronicle*, XII (1804), 313, 488.

10. See Viscount Castlereagh, *Correspondence, Dispatches, and Other Papers of Viscount Castlereagh, Second Marquess of Londonderry*, ed. by Charles William Vane (12 vols.; London, 1848–1853), V, 83–160.

11. *Naval Chronicle*, XIV (1805), 339, 343.

12. Fulton to "Mamy" West, 16 October 1805, New York Historical Society, Robert Fulton Papers, Box 1; Castlereagh, *Correspondence*, V, 119–20, 124–25. According to Wallace Hutcheon ("Robert Fulton and Naval Warfare," pp. 107–8), Fulton was at the height of his powers in England following the demonstration against the *Dorothea*.

13. Castlereagh, *Correspondence*, V, 131–40.

14. Dickinson, *Fulton*, p. 194.

15. Robert Fulton, *Torpedo War, and Submarine Explosions* (Washington, 1810; reprint ed., Chicago, 1971), p. 7n.

16. Berkeley to James Barry, 14 September 1807, in Historical Society Of Pennsylvania, Autograph Collection of Simon Gratz, Case 4, Box 36.

17. There is little published material available on Fulton's underwater warfare activities in the United States beyond the brief account in Dickinson, *Fulton*, pp. 206–10. The fullest account now available is Hutcheon, "Robert Fulton and Naval Warfare," chaps. 4, 5.

18. Compare the cost effectiveness presentation in *Torpedo War*, pp. 22–31, 46–50 with (Colonel William) Congreve, *The Details of the Rocket System* . . . (London, 1814; reprint ed., Ottawa, Ontario, 1970), pp. 57–61.

19. *State Papers, Naval Affairs*, Vol. I, pp. 234–45, 11th Cong., 3d sess.

20. Fulton to Paul Hamilton, 3 May 1810, in New York Public Library, Robert Fulton Papers, Box 1. The commission members were: Cadwallader D. Colden (1769–1834), John Kemp (1763–1812), Morgan Lewis (1754–1844), Robert R. Livingston (1746–1813), Jonathan Williams (1750–1815), Oliver Wolcott (1760–1833), and John Garnett (?). Information on all but the last is available in *Dictionary of American Biography*.

21. *DAB*, XVI, 77.

22. *Torpedo War*, p. 57.

23. New York Historical Society, Commodore John Rodgers Papers (microfilm), reel 1.

24. Fulton, "Reflections on Torpedoes," [1810].

25. *State Papers, Naval Affairs*, I, 243.

26. See Howard I. Chapelle, "Fulton's 'Steam Battery': Blockship and Catamaran," *United States National Museum Bulletin 240: Contributions from the Museum of History and Technology* Washington, 1964), pp. 137–76.

27. Fulton to General Wm Duane, 1 March 1813, quoted in editor's preface to *Torpedo War, and Submarine Explosions*, "Being Extra No. 35 of *The Magazine of History with Notes and Queries*" (New York, 1914), p. 173.

28. See New York Public Library, Robert Fulton Papers; and United States

Naval Academy Museum, Robert Fulton Papers, Diary of round trip from New York to Washington, 1–12 September 1814.

29. See Historical Society of Pennsylvania, The Dreer Collection, Vol. 168: Robert Fulton Papers.

30. Ibid., pp. 159–65, 166–74.

31. Parsons, *Fulton and the Submarine*, p. 106.

32. Ibid., p. 144.

33. New York Historical Society, Robert Fulton Papers, Box 1.

CHAPTER IX: IN FULTON'S FOOTSTEPS

1. Royal Bird Bradford, *History of Torpedo Warfare* (Newport, R.I., 1882), p. 25.

2. *The Art of War in Seven Books Written by Nicholas Machiavel, Secretary of State, To the Republic of Florence. To Which Is Added "Hints Relative to Warfare," by a Gentleman of the State of New York* (Albany, 1815), pp. 323–49.

3. Ibid., p. 348.

4. On Mix, see the references cited in the letter from D. W. Knox to David Thomson, 11 March 1944, in NA RG 45, Subject File BM, Box 1. See also Bradford, *Torpedo Warfare*, p. 25; and *Niles Register*, IV (7 August 1813), 366. On Fulton's ties to Mix, see the draft of the letter from Fulton to Stephen Decatur prepared between 5 August and 12 September 1813, in U.S. Naval Academy Museum, Robert Fulton Papers.

5. *Niles' Register*, VI (9 July 1814), 318.

6. Ibid., IV (17 July 1813), 326–27.

7. Bradford, *Torpedo Warfare*, pp. 25–26; Fulton to Decatur, 5 August to 12 September 1813.

8. *Niles' Register*, IV (7 August 1813), 365.

9. Quoted in F. von Ehrenbrook, "History of Submarine Mining and Torpedoes," trans. Frederick Martin, No. 1 in U.S. Engineer School of Application, *Professional Papers* (Willets Point, N.Y., 1881–1882), 14.

10. *Niles' Register*, IV (3 July 1813), 293; Arnold S. Lott, *Most Dangerous Sea: A History of Mine Warfare, and an Account of U.S. Navy Mine Warfare Operations in World War II and Korea* (Annapolis, 1959), p. 7.

11. Norfolk *Herald*, 27 July 1813, quoted in *Niles' Register*, IV (7 August 1813), 365.

12. *Niles' Register*, IV (7 August 1813), 265. Italics in original.

13. *Naval Chronicle*, XII (January–June 1809), 408–12.

14. Ibid., XXII (July–December 1809), 27–29.

15. Ibid., pp. 31–32.

16. Ibid., pp. 100–102.

17. Ibid., pp. 196–99.

18. A copy of this drawing is attached inside the front cover of one of John S. Barnes's two personal copies of *Submarine Warfare* (New York, 1869), now in the New York Historical Society.

19. *Naval Chronicle*, XXI (January–June 1809), 410.

20. Fulton to Stanhope, 3 April 1810, New York Public Library, Robert Fulton Papers.

21. Cited in H. Dircks, *The Life, Times, and Scientific Labors of the Second Marquis of Worcester; to which is added a Reprint of his "Century of Inventions," 1663, with a Commentary thereon* (London, 1865), pp. 402–3.

22. *Naval Chronicle*, XX (July–December 1808), 452–53.

23. Charles James, *A New and Enlarged Military Dictionary* . . . (3d ed.; 2 vols.; London, 1810), I, s.v. "Turtle."

24. William Burney, ed., *A New Universal Dictionary of the Marine* . . . [i.e., "Falconers Marine Dictionary," 2d ed.] (London, 1815), pp. 570–71, 510, 125.

25. Fulton to Volney, Monge, Laplace, 12 March 1810, New York Public Library, Robert Fulton Papers.

26. Ibid.

27. Maurice Delpeuch, *Les Sous–marins à travers les siècles* (Paris, 1907), chap. 8; G.-L. Pesce, *La Navigation sous–marine* (Paris, 1906), chaps. 22–24.

28. Jacques-Philippe Mérigon de Montgery, *Mémoire sur les mines flottantes et les petards flottans, ou machines infernales maritimes* (Paris, 1819).

29. Ibid., pp. 12–32.

30. Ibid., pp. 50–71.

31. Ibid., 70–72. Montgéry also included earlier (pp. 41–42) a refreshing interpretation of why governments fail to adopt new weapons. He maintained that persons in positions of power were accustomed to quickly discern flaws in proposals made to them, but they seldom had either the time or the perseverence to work out corrections for these flaws.

32. A. A. Samarov and F. A. Petrov, eds., *Development of Mine Material in the Russian Navy: A Collection of Documents*, compiled by S. V. Rogulin and M. N. Varfolomeev. Available in English as U.S. Navy Bureau of Ships Translation 611, trans. by Lloyd G. Robbins, ed. by R. A. Raven and M. W. Raven (n.p., 1956). Personal copy obt ined through Naval Ordnance Systems Command, Washington, D.C.

33. Ibid., p. 2.

34. Ibid., pp. 46, 48, 51.

35. Ibid., pp. 60ff.

36. Philip K. Lundeberg, "Undersea Warfare and Allied Strategy in World War I, Part I: to 1916," reprinted from *The Smithsonian Journal of History*, I (Autumn 1966), p. 4.

37. Samarov and Petrov, *Documents*, p. 70.

38. Ibid., p. 203.

39. Ibid., pp. 136–72. See also Bradford, *Torpedo Warfare*, pp. 37–40.

40. Samarov and Petrov, *Documents*, pp. 173–201.

41. Alan H. Burgoyne, *Submarine Navigation: Past and Present* (2 vols.; London and New York, 1903), I, 127. The following account of Bauer is from pp. 127–34.

42. Nor has his conceptualization of a David and Goliath analogy received much attention. See Pesce, *La Navigation*, p. 281.

43. Ragnar Sohlman and Henrick Schuck, *Nobel: Dynamite and Peace*, trans. by Brian and Beatrix Lunn (New York, 1929), pp. 36–41.

44. I am indebted to Mr. James W. Cheevers, Curator of the U.S. Naval Academy Museum, for this information. See the letter to him from Mr. Ole Lisberg Jensen of the Marinmuseum, Karlskrona, Sweden, dated 10 October 1972.

45. Robert Fulton Papers, Box 2.

46. Most probably this was Augustin de Bathencourt y Molina (1760–1826). See *Nouvelle biographie generale* (46 vols.; Paris, 1853–1866), V, 834.

CHAPTER X: SAMUEL COLT AND THE ELECTRICAL CONNECTION

1. Quoted in full in John S. Barnes, *Submarine Warfare* (New York, 1869), pp. 229–30.

2. Jack Rohan, *Yankee Arms Maker: The Incredible Career of Samuel Colt* (New York and London, 1935), p. 12.

3. Colt's own version of his activities in underwater warfare is spelled out in three letters in the Samuel Colt Papers, Box 5–6, in the Connecticut Historical Society [hereafter referred to as *Colt Papers*]; Colt to Abel P. Upshur, 12 November 1841 (copy); Colt to Henry C. Murphy, 3 June 1844 (copy); and Colt to the "Honorable Members of the Senate and House of Representatives in Congress Assembled," 31 March 1846 (draft). The most complete secondary account is Philip K. Lundeberg, *Samuel Colt's Submarine Battery: The Secret and the Enigma*, Smithsonian Studies in History and Technology, Number 29 (Washington, 1974).

4. This letter is quoted in full in Lundeberg *Colt's Submarine Battery*, pp. 59–60.

5. Colt's plans, as finally matured, are contained in a collection of papers entitled "S. Colt's Submarine Battery," now in the Connecticut State Library [hereafter cited as *Colt Plans*]. On contemporary work in underwater detonation, see Royal Bird Bradford, *History of Torpedo Warfare* (Newport, R.I., 1882), p. 34; John P. Merrell, *Lecture on Galvanic Batteries and Electrical Machines, as Used in Torpedo Operations, Arranged in Three Parts. Part I. Galvanic Batteries* (Newport, R.I., 1874), p. 3; and U.S., Congress, House, *Colt's Submarine Battery*, H. Doc. 127, 28th Cong., 2d sess., 1845, pp. 6–8, 12–17, 22–23 [hereafter cited as H. Doc. 127].

6. See U.S., Congress, House, *Samuel Colt*, H. Rept. 46. To Accompany H. 519, 28th Cong., 2d sess., 1845. This report is printed in full in H. Doc. 127, pp. 18–24. Hereafter the latter source will be cited, as it provides in one place more of the essential information on Colt's dealings with the government.

7. See the note signed by Southard, dated 24 September 1841, in *Colt Papers*. An undated subscription list for Colt's battery also contains Southard's name.

8. See *General Register of the United States Navy and Marine Corps . . . (1782–1882)* . . ., ed. by Thomas H. S. Hamersley (Washington, 1882), p. 1, for the terms of these secretaries of the navy.

9. Colt to Badger, 8 October 1841; and Colt to McNeil, 9 October 1841; *Colt Papers*.

10. Colt to Upshur, 11 November 1841, ibid.

11. Colt to Upshur, 24 November 1841, ibid.

12. Colt to Southard, 2 January [1842], ibid. This letter is mistakenly dated 1841. Here, as elsewhere in this chapter, Colt's atrocious spelling is left uncorrected.

13. Letter from Fourth Auditor's Office, Treasury Department, to Colt, 9 December 1844, ibid.

14. See the letters between Colt and Upshur from 9 March 1842 through 5 July 1842, ibid.

15. Barnes, *Submarine Warfare*, p. 56. Colt wrote to Adams on 11 August 1842 asking for an interview, but he received no answer. See copy of this letter, *Colt Papers*.

16. For some of the debate on this bill see *Congressional Globe*, Vol. XI, 27th Cong., 2d sess., pp. 941, 949–50, 962, and 977. For the resolution itself, see *The Public Statutes at Large of the United States* . . . , Vol. V (Boston, 1845), p. 584.

17. Colt to John D. Simms, 12 September 1842 (copy), *Colt Papers*.

18. Connecticut Historical Society, MS 73555.

19. Colt to Partridge, 5 August 1841; Sargent to Colt, 21 February 1842; and Colt to Southard, 23 February 1842; *Colt Papers*.

20. H. Doc. 127, pp. 13, 22–23, in which the articles are reprinted. See also Colt to Draper, 10 March 1842, *Colt Papers*.

21. Colt to Henshaw, 7 September 1843, *Colt Papers*. See also Henshaw's letters to Colt during the two previous months, ibid.

22. The target ship was commanded by a Lieutenant Boyle. Bradford, *Torpedo Warfare*, p. 32. The proper year is 1844, not 1843 as reported in Barnes, *Submarine Warfare*, p. 56.

23. Colt to McNeil, 22 April 1844 (draft), *Colt Papers*.

24. H. Doc. 127, p. 1.

25. Quoted in ibid., p. 4. Italics in original.

26. Ibid., pp. 4–5.

27. See exchange of letters between 22 April and 1 May 1842, *Colt Papers*.

28. Mason to William Parmenter, 7 May 1844, *Colt Papers*.

29. Wilkin's report, with enclosures, appears in H. Doc. 127, pp. 1–17.

30. See Wilkins to Joseph Henry, 29 April 1844, ibid., p. 11.

31. Ibid., p. 8.

32. Ibid., p. 9.

33. Ibid., p. 10.

34. Ibid., p. 3.

35. Ibid., p. 5.

36. Jones to Colt, 14 June 1844, *Colt Papers*. This letter is printed in H. Doc. 127, p. 24; and an account of the transactions between Colt and the Committee on Naval Affairs appears on pp. 18–20. The patent application, dated 8 June 1844, is in *Colt Papers*, as are other documents pertinent to the petition.

37. H. Doc. 127, p. 22.

38. Ibid.

39. Samuel Southard died in 1842 and Abel P. Upshur was killed in the explosion aboard the U.S.S. *Princeton* in 1844; McNeil was retired at the outset and

Badger was between jobs in 1845; Thomas P. Jones was a private citizen and Henry Ellsworth, Commissioner of Patents, could not assume an advocate role; Henry Wise was in Rio de Janeiro. See *DAB* and U.S., Congress, House, *Biographical Directory of the American Congress, 1774–1961*, H. Doc. 442, 85th Cong., 2d sess., 1961.

40. Mason to John Stewart, 13 February 1845, *Colt Papers.*

41. Treasury Department to Colt, 23 August 1850; and Colt to Secretary of the Navy, 3 December 1859; *Colt Papers.*

CHAPTER XI: MATTHEW FONTAINE MAURY AND THE FINAL CONNECTION

1. Frances Leigh Williams, *Matthew Fontaine Maury: Scientist of the Sea* (New Brunswick, N.J., 1963), chaps. 18 and 19. Unless otherwise indicated, information on Maury is derived from this model biography.

2. Ibid., p. 368.

3. Interview, Washington, D.C., 3 January 1973.

4. Upshur to Maury, 31 August 1842, *Colt Papers.*

5. Williams, *Maury*, pp. 146–48; Colt to McNeil, 26 July 1841, *Colt Papers.*

6. Morse's comment was in a letter to Henry C. Deming, 25 March 1861, Connecticut Historical Society MS 73556. On Maury's connection with the transatlantic cable, see Williams, *Maury*, chap. 12.

7. "Annual Address delivered before the Maryland Institute," 25 October 1855, quoted in Williams, *Maury*, p. 227.

8. Williams, *Maury*, pp. 367–68, 370, 372–73, 376–79; and Milton F. Perry, *Infernal Machines: The Story of Confederate Subm ine and Mine Warfare* ([Baton Rouge, La.,] 1965), pp. 5–8. On the discord between Maury and Mallory, see Williams, *Maury*, chaps 14 and 15. The evidence here of bad feelings between the two men outweigh's Charles Lee Lewis's judgement that Mallory's action was free of "personal animus." *Matthew Fontaine Maury: The Pathfinder of the Seas* (Annapolis, 1927), p. 114.

9. Williams, *Maury*, pp. 380–96.

10. For Williams's argument on this point see *Maury*, pp. 394 and 620. See also Richard L. Maury, *A Brief Sketch of the Work of Matthew Fontaine Maury during the War 1861–1865* (Richmond, Va., 1915), for a son's eulogistic operational account of his father's claim to first position in the introduction of modern torpedo warfare.

11. Perry, *Infernal Machines*, chap. 3.

12. Gabriel J. Rains, "Torpedoes," *Southern Historical Society Papers*, III (May and June 1877), 259.

13. Rains to Maj. Gen. D. H. Hill, 14 May 1862, in *The War of the Rebellion: A Compilation of the Official Records of the Union and Confederate Armies* (70 vols.; Washington, 1881–1901), ser. i, vol. XI, part iii. p. 516. [Hereafter cited as *O.R.A.*]

14. Hunter Davidson also laid claim to precedence in Confederate mining

and ridiculed Rains's assertions in the process. However, his discounting of Maury's importance was less convincing. Hunter Davidson, "The Electrical Submarine Mine, 1861–1865," *Confederate Veteran*, XVI (September 1908), 456–59.

15. Royal Bird Bradford, *History of Torpedo Warfare* (Newport, R.I., 1882), p. 44; and Perry, *Infernal Machines*, p. 8.

16. Victor Ernest Rudolph von Scheliha, *A Treatise on Coast Defence* . . . (London, 1868), p. 220.

17. Perry, *Infernal Machines*, p. 31. Unfortunately the records of these bureaus were destroyed just before the war ended and only the most fragmentary evidence of their structure remains. For a suggestive insight into the day-to-day workings of the Navy "Torpedo Division," see the postwar reminiscences of one of the electricians: R. O. Crowley, "The Confederate Torpedo Service," *Century*, XLVI (May 1898), 290–300.

18. Compare John S. Barnes's argument that underwater warfare was adopted by the Confederacy because: (1) ironclads were vulnerable only below the waterline, and (2) the South was the weaker naval power. *Submarine Warfare* (New York, 1869), pp. 61–62.

19. Davidson, "Electrical Submarine Mine," p. 5.

20. Crowley, "Torpedo Service," p. 300.

21. Quoted in Bradford, *Torpedo Warfare*, p. 72.

22. *O.R.A.*, ser. i, vol. XI, part iii, pp. 509–11, 516, 517.

23. George Smith, *An Universal Military Dictionary* . . . [1799] (Ottawa, Ontario, 1969), p. 108. Compare H. L. Scott's interpretation that fougasses are "placed at the bottom of a pit or shaft dug in the ground over which an enemy must pass to attack." *Military Dictionary* . . . (New York, 1861), p. 317.

24. Quoted in Robert V. Johnson and Clarence C. Buel, eds., *Battles and Leaders of the Civil War* (4 vols.; New York, 1887–1888), II, 201. The analogy to underwater warfare is striking, yet I have found only two references to an "underwater fougasse"—in reports by the Russian Committee on Underwater Experiments in 1840 and again in 1842. A. A. Samarov and R. A. Petrov, eds., *Development of Mine Material in the Russian Navy: A Collection of Documents*, compiled by S. V. Rogulin and M. N. Varfolomeev; U. S. Navy Bureau of Ships Translation 611, trans. by Lloyd G. Robbins, ed. by F. A. Raven and M. W. Raven (n.p., 1956), pp. 67, 81. It seems strange that army officers were quick to perceive the difference between a fougasse (fixed position, fixed time of detonation) and a land mine as used by Rains (random position, contact detonated—hence clandestine), while naval officers classed all underwater weaponry as clandestine.

25. Rains to Secretary of War James A. Seddon, 29 October 1864, *O.R.A.*, ser. i, vol. XLII, part iii, pp. 1181–82; and Rains to Seddon, 18 November 1864, ibid., p. 1220.

26. R. Delafield, *Report on the Art of War in Europe in 1854, 1855, and 1856* [U.S., Congress, House, Executive Doc. 59, 36th Cong., 2d sess., 1861] (Washington, 1861), p. 111 and *passim*.

27. Rains to Maj. Gen. Hill, 30 May 1863, *O.R.A.*, ser. i, vol. XVIII, p. 1082.

28. Secretary Seddon to Gen. Joseph E. Johnston, 27 May 1863, ibid., pp. 1082–83.

29. Francis Lieber, "A Code for the Government of Armies in the Field, as Authorized by the Laws and Usages of War on Land, Printed as manuscript for the Board appointed by the Secretary of War [Special Orders, No. 399] To Propose Amendments or Changes in the Rules and Articles of War . . . ," February 1863, Duke University Library. Compare with Henry Wheaton, *Elements of International Law: The Literal Reproduction of the Edition of 1866 by Richard Henry Dana, Jr.*, ed. by George Grafton Wilson, No. 19 of The Classics of International Law, ed. by James Brown Scott (Oxford, 1936), pp. 358–59.

30. It is also ironic that the mines that sank her were simple glass demijohns in wicker baskets operated from shore by friction fuses, very much like the weapons made in the decades before 1860, or for that matter like those used in the rivers of the Mekong Delta during the recent Vietnam conflict.

31. *Official Records of the Union and Confederate Navies in the War of the Rebellion* (31 vols.; Washington, 1894–1927), ser. i, vol. XXIII, p. 545. [Hereafter cited as *O.R.N.*] Times were changing though. The act of idolization was not now as strong and not every David in the Southern camp insisted on the largest Goliath. One torpedoist named Stephen Elliott, when asked if he would take his invention against the massive U.S.S. *New Ironsides*, replied: "I shall not hunt the field for a Harold, Colonel; any one of them is worth the attempt." J. A. Hamilton, "General Stephen Elliott, Lietenant James A. Hamilton, and Elliott's Torpedoes," *Southern Historical Society Papers*, X (April 1882), 185.

32. Beauregard to Stephen Mallory, 31 October 1862, *O.R.A.*, ser. i, vol. XIV, p. 661; and Beauregard to Representative W. Porcher Niles, 2 May 1863, ibid., p. 924.

33. On Francis Lee's efforts, see Perry, *Infernal Machines*, chaps. vii and viii. Quotations are from Crowley, "Torpedo Service," p. 294; and *O.R.A.*, ser. i, vol. XL, part iii, p. 764.

34. Perry, *Infernal Machines*, pp. 4, 199–201.

35. Quoted in ibid., p. 172. Ironically, he made this observation after U.S.S. *Harvest Moon* was blown out from under him in 1865.

36. Dahlgren to Secretary of War Gideon Welles, 19 February 1864, *O.R.N.*, ser. i, vol. XV, p. 330.

37. Dahlgren to Welles, 6 April 1864, ibid., p. 394; and diary entry for 10 October 1863, ibid., p. 19.

38. Perry, *Infernal Machines*, p. 84.

39. 7 October 1863, *O.R.N.*, ser. i, vol. XV, pp. 13–14.

40. Quoted in Bradford, *Torpedo Warfare*, p. 72.

41. Dahlgren to Welles, 17 October 1863, *O.R.N.*, ser. i, vol. XV, p. 48.

42. E. Beidernanny to Gideon Welles, 30 December 1861, NA, RG 45, Subject File AD, Box 6.

43. Louis H. Bolander, "The Alligator: First Federal Submarine of the Civil War," *United St tes Naval Institute Proceedings*, LXIV (June 1938), 845–54.

44. See, for example, Maj. Gen. S. A. Hurlbut to Gideon Welles, 12 April 1864, *O.R.N.*, ser. i, vol. XXI, p. 187.

45. Williams, *Maury*, p. 393.

46. For examples of this literature see NA, RG 45, Subject File BM, Box 1 and Subject File AD, Box 6. See also Perry, *Infernal Machines*, p. 91.

47. Mitchell to Mallory, 21 October 1864, *O.R.N.*, ser. i, vol. X, p. 791.

48. Hardee to Maj. Gen. J. F. Gilmer, 7 November 1864, ibid., vol. XVI, p. 460.

49. *Elements of Intern tional Law*, p. 371. Compare Lieber, *Code*, p. 5.

50. See Maury to B. F. Minor, 19 July 1861, quoted in Williams, *Maury*, p. 379; and Perry, *Infernal Machines*, p. 42.

51. Quoted in J. Thomas Scharf, *History of the Confederate States Navy* . . . (New York, 1887), p. 765.

CHAPTER XII: DAVID TRIUMPHANT

1. John S. Barnes, *Submarine Warfare* (New York, 1869), p. 225.

2. (Washington, 1866). Quotes are from pp. 59, i, and title page.

3. Pp. 86–87.

4. P. 971

5. From Willets Point issued the U.S. Engineer School *Professional Papers*, in which were included the works of Abbot and von Ehrenkrook, cited earlier. From Newport issued a series of important published lectures including such works as Royal Bird Bradford, *History of Torpedo Warfare* (1882) and *Notes on the Spar Torpedo* (1882); and Francis Morgan Barber, *Lecture on Drifting and Automatic Movable Torpedoes, Submarine Guns, and Rockets* (1874) and *Lecture on Submarine Boats and Their Application to Torpedo Operations* (1875).

6. *Report on Active Obstructions for the Defence of Harbours and Channels, & c., and on the Employment of Torpedoes for Purposes of Attack* . . . (London, 1868).

7. Ibid., P. xi.

8. Frances Leigh Williams, *Matthew Fontaine Maury: Scientist of the Sea* (New Brunswick, N.J., 1963), pp. 442 ff. Ms. Williams was not aware that the Russians also availed themselves of Maury's course. See A. A. Samarov and F. A. Petrov, eds., *Development of Mine Material in the Russian Navy: A Collection of Documents*, compiled by S. V. Rogulin and M. N. Varfolomeev; U.S. Navy Bureau of Ships Translation 611, trans. by Lloyd G. Robbins, ed. by F. A. Raven and M. W. Raven (n.p., 1956), pp. 243–50. Their rejection of his system on grounds that it was inferior to their own is more than a little suspect. As the American translators of the *Documents* have pointed out, the final refusal was signed by "Comrade Inspector-General for the Engineering Section," a strange title for one of the Czar's officers in 1866.

9. P. 299. Scheliha's volume was subtitled: *Based on the Experiences Gained by Officers of the Corps of Engineers of the Army of the Confederate States, and Compiled from Official Reports of Officers of the Navy of the United States, Made during the Late North American War from 1861 to 1865* (London, 1868). See also Philip K. Lundeberg, "Undersea Warfare and Allied Strategy in World War I, Part I: to 1916," reprinted from *The Smithsonian Journal of History*, I (Autumn, 1966), p. 2; and

Milton F. Perry, *Infernal Machines: The Story of Confederate Submarine and Mine Warfare* ([Baton Rouge, La.,] 1965), pp. 182–84.

10. Hunter Davidson, "Electrical Torpedoes as a System of Defense," *Southern Historical Society Papers*, II (July 1876), p. 3.

11. Henry Wheaton, *Elements of International Law: The Literal Reproduction of the Edition of 1866 by Richard Henry Dana, Jr.*, ed. by George Grafton Wilson, No. 19 of The Classics of International Law, ed. by James Brown Scott (Oxford, 1936), p. 360n.

12. Quoted in Committee on Floating Obstructions . . . , *Report*, p. 43.

13. George H. Waltz, Jr., *Jules Verne: The Biography of an Imagination* (New York, 1943), chap. 1; and Jules Verne, *Twenty Thousand Leagues Under the Sea* [1870], trans. by Walter James Miller, assisted by Judith Ann Tirsch (New York, 1965), p. viii.

14. Verne, *Twenty Thousand Leagues*, pp. 3–22.

15. "Space being (don't forget to remember) Curved," *Poems 1923–1954* (New York, 1954), p. 227.

16. In his *Ideas and Weapons*, I. B. Holley, Jr. has demonstrated that the full and successful integration of an innovative weapon into a military organization requires a comprehensive doctrine on how the weapon will be used. However, the doctrine can only be formulated by the military experts, and they are unlikely to address the subject until the weapon has once been adopted. It was only after underwater warfare had proved its worth in the Civil War that the professionals at Willets Point and Newport began the process of building a doctrine. Doctrine is essential to the effective utilization of a weapon, but not to its adoption. See Irving B. Holley, Jr., *Ideas and Weapons: Exploitation of the Aerial Weapon by the United States during World War I; A Study in the Relationship of Technological Advance, Military Doctrine, and the Development of Weapons*, Yale Historical Publications, Miscellany: LVII (New Haven, 1953).

SELECTED BIBLIOGRAPHY

BIBLIOGRAPHIC GUIDES

Albion, Robert Greenhalgh. *Naval and Maritime History: An Annotated Bibliography*. 3d ed., rev. and exp. Mystic, Conn.: Marine Historical Association, 1963.

Anderson, Frank J. *Submarines, Submariners, Submarining: A Checklist of Submarine Books in the English Language*. Hamden, Conn.: Shoe String Press, 1963.

Committee on Undersea Warfare of the National Academy of Sciences, National Research Council. *An Annotated Bibliography of Submarine Technical Literature, 1557 to 1953*. Washington, D.C.: n.p., 1954.

Ellis, William A. *Torpedoes: A List of References to Material in the New York Public Library*. New York: n. p., 1917.

Ferguson, Eugene S. *Bibliography of the History of Technology*. Cambridge, Mass. and London: Society for the History of Technology, 1968.

Jameson, Mary Ethel. *Submarines: A List of References in the New York Public Library*. New York: n.p., 1918.

London, Imperial War Museum. *Bibliography of Submarine Warfare*. London: n.p., 1953.

Paine, T. O. *Submarining: Three Thousand Books and Articles*. Santa Barbara, Calif.: General Electric Co., 1971.

Rushmore, David B., assisted by William H. Lanman and Eric A. Lof. "Bibliography of the Literature of Submarines, Mines and Torpedoes," *General Electric Review*., 20 (August 1917), 675–85.

(United States Navy Department, Naval History Division). *United States Naval History: A Bibliography*. 5th ed. Washington, D.C.: Government Printing Office, 1969.

ARCHIVE AND MANUSCRIPT COLLECTIONS

Annapolis, Md. United States Naval Academy Museum.
Letter from Ole Lisberg Jensen to James W. Cheevers, 10 October 1972.
Robert Fulton Papers.

Cambridge, Mass. Harvard College Library. The Houghton Library.
Joel Barlow Papers.

Durham, N.C. Duke University Library.
Lansen Collection Pamphlets. Vol. 153, no. 4.

Hartford, Conn. Connecticut Historical Society.
Samuel Colt Papers. MSS. 65910, 73555, 73556.

Hartford, Conn. Connecticut State Library.
"S. Colt's Submarine Battery."

London. National Maritime Museum.
N.E. Upham, Assistant Keeper I, Curator of Models, Department of Ships, to D. Shaw, 28 October 1976.

New Haven, Conn. Yale University Library. Beinecke Rare Book and Manuscript Library.
Card Catalogue of the 1742 Library.
Joel Barlow Papers (Pequot Library Collection).
Nathan Hale, List of Books in Linonian Library, MS Vault, Section 1, Drawer 1.
New Haven, Conn. Yale University Library. Sterling Memorial Library, Manuscript Division.
MSS., Miscellaneous B, David Bushnell Folder.
MSS. (Stokes), Group 402, Series I, Box 2, Folder 93.
Records of the Linonian Society, 1768–1790.
New York. New York Historical Society.
Commodore John Rodgers Papers.
Robert Fulton Papers.
Robert R. Livingston Papers.
New York. New York Public Library.
James Monroe Papers.
Robert Fulton Papers.
William Barclay Parsons Collection.
Philadelphia. Historical Society of Pennsylvania.
Autograph Collection of Simon Gratz, Case 4, Box 36.
Dreer Collection, Vol. 168: Robert Fulton Papers.
Washington, D.C. Library of Congress. Manuscript Division.
Matthew Fontaine Maury Papers.
Washington, D.C. National Archives.
General Records of the Department of State. Record Group 59. Entry 807. Robert Fulton Papers.
Naval Records Collection of the Office of Naval Records and Library. Record Group 45. Subject File AC; AD, Boxes 3½, 4, 5, 6, 11; AH, 1; AV, 1, 2; BM, 1, 2.

PUBLIC DOCUMENTS

Biographical Directory of the American Congresses, 1774–1961. (U.S., Congress, House, H. Doc. 492, 85th Cong., 2d sess.) Washington: Government Printing Office, 1961.

Committee on Floating Obstructions and Submarine Explosive Machines. *Report on Active Obstructions for the Defence of Harbours and Channels, &c., and on the Employment of Torpedoes for Purposes of Attack. . . .* London: George Edward Eyre and William Spottiswood, 1868.

General Register of the United States Navy and Marine Corps . . . (1782–1882). . . . Edited and published by Thomas H. S. Hamersley. Washington: Thomas H. S. Hamersley, 1882.

Great Britain. Public Record Office. *Calendar of State Papers, Domestic Series, of the Reign of Charles I.* 23 vols. London: Longman, Brown, Green, Longmans, & Roberts, 1858–97.

______. *Calendar of State Papers, Domestic Series, of the Reign of Charles II.* 28 vols. London: Longman, Longman, Green, Longman, & Roberts, 1860–1939.

Hinman, Royal R. *A Historical Collection, from Official Records, Files, & c., of the Part Sustained by Connecticut, during the War of the Revolution.* Hartford, Conn.: E. Gleason, 1842.

Official Records of the Union and Confederate Navies in the War of the Rebellion. 31 vols. Washington, D.C.: Government Printing Office, 1894–1927.

Public Records of the State of Connecticut. 9 vols. Hartford: Press of the Case, Lockwood & Brainard Co., 1894–1953.

The Public Statutes at Large of the United States. . . . Vol. V, Boston: Charles C. Little and James Brown, 1845.

U. S., Congress. House. *Colt's Submarine Battery.* H. Doc. 127, 28th Cong., 2d sess., 1845.

______. *Samuel Colt.* H. Rept. 46 to Accompany H. 519, 28th Cong., 2d sess., 1845.

U.S., Congress. *State Papers, Naval Affairs*, Vol. I, pp. 211–27, 234–45. 11th Cong., 3d sess., 1811.

The War of the Rebellion: A Compilation of the Official Records of the Union and Confederate Armies. 70 vols. Washington, D.C.: Government Printing Office, 1881–1901.

BOOKS AND ARTICLES

Abbott, Henry L. *The Beginning of Modern ubmarine Warfare, under Captain-Lieutenant David Bushnell, Sappers and Miners, Army of the Revolution.* Professional Papers, no. 3. U.S. Engineer School of Application. Willets Point, N.Y.: U.S. Engineer School, 1881–1882.

Alexander, W. A. "Thrilling Chapter in the History of the Confederate States Navy: Work of Submarine Boats." *Southern Historical Society Papers*, 30 (1902), 64–74.

Allen, Gardner Weld. *A Naval History of the American Revolution.* 2 vols. Boston and New York: Houghton Mifflin Co., 1913.

Archibald, E. H. H. *The Wooden Fighting Ship in the Royal Navy, AD 897–1860.* London: Blanford Press, 1968.

The Art of War in Seven Books Written by Nicholas Machiavel, Secretary of State, to the Republic of Florence. To Which is Added "Hints Relative to Warfare," by a Gentleman of the State of New York. Albany: Henry C. Southwick, 1815.

Aubry, Paul V. *Monge: Le savant ami de Napoléon Bonaparte, 1746–1818.* Paris: Gauthiers-Villars, 1954.

Ayala, Balthazar. *Three Books on the Law of War And on the Duties Connected with War And on Military Discipline.* (1582) Translated by John Pawley Bate. Edited by John Westlake. (no. 2, Vol. 2 of The Classics of International Law, edited by James Brown Scott.) Washington, D.C.: Carnegie Institution, 1912.

Bacon, Francis. *New Atlantis.* (The Harvard Classics, edited by Charles W. Eliot, vol. 3). Regular ed. New York: P. F. Collier & Son, 1937, pp. 141–81.

Ballis, William. *The Legal Position of War: Changes in Its Practice and Theory from Plato to Vattel*. The Hague: M. Nijhoff, 1937.

Barber, Francis Morgan. *Lecture on Drifting and Automatic Movable Torpedoes, Submarine Guns, and Rockets*. Newport, R.I.: U.S. Torpedo Station, 1874.

——. *Lecture on Submarine Boats and Their Application to Torpedo Operations*. Newport, R.I.: U.S. Torpedo Station, 1875.

Barber, John Warner. *Connecticut Historical Collections, Containing a General Collection of Interesting Facts, Traditions, Biographical Sketches, Anecdotes, &c., Relating to the Histories and Antiquities of Every Town in Connecticut, with Geographical Descriptions*. New Haven: Durrie & Peck, 1838.

Barnes, John S. *Submarine Warfare*. New York: D. Van Nostrand, 1869.

Bates, Ralph S. *Scientific Societies in the United States*. 2d ed. New York: Columbia University Press, 1958.

Baxter, James Phinney. *The Introduction of the Ironclad Warship*. Cambridge, Mass.: Harvard University Press, 1933.

Beauregard, Pierre Gustave Toutant de. "Torpedo Service in the Harbor and Water Defenses of Charleston," *Southern Historical Society Papers*, 5 (April 1878), 145–61.

Bishop, Farnham. *The Story of the Submarine*. Revised & enlarged. New York: Century Co., 1929.

Bishop, J. Leander. *A History of American Manufactures from 1608 to 1860*. . . . 2 vols. Philadelphia: Edward Young & Co., 1864.

Bolander, Louis H. "The Alligator: First Federal Submarine of the Civil War." *United States Naval Institute Proceedings*. 64 (June 1938), 845–54.

Borelli, Joh. Alphonsi. *De Motu Animalum* (1680). Bound with Daniel LeClerc and I. Iacobus Mangetus. *Bibliotheca Anatomica sive recens in anatomia inventorum Thesaurus locupletissimus* . . . . 2 vols. Genevae: Joannis Anthonii Chovët, 1685. pp. 812–1044.

Bourne, William. *The Art of Shooting in Great Ordnance; Contayning very necessary matters for all sortes of Servitoures eyther by Sea or by Lande*. London: Thomas Woodcocke, 1587.

——. *A Book called the Treasure for Traveilers . . . Contayning Very Necessary matters, for all sortes of Travailers, eyther by Sea or by Lande*. London: Thomas Woodcocke, 1578.

——. *Inuentions or Deuices. Very necessary for all Generalles and Captains, or Leaders of men, as wel by Sea as by Land*. (c. 1578) London: Printed for Thomas Woodcocke, (c. 1590).

——. *A Regiment for the Sea* (1574) *and Other Writings on navigation*. Edited by E. G. R. Taylor. (Works Issued by the Hakluyt Society, second series, no. 121.) Cambridge: University Press, 1963.

Boyle, Robert. *New Experiments Physico-Mechanicall, Touching The Spring of Air*. . . . Oxford: Printed by H. Hall for Tho. Robinson, 1660.

——. *Tracts*. . . . London: Richard Davis, 1672.

——. *The Works of the Honourable Robert Boyle*. . . . Edited by Thomas Birch. 5 vols. London: A. Millar, 1744.

______. *The Works of the Honourable Robert Boyle. In Six Volumes. To Which Is Prefixed the Life of the Author.* 6 vols. London: Printed for J. and F. Rivington, 1772.

Bradford, Royal Bird. *History of Torpedo Warfare.* Newport, R. I.: U.S. Torpedo Station, 1882.

______. *Notes on the Spar Torpedo.* Newport, R.I.: U.S. Torpedo Station, 1882.

Brasch, Frederick E. "The Newtonian Epoch in the American Colonies, 1680–1783." *Proceedings of the American Antiquarian Society*, 2d ser. 49 (October 1939), 314–32.

______. "The Royal Society of London and Its Influence upon Scientific Thought in the American Colonies." *Scientific Monthly*, 33 (1931), 337–55, 448–69.

Brodie, Bernard. *Sea Power in the Machine Age.* Princeton: Princeton University Press, 1941.

______, and Fawn Brodie. *From Crossbow to H-Bomb: The Evolution of the Weapons and Tactics of Warfare.* New York: Laurel Science Series, 1962. Rev. and enl. ed., Bloomington and London: Indiana University Press, 1973.

Brown, H. D. "The First Successful Torpedo and What It Did." *Confederate Veteran*, 18 (April 1910), 169.

Brown, Harcourt. *Scientific Organizations of 17th Century France (1620–1680).* (History of Science Publications, New Series 5.) Baltimore: William I. Wilkins Co., 1934.

Brown, W. Baker. *History of Submarine Mining in the British Army.* Chatham, England: W. & J. Mackay & Co., 1910.

Bucknill, John Townsend. *Submarine Mines and Torpedoes as Applied to Harbour Defence.* New York: John Wiley & Sons, 1889.

Burgoyne, Alan H. *Submarine Navigation: Past and Present.* 2 vols. London: Grant Richards, and New York: E. P. Dutton & Co., 1903.

Burney, William (ed.) *A New Universal Dictionary of the Marine. . . .* (i.e., "Falconers Marine Dictionary," 2d ed.) London: T. Caldwell and W. Davies, 1815.

(Bushnell, David). "General Principles and Construction of a Sub-marine Vessel, communicated by D. Bushnell of Connecticut, the inventor, in a letter of October, 1787, to *Thomas Jefferson*, then Minister Plenipotentiary of the United States at Paris," *Transactions of the American Philosophical Society, Held at Philadelphia for Promoting Useful Knowledge*, 4 (1799), 303–12.

Butterfield, H(erbert). *The Origins of Modern Science, 1300–1800.* 2d ed. New York: Macmillan Co., 1957.

Bynkershoek, Cornelius van. *Quaestionum Juris Publici libri Duo.* Translated by Tenney Frank. (No. 14, vol 2 of The Classics of International Law, edited by James Brown Scott.) Oxford Clarendon Press, 1930.

Castlereagh, Viscount. *Correspondence, Despatches, and Other Papers of Viscount Castlereagh, Second Marquess of Londonderry.* Edited by Charles William Vane. 12 vols. London: John Murray, 1848–53.

Catalogue of Books in the Library of Yale-College, New-Haven. N.p.: T & S. Green, 1791.

A Catalogue of the Books in the Library of Yale-College in New-Haven. N.p.: n.p., 1790.

Catalogue of the Library of the Linonian Society, Yale College. New Haven: J. H. Benham, 1846.

Catalogue of the Library of the Society of the Brothers in Unity, Yale College. New Haven: B. L. Hamlen, 1846.

Cervantes Saavedra, Miguel de. *The First Part of the Life and Achievements of the Renowned Don Quixote de la Mancha.* (1605) Translated by Peter Motteux. New York: Random House, 1941.

Chambard, Claude. *Les Sous-marins.* Paris: Editions France-Empire, 1968.

Chapelle, Howard I. "Fulton's 'Steam Battery': Blockship and Catamaran." *United States National Museum Bulletin 240: Contributions from the Museum of History and Technology.* Washington: Smithsonian Institution, 1964. pp. 137–76.

Cipolla, Carlo M. "The Diffusion of Innovations in Early Modern Europe." *Comparative Studies in Social History,* 14 (January, 1972), 46–52.

Clap, Thomas. *The Annals or History of Yale-College, In New-Haven, In the Colony of Connecticut, from the First Founding Thereof, in the Year 1700, to the Year 1766. . . .* New Haven: Printed for John Hotchkiss and B. Mecom, 1766.

(———). *A Catalogue of Books in the Library of Yale-College in New Haven.* New Haven: James Parker, 1755.

———. *A Catalogue of the Library of Yale-College in New-Haven.* New London, Conn.: T. Green, 1743.

Clark, Austin H. "Background and Origin of the American Association for the Advancement of Science." American Association for the Advancement of Science, June, 1929–January, 1934. *Summarized Proceedings,* vols. 82 to 86 (1934), 15–20.

Clark, G. N. *Science and Social Welfare in the Age of Newton.* Oxford: Clarendon Press, 1937.

Clark, William Bell. *George Washington's Navy: Being an Account of His Excellency's Fleet in New England Waters.* Baton Rouge, La.: Louisiana State University Press, 1960.

Clark, William Bell (ed.). *Naval Documents of the American Revolution.* 5 vols. to date. Washington, D.C.: Government Printing Office, 1964–70.

Cobban, Alfred. *A History of Modern France.* Vol. 1: *Old Regime and Revolution, 1715–1799.* Penguin Books. 3d ed. Harmondsworth, England: Penquin Books, 1963.

Coblentz, Stanton H. *From Arrow to Atom Bomb: The Psychological History of War.* New York: Beechhurst Press, 1953.

Coggins, Jack. *Ships and Seamen of the American Revolution: Vessels, Crews, Weapons, Gear, Naval Tactics, and Actions of the War for Independence.* Harrisburg, Pa.: Stackpole Books, 1969.

Colden, Cadwallader D. *The Life of Robert Fulton, by His Friend Cadwallader D. Colden. . . .* New York: Kirk & Mercein, 1817.

Collections of the Connecticut Historical Society. 31 vols. Hartford: The Society, 1860–1967.

Concordance des calendriers grégorien et républicain. Paris: Libraire Historique R. Clavreuil, 1963.

Congreve, (William). *The Details of the Rocket System. . . .* (1814) Ottawa, Ontario: Museum Restoration Service, 1970.

Correspondance de Napoléon Ier. 32 vols. Paris: H. Plon, J. Dumaine, 1858–70.

Cotgrave, Randle. *A dictionaire of the French and English tongues.* (1611) Columbia, South Carolina: University of South Carolina Press, 1950.

Cowie, J. S. *Mines, Minelayers and Minelaying.* London: Oxford University Press, 1949.

Crowley, R. O. "The Confederate Torpedo Service," *Century.* 46 (May 1898), 290–300.

cummings, e.e. *Poems 1923–1954.* New York: Harcourt, Brace, 1954.

Davidson, Hunter. "The Electrical Submarine Mine, 1861–1865," *Confederate Veteran,* 16 (September 1908), 456–59.

______. "Electrical Torpedoes as a System of Defense," *Southern Historical Society Papers.* 2 (July 1876), 1–6.

Davies, C. M. *History of Holland, From the Beginning of the Tenth to the End of the Eighteenth Century.* 3 vols. London: John W. Parker, 1841–44.

Delafield, R(ichard). *Report on The Art of War in Europe in 1854, 1855, and 1856.* (U.S., Congress, House, Executive Doc. #59, 36th Cong., 2d sess.) Washington: Government Printing Office, 1861.

Delpeuch, Maurice. *Les Sous-marins à travers les siècles.* Paris, 1907.

Denny, Margaret. "The Royal Society and American Scholars." *Scientific Monthly.* 65 (November 1947), 415–27.

Desbrière, Edouard. *Projets et tentatives de débarquement aux Isles Brittaniques: 1793–1805.* 5 vols. Paris: Libraire Militaire R. Chapelot, 1900–1902.

Dexter, Franklin Bowditch (ed.) *Documentary History of Yale University Under the Original Charter of the Collegiate School of Connecticut 1701–1745.* New Haven: Yale University Press, 1916.

Dickinson, H(enry). W(inram). *Robert Fulton, Engineer and Artist: His Life and Work.* (1913) Freeport, N.Y.: Books for Libraries Press, 1971.

Dictionary of American Biography. 20 vols.; New York: C. Scribner's Sons, 1928–36. 2 supplements. 1944, 1958.

The Dictionary of National Biography. 21 vols. and 1 vol. supplement (1885–1901) London: Oxford University Press, 1921–22.

Dictionnaire de biographie française. 12 vols. to date. Paris: Libraire Letouzey et Ané, 1933–1970.

Dircks, H(enry). *A Biographical Memoir of Samuel Hartlib. . . .* London: John Russel Smith, n.d.

______. *The Life, Times, and Scientific Labors of the Second Marquis of Worcester; to which is added a Reprint of his "Century of Inventions," 1663, with a Commentary thereon.* London: Bernard Quaritch, 1865.

Donne, John. *The Works of John Donne, DD., Dean of St. Paul's 1621–1631, with a Memoir of His Life.* Edited by Henry Alford. 6 vols. London: J. W. Parker, 1839.

Drayton, Michaell. *The Battaille of Agincourt. . . .* London: Printed by A. M. for William Lee, 1631.

Drebbel, Cornelius. "Deux traitez philosophiques de Corneille Drebel," in *Divers traitez de la philosophie naturelle. . . .* Paris: Jean d'Houry à l'Image S. Jean, 1672, pp. 175–273.

Duncan, Robert C. *America's Use of Sea Mines.* Silver Spring, Md.: U.S. Naval Ordnance Laboratory, 1962.

"Early Days of Submarine Warfare," *Scientific American*, 103 (8 October 1910), 227, 285–86.

Ehrenkrook, F. von. *History of Submarine Mining and Torpedoes.* Translated by Frederick Martin. Professional Papers, no. 1. U.S. Engineer School of Application. Willets Point, N.Y.: U.S. Engineer School, 1881–1882.

Emery, Clark. "A Further Note on Drebbel's Submarine." *Modern Language Notes*, 57 (June 1942), 451–55.

Fayet, Joseph. *La revolution française et la science, 1789–1795.* Paris: Libraire Marcel Rivière & Cie, 1960.

Feuer, Lewis S. *The Scientific Intellectual: The Psychological and Sociological Origins of Modern Science.* New York and London: Basic Books, 1963.

Field, Cyril. *The Story of the Submarine: From the Earliest Ages to the Present Day.* London: Sampson, Low, Marston & Company, Ltd., 1908.

Florio, John. *A World of Wordes, or Most Copious, and Exact Dictionairie in Italian and English.* London: Printed by Arnold Hatfield for Edw. Blount, 1598.

Fournier, Georges. *Hydrographie contenant la théorie et la practique de toutes les parties de la navigation.* 2d ed. Rev., corr., & aug. Paris: Jean Du Puis, 1667.

Franklin, Benjamin. *The Writings of Benjamin Franklin.* Edited by Albert Henry Smyth. 10 vols. New York: Macmillan Company, 1905–1907.

Frazer, James George. *The Golden Bough: A Study in Magic and Religion.* 1 vol. abr. ed. New York: Macmillan Company, 1944.

Fulton, Robert. *Torpedo War, and Submarine Explosions.* (1810) ("Being Extra No. 35 of *The Magazine of History with Notes and Queries*," pp. 171–225.) New York: William Abbott, 1914.

———. *Torpedo War, and Submarine Explosions.* (1810) Chicago: Swallow Press, 1971.

———. *A Treatise on the Improvement of Canal Navigation. . . .* London: I & J. Taylor, 1796.

Furber, Holden. "Fulton and Napoleon in 1800: New Light on the Submarine Nautilus." *American Historical Review.* 39 (April 1934), 489–94.

Fyfe, Herbert C. *Submarine Warfare: Past, Present, and Future.* London: Grant Richards, 1902.

Gaget, Maurice. *La Navigation sous-marine.* Paris: Libraire Polytechnique Ch. Béranger, 1901.

Gates, Gilman C. *Saybrook at the Mouth of the Connecticut: The First One Hundred*

Years. Orange and New Haven, Conn.: Wilson H. Lee Co., 1935.

Gay, Peter. *The Enlightenment: An Interpretation*. Vol. I: *The Rise of Modern Paganism*. Vintage Books. New York: Random House, 1968. vol. 2: *The Science of Freedom*. New York: Alfred A. Knopf, 1969.

de Gaya (, Louis, Sieur de Treville). *Traite des armes, des machines de guerre, des feux d'artifice, des enseignes & des instrumens militaires anciens & modernes*. . . . (1678) Edited by Charles Ffoulkes. London: Clarendon Press, 1911.

Gentili, Alberico. *De Iure Belli Libri Tres*. (1612) Translated by John C. Rolfe. (No. 16, vol. 2 of The Classics of International Law, edited by James Brown Scott.) Oxford: Clarendon Press, 1933.

Gentleman's Magazine and Historical Chronicle. 303 vols. London, 1731–1907.

Gilfillan, S. C. *The Sociology of Invention*. Chicago: Follett Publishing Co., 1935.

Grose, Francis. *Military Antiquities Respecting a History of the English Army from the Conquest to the Present Time*. 2 vols. London: S. Hooper, 1788.

Guerlac, Henry. "Some Aspects of Science during the French Revolution." *Scientific Monthly*, 80 (February 1955), 93–101.

Hahn, Roger, *The Anatomy of a Scientific Institution: The Paris Academy of Sciences (1666–1803)*. Berkeley, Calif.: University of California Press, 1971.

Hall, A. R. *Ballistics in the Seventeenth Century: A Study in the Relations of Science and War with Reference Principally to England*. Cambridge: University Press, 1952.

Hamilton, J. A. "General Stephen Elliott, Lieutenant James A. Hamilton, and Elliott's Torpedoes." *Southern Historical Society Papers*, 10 (April 1882), 183–86.

Harris, L. E. *The Two Netherlanders: Humphrey Bradlee and Cornelis Drebbel*. Leiden: E. J. Brill, 1961.

Harsdorffer, George Philip. *Delitiae Philosophicae et Mathematicae*. 3 vols. Nurnberg: J. Dümler, 1636–92.

Hennebert (, Eugene). *Les Torpilles*. Paris: Libraire Hachette et Cie, 1888.

Hindle, Brooke. *The Pursuit of Science in Revolutionary America, 1735–1789*. Chapel Hill, N.C.: University of North Carolina Press, 1956.

History of Middlesex County, Connecticut: With Biographical Sketches of Its Prominent Men. New York: J. B. Beers & Co., 1884.

Hoar, Allen. *The Submarine Torpedo Boat: Its Characteristics and Modern Development*. New York: D. Van Nostrand, 1916.

Holley, Irving B., Jr. *Ideas and Weapons: Exploitation of the Aerial Weapon by the United States during World War I: A Study in the Relationship of Technological Advance, Military Doctrine, and the Development of Weapons*. (Yale Historical Publications, Miscellany 57.) New Haven: Yale University Press, 1953.

Holtman, Robert B. *The Napoleonic Revolution*. Philadelphia: J. B. Lippincott Co., 1967.

Hooke, Robert. *The Posthumous Works of Robert Hooke*. (1705) Edited by Richard Waller, (The Sources of Science, no. 73.) New York and London: Johnson Reprint Corporation, 1969.

Hornberger, Theodore. *Scientific Thought in the American Colleges, 1638–1800*. Austin, Texas: University of Texas Press, 1945.

Huizinga, J. *The Waning of the Middle Ages: A Study of the Forms of Life, Thought and Art in France and the Netherlands in the XIVth and XVth Centuries*. London: Edward Arnold, 1924.

Humphreys, David. *An Essay on the Life of the Honourable Major General Israel Putnam. Addressed to the State Society of the Cincinnati in Connecticut, and first published by their order. . . .* Boston: Samuel Avery, 1818.

Hutcheon, Wallace S., Jr., "Robert Fulton and Naval Warfare." Unpublished Ph.D. dissertation, George Washington University, 1975.

James, Charles. *A New and Enlarged Military Dictionary* . . . 2 vols. 2d ed. London: T. Egerton, 1805.

———. *A New and Enlarged Military Dictionary*. . . . 2 vols. 3d ed. London: T. Egerton, 1810.

Jameson, Sir William. *The Most Formidable Thing: The Story of the Submarine from Its Earliest Days to the End of World War I*. London: Rupert Hart-Davis, 1965.

Jefferson, Thomas. *The Papers of Thomas Jefferson*. Edited by Julian P. Boyd. 20 vols. to date. Princeton: Princeton University Press, 1950–74.

Jewkes, John, David Sawers, and Richard Stillerman. *The Sources of Invention*. London: Macmillan & Co., Ltd. and New York: St. Martin's Press, 1958.

Johnson, Robert U. and Clarence C. Buel (eds.). *Battles and Leaders of the Civil War*. 4 vols. New York: Century Co., 1887–88.

Johnston, Henry P. "Sergeant Lee's Experience with Bushnell's Submarine Torpedo in 1776." *Magazine of American History with Notes and Queries*, 29 (March 1893), 262–66.

———. *Yale and Her Honor-Roll in the American Revolution, 1775–1783: Including Original Letters, Record of Service, and Biographical Sketches*. New York: Privately Printed, 1888.

Jonson, Ben. *The Works of Ben Jonson with a Biographical Memoir by William Gifford*. New York: D. Appleton & Co., 1869.

Keen, Maurice H. *The Laws of War in the Late Middle Ages*. London: Routledge & Kegan Paul, 1965.

The Keith Papers III (1803–1815). Edited by Chrisopher Lloyd. Publications of the Navy Record ociety, vol. 96. (London): Printed for the Navy Records Society, 1955.

Keogh, Andrew. "Bishop Berkeley's Gift of Books in 1733." *The Yale University Library Gazette*, 8 (July 1933), 1–25.

Keynes, (John Maynard). "Newton, the Man," in *The Royal Society Newton Tercentenary Celebration*. Cambridge: University Press, 1947.

King, W. R. *Torpedoes: Their Invention and Use, from the First Application to the Art of War to the Present Time*. Washington, D.C.: n.p., 1866.

Knight, R. J. B. "The Introduction of Copper Sheathing into the Royal Navy, 1779–1786." *Mariner's Mirror*. 59 (August 1973), 299–309.

Kranzberg, Melvin and Carroll W. Pursell, Jr. (eds.). *Technology in Western Civilization*. Vol. I: *The Emergence of Modern Industrial Society, Earliest Times to 1900*. New York: Oxford University Press, 1967.

Kuethe, J. Louis. "Mechanical Features of a Seventeenth Century Submarine." *Modern Language Notes*, 56 (March 1941), 202–204.

La Chesnaye-Desbois, Francois Alexandre Aubert. *Dictionnaire militaire: ou, Recueil alphabétique de tous les termes propres à l'art de la guerre.* . . . 3 vols. Rev., corr., and aug. Paris: Gissey, 1745–46.

Le Masson, Henri. *Du Nautilus (1800) au Redoubtable: Histoire critique du sous-marin dans la marine française.* Paris: Presses de la Cité, 1969.

Lenoble, Robert. *Mersenne ou la naissance du mécanisme.* ("Bibliothèque d'histoire de la philosophie.") Paris: Libraire Philosophique J. Vrin, 1943.

Lepotier, A. *Mer contre terre.* ("Les lecons de l'histoire (1861–1865).") Paris: Editions Mirambeau, (1945).

Lewis, Charles Lee. *Matthew Fontaine Maury: The Pathfinder of the Seas.* Annapolis, Md.: United States Naval Institute, 1927.

Lieber, Francis. "A Code for the Government of Armies in the Field, as Authorized by the Laws and Usages of War on Land." Manuscript prepared for U. S. Secretary of War, February, 1863. In Duke University Library.

Lott, Arnold S. *Most Dangerous Sea: A History of Mine Warfare, and an Account of U.S. Navy Mine Warfare Operations in World War II and Korea.* Annapolis: U.S. Naval Institute, 1959.

Low, Archibald Montgomery. *Mine and Countermine.* New York: Sheridan House, 1940.

Lundeberg, Philip K. *Samuel Colt's Submarine Battery: The Secret and the Enigma.* Smithsonian Studies in History and Technology, number 29. Washington: Smithsonian Institution Press, 1974.

(———). "Undersea Warfare and Allied Strategy in World War I, Part I: to 1916," *The Smithsonian Journal of History*, 1 (Autumn 1966), 1–30.

McKeehan, Louis W. *Yale Science: The First Hundred Years, 1701–1801.* New York: Henry Schuman, 1947.

Mahan, Alfred Thayer. *The Influence of Sea Power upon the French Revolution and Empire, 1793–1812.* 2 vols. 9th ed. Boston: Little, Brown, and Co., 1898.

Masson, Philippe and José Muracciole. *Napoléon et la marine.* Paris: J. Peyronnet & Cie, 1968.

Mattingly, Garrett. *The Armada.* Boston: Houghton Mifflin, (1959).

Maury, Richard L. *A Brief Sketch of the Work of Matthew Fontaine Maury during the War 1861–1865.* Richmond, Va.: Whittet & Shepperson, 1915.

Merrell, John P. *Lecture on Galvanic Batteries and Electrical Machines, as Used in Torpedo Operations, Arranged in Three Parts. Part I. Galvanic Batteries.* Newport, R.I.: U.S. Torpedo Station, 1874.

Mersenne, Marin. *Cogitata Physico-mathematica.* . . . Paris: Sumptibus A. Bertier, 1644.

Middlebrook, Louis F. *History of Maritime Connecticut during the American Revolution, 1775–1783.* 2 vols. Salem, Mass.: Essex Institute, 1925.

Minsheu, John. *A Dictionarie in Spanish and English, First Published into the English*

Tongue by Ric. Percivale Gent. Now Enlarged and Amplified. . . . London: Edm. Bollifant, 1599.

Montgéry (, Jacques-Philippe Mérigon de). *Mémoire sur les mines flottantes et les petards flottans, ou machines infernales maritimes.* Paris: Bachelier, Libraire pour la Marine, 1819.

Montross, Lynn. *War through the Ages.* New York and London: Harper and Brothers, 1944.

Morris, Edward P. "A Library of 1742." *The Yale University Library Gazette,* 9 (July 1934), 3–11.

Motley, John Lothrop. *History of the United Netherlands from the Death of William the Silent to the Twelve Years' Truce – 1609.* 4 vols. New York: Harper and Brothers, 1867.

Mumford, Lewis. *Technics and Civilization.* New York: Harcourt, Brace, 1934.

The Naval Chronicle . . . Containing a General and Biographical History of the Royal Navy of the United Kingdom; with a Variety of Original Papers on Nautical Subjects. 40 vols. London, 1799–1818.

Nef, John U. *War and Human Progress: An Essay on the Rise of Industrial Civilization.* Cambridge, Mass.: Harvard University Press, 1950.

Newbolt, Henry. *A Note on the History of Submarine War.* New York: George H. Doran Co., (c. 1916).

______. *Submarine and Anti-Submarine.* London: Longmans, Green and Co., 1918.

Newman, James R. *The Tools of War.* Garden City, N.Y.: Doubleday, Doran & Co., 1942.

Niles' National Register, Containing Political, Historical, Geographical, Scientifical, Statistical, Economical, and Biographical Documents, Essays and Facts: Together with Notices of the Arts and Manufactures, and a Record of the Events of the Times. 76 vols. Philadelphia, 1811–1849.

Noalhat, Henri. *Les Torpilles et les mines sous-marines.* Paris and Nancy: Berger-Levrault & Cie, 1905.

Nouvelle biographie generale despuis les temps les plus recules jusqu' à nos jours, avec les renseignements bibliographiques et l'indication des sources à consulter. 46 vols. Paris: Firmin Didot frères, 1853–66.

Oliver, John W. *History of American Technology.* New York: Ronald Press Co., 1956.

Ornstein, Martha. *The Rôle of Scientific Societies in the Seventeenth Century.* Chicago: University of Chicago Press, 1928.

Osterweis, Rollin G. *Three Centuries of New Haven, 1638–1938.* New Haven: Yale University Press, 1953.

Oviatt, Edwin. *The Beginnings of Yale (1701–1726).* New Haven: Yale University Press, 1916.

Palmer, R. R. *The World of the French Revolution.* New York and Evanston: Harper & Row, 1971.

______, and Joel Colton. *A History of the Modern World.* 4th ed. New York: Alfred A. Knopf, 1971.

Papin, D(enis). *Recueil de diverses Pieces touchant quelques nouvelles Machines. . . .* Cassel: Jacob Estienne Marchaud Libraire, 1695.

Parker, Harold T. "French Administrators and French Scientists during the Old Regime and the Early Years of the Revolution." *Ideas in History: Essays Presented to Louis Gottschalk by His Former Students.* Edited by Richard Herr and Harold T. Parker. Durham, N.C.: Duke University Press, 1965.

Parks, E. Taylor. "Robert Fulton and Submarine Warfare." *Military Affairs*, 25 (February 1962), 177–82.

Parsons, William Barclay. *Robert Fulton and the Submarine.* New York: Columbia University Press, 1922.

Paullin, Charles Oscar. *The Navy of the American Revolution: Its Administration, Its Policy, and Its Achievements.* Cleveland: Burrows Brothers Co., 1906.

Pepys, Samuel. *The Diary of Samuel Pepys M.A. F.R.S. . . .* Edited by Henry B. Wheatley. 10 vols. London: G. Bell and Sons, 1923–24.

Perry, Milton F. *Infernal Machines: The Story of Confederate Submarine and Mine Warfare.* (Baton Rouge, La.): Louisiana State University Press, 1965.

Pesce, G.-L. *La Navigation sous-marine.* Paris: Viubert & Mony, 1906.

Pratt, Anne S. and Andrew Keogh. "The Yale Library of 1742." *The Yale University Library Gazette*, 15 (October 1940), 29–40.

Purver, Margery. *The Royal Society: Concept and Creation.* Cambridge, Mass.: M.I.T. Press, 1967.

Rains, Gabriel J. "Torpedoes," *Southern Historical Society Papers*, 3 (May and June 1877), 255–60.

Roberts, Michael. "The Military Revolution, 1560–1660." *Essay in Swedish History.* London: Weidenfeld & Nicholson, , 1967.

Robison, Georgia. *Révellière-Lépeaux, Citizen Director, 1753–1824.* New York: Octagon Books, 1972.

Rohan, Jack. *Yankee Arms Maker: The Incredible Career of Samuel Colt.* New York and London: Harper & Brothers, 1935.

Ropp, Theodore. *War in the Modern World.* New, rev. ed. New York: Collier Books, 1962.

Rossi, Paolo. *Philosophy, Technology, and the Arts in the Early Modern Era* [1962]. Translated by Salvator Attanasio, Edited by Benjamin Nelson. Torchbook Library ed. New York: Harper and Row, 1970.

Royal Society of London. *Philosophical Transactions.* (117 vols. London, 1665–1886.) Amsterdam, 1963–64.

Rush, C. W., W. C. Chabliss, and H. J. Gempel. *The Complete Book of Submarines.* Cleveland and New York: World Publishing Co., 1958.

Samarov. A.A. and F. A. Petrov (eds.). *Development of Mine Material in the Russian Navy: A Collection of Documents.* Compiled by S. V. Rogulin and M. N.

Varfolomeev. (U. S. Navy Bureau of Ships Translation 611.) Translated by Lloyd G. Robbins. Edited by F. A. Raven and M. V. Raven. N.p.: n.p., 1956.

Savant, Jean. *Les ministres de Napoléon.* (Paris:) Hachette, 1959.

Scharf, J. Thomas. *History of the Confederate States Navy. . . .* New York: Rogers and Sherwood, 1887.

Scheliha, Victor Ernest Rudolph von. *A Treatise on Coast Defence: Based on the Experiences Gained by Officers of the Corps of Engineers of the Army of the Confederate States, and Compiled from Official Reports of Officers of the Navy of the United States, Made during the Late North American War from 1861 to 1865.* London: E. & F. N. Spon, 1868.

Schiller, Friedrich. *The Revolt of the Netherlands.* Translated by E. B. Eastwick and A. J. W. Morrison. Vol. V of *The Works of Friedrich Schiller.* Edited by Nathan Haskell Dole. 10 vols. New York: Bigelow, Brown & Co., 1901.

Schott, Gaspar. *Technica Curiosa, sive Mirabilia artis, libris XII. comprehensa. . . .* Nuremberg: J. A. Endteri & Wolfgangi, 1664.

Scott, H. L. *Military Dictionary: Comprising Technical Definitions; Information in Raising and Keeping Troops; Actual Service; Including Makeshifts and Improved Material; and Law, Government, Regulation, and Administration Relating to Land Forces.* New York: D. Van Nostrand, 1861.

Seymour, George Dudley. *A Documentary Life of Nathan Hale.* New Haven: Privately printed for the author, 1941.

Shores, Louis. *Origins of the American College Library, 1638–1800.* Nashville, Tenn.: George Peabody College for Teachers, 1934.

Simes, Thomas. *The Military Guide for Young Officers.* 2 vols. Philadelphia: J. Humphreys, D. Bell, and R. Aitken, 1776.

Six, Georges. *Dictionaire biographique des généraux & amiraux français de la Révolution et de l'Empire (1792–1814).* 2 vols. Paris: Libraire Historique et Nobilaire, 1934.

Sleeman, Charles William. *Torpedoes and Torpedo Warfare.* 2d ed. Portsmouth, England: Griffin & Co., 1889.

Smith, George. *An Universal Military Dictionary, or A Copious Explanation of the Technical Terms & c. Used in the Equipment, Machinery, Movements, and Military Operations of an Army.* (1799) Ottawa, Ontario: Museum Restoration Service, 1969.

Sohlman, Ragnar and Henrick Schuck. *Nobel: Dynamite and Peace.* Translated by Brian and Beatrix Lunn. New York: Cosmopolitan Book Corporation, 1929.

Sprat, Thomas. *The History of the Royal-society of London, for the Improving of Natural Knowledge.* London: Printed by T. R. for J. Martyn and J. Allistry, 1667.

Sprout, Harold and Margaret. *The Rise of American Naval Power: 1776–1918.* Rev. ed. Princeton: Princeton University Press, 1942.

Stearns, Raymond P. *Science in the British Colonies of America.* Urbana, Ill.: University of Illinois Press, 1970.

Stotherd, Richard Hugh. *Notes on Torpedoes, Offensive and Defensive.* Washington, D.C.: Government Printing Office, 1872.

Struik, Dirk J. *Yankee Science in the Making.* Boston: Little, Brown, 1948.

Sueter, Murray F. *The Evolution of the Submarine Boat Mine and Torpedo from the Sixteenth Century to the Present Time.* Portsmouth, England: J. Griffin and Co., 1907.

Supplee, Henry Harrison. "Fulton in France," *Cassier's Magazine*, 32 (September 1908), 780–94.

Sutcliffe, Alice Crary. *Robert Fulton and the "Clermont."* New York: Century Co., 1909.

———. "The Early Life of Robert Fulton," *Century*, 76 (September 1908), 780–94.

———. "Robert Fulton in France," *Century*, 76 (October 1908), 931–45.

Taton, René (ed.). *History of Science.* Vol. 2: *The Beginnings of Modern Science: From 1450 to 1800.* Translated by A. J. Pomerans. New York: Basic Books, 1964.

Taylor, E.G.R. *The Mathematical Practitioners of Tudor and Stuart England.* Cambridge: Published for the Institute of Navigation at the University Press, 1954.

———. *Tudor Geography, 1485–1583.* London: Methuen & Co., 1930.

Thacher, James. *A Military Journal during the American Revolutionary War, from 1775 to 1783, Describing Interesting Events and Transactions of this Period, with Numerous Historical Facts and Anecdotes from the Original Manuscript. To Which Is Added an Appendix, Containing Biographical Sketches of Several General Officers.* Boston: Richard on and Lord, 1823.

Thomson, David Whittet. "Robert Fulton and the French Invasion of England," *Military Affairs*, 18 (July 1954), 57–63.

Thorndike, Lynn. *A History of Magic and Experimental Science.* 8 vols. New York: Columbia University Press, 1929–58.

Tierie, Gerrit. *Cornelis Drebbel, 1572–1633.* Amsterdam: H. J. Paris, 1932.

Todd, Charles Burr. *Life and Letters of Joel Barlow, LL.D.: Poet, Statesman, Philosopher.* New York and London: G. P. Putnam's Sons, 1886.

Toynbee, Arnold J. *War and Civilization.* Selected by Albert V. Fowler from *A Study of History.* New York: Oxford University Press, 1950.

Vattel, E(mer or merrich). de. *The Law of Nations or the Principles of Natural Law Applied to the Conduct and to the Affairs of Nations and of Sovereigns.* (1758) Translated by Charles G. Fenwick. (No. 4, vol. 3 of The Classics of International Law, edited by James Brown Scott.) Washington, D.C.: Carnegie Institution, 1916.

de Veillechèze, Francois, de la Mardière. *L'Evolution historique du controle de la marine.* Poitiers: Société Française D'Imprimerie et de Libraire, 1912.

Verne, Jules. *Twenty Thousand Leagues Under the Sea.* Translated by Walter James Miller, assisted by Judith Ann Tirsch. New York: Washington Square Press, 1965.

Wagner, Frederick. *Submarine Fighter of the American Revolution: The Story of David Bushnell.* New York: Dodd, Mead & Company, 1963.

Waller, John Francis. (ed.). *The Imperial Dictionary of Universal Biography: A Series of Original Memoirs of Distinguished Men, of All Ages and All Nations by Writers of Eminence in the Various Branches of Literature, Science and Art.* 14 vols. London: William MacKenzie, (c.1863).

Walsh, James J. "Scholasticism in the Colonial Colleges," *New England Quarterly*. 5 (July 1932), 483–532.

Waltz, George H., Jr. *Jules Verne: The Biography of an Imagination.* New York: Henry Holt and Company, 1943.

Wegg, Jervis. *The Decline of Antwerp under Philip of Spain.* London: Methuen & Co., 1924.

Weld, Charles Richard. *A History of the Royal Society, with Memoirs of the Presidents, Compiled from Authentic Documents.* 2 vols. London: John W. Parker, 1848.

Wheaton, Henry. *Elements of International Law: The Literal Reproduction of the Edition of 1866 by Richard Henry Dana, Jr..* Edited by George Grafton Wilson (No. 19 of The Classics of International Law, edited by James Brown Scott.) Oxford: Clarendon Press, 1936.

Wheeler, H. F. B. and A. M. Broadley. *Napoleon and the Invasion of England: The Story of the Great Terror.* 2 vols. New York and London: John Lurre, 1908.

"When Fulton Suggested Submarine Warfare." *Scientific American*, 115 (18 November 1916), 458 ff.

White, Lynn, Jr. "Jacopo Aconcio as an Engineer." *American Historical Review*, 72 (January 1967), 425–44.

Wiener, Philip P. and Aaron Noland (eds.). *The Roots of Scientific Thought: A Cultural Perspective.* New York: Basic Books, 1957.

Wilkins, John. *Mathematical Magick: or the Wonders that May Be Performed by Mechanical Geometry. . . .* (5th ed., 1707) in *The Mathematical and Philosophical Works of the Right Reverend John Wilkins, Late Lord Bishop of Chester.* London: J. Nicholson, 1708.

Williams, Frances Leigh. *Matthew Fontaine Maury: Scientist of the Sea.* New Brunswick, N.J.: Rutgers University Press, 1963.

Williams, L. Pearce. "Science, Education and the French Revolution." *Isis*, 44 (December 1953), 311–30.

Winterbotham, W(illiam). *An Historical Geographical, Commercial and Philosophical View of the American United States. . . .* 4 vols. London: J. Ridgway, H. D. Symonds, and D. Holt, 1795.

Wintringham, T. *The Story of Weapons and Tactics from Troy to Stalingrad.* Boston: Houghton Mifflin Co., 1943.

Wolf, A. *A History of Science, Technology, and Philosophy in the Eighteenth Century.* New York: Macmillan Co., 1939.

———. *A History of Science, Technology, and Philosophy in the 16th & 17th Centuries.* New York: Macmillan Co., 1935.

Wolff, Christian. *Jus Gentium Methodo Scientifica Pertractatum.* (1764 ed.) Translated by Joseph H. Drake. (No. 13, vol. 2 of The Classics of International Law, edited by James Brown Scott.) Oxford: Clarendon Press, 1934.

Worcester, (Edward Somerset, Second) Marquis of. *A Century of the Names and Scantlings of Such Inventions. . . .* (1655) Glasgow: R. and A. Foulis, 1767.

Wright, Quincy. *A Study of War*. 2d ed. Chicago: University of Chicago Press, 1965.

Zunder, Theodore Albert. *The Early Days of Joel Barlow, a Connecticut Wit . . . from 1754 to 1787*. New Haven: Yale University Press, 1934.

Index